A Literary Journal [Ed. by J.P. Droz]. (1745)

A

LITERARY

JOURNAL,

For *Octob. Novem. Decem.* 1744.

A

LITERARY

JOURNAL.

October, November, December, 1744.

VOL. I.

PART I.

DUBLIN:

Printed by S. POWELL, for the AUTHOR,

MDCCXLIV.

ADVERTISEMENT.

INſtead of a Preface, which the Reader probably expects, I give here the Advertiſement, I publiſh'd ſome time ago, which contains every material thing, I cou'd ſay in a Preface.

As Foreign Books are only known from the French Journals, publiſh'd abroad, underſtood by few, and read by fewer, my Intention is to give Engliſh Abſtracts of the moſt important foreign Books, German, Dutch, French, or Latin.

To execute this Scheme, I ſhall chuſe the beſt Abſtracts to be found in the great Variety of foreign Journals; give them either whole or in part, according to the Importance of the Subject; enlarge upon what ſhall be judged to be of the greateſt Moment; and ſuppreſs what ſhall appear to be of ſmall Uſe.

A 3   1

ADVERTISEMENT.

I shall also venture some short Remarks of my own, when necessary to the better understanding of the Subject in hand, and sometimes give Abstracts not to be met with in any Journal: In short, I shall use my best Endeavours that nothing be omitted, that may render this Work agreeable or useful to the Public.

Tho' my principal Design is to give Information of foreign Books, yet I do not mean so to confine my self as never to take notice of English Writers, who treat of Matters either entirely new, or remarkably curious. I shall speak of them, as of every other, in as concise a manner as possible, free from Flattery or Malignity. Satyr, personal Reflections, and whatever might reasonably give Offence, shall be totally excluded from these Papers. I shall most industriously avoid whatever may directly or indirectly affect the Government, we have the Happiness of living under, or be in any way repugnant to the Respect we owe those intrusted with it.

As Liberty in religious Matters is the right of every Rational Being, I shall make use of mine, but in such a manner as will not, I hope, prejudice the Cause of true Christianity.

I will

ADVERTISEMENT.

I will receive with Gratitude friendly Advice, and Differtations upon any Literary Subject, and will infert them in this Journal, provided their Authors keep within the Bounds I have prefcribed to my felf.

The Author of any Abftract, of any Differtation, or of any particular Remark inferted in an Abftract, fhall not be named, without his exprefs Confent ; but fuch Remarks fhall be fo diftinguifh'd, as not to be miftaken for mine. A Writer who aims at public Utility alone, is fatisfied and fufficiently rewarded if his Performance be approved of; fhould the contrary happen, he has Reafon to keep himfelf concealed,

The favourable Reception of this Undertaking muft neceffarily depend on the Execution ; the Public muft decide it's Fate. Succefs will encourage me to go on, and to give Four Parts, Octavo, every Year, one each Quarter, containing about Fourteen Sheets, at the rate of One Shilling and Sixpence Englifh Money, each Part. The want of Succefs fhall be afcribed to my want of proper Abilities, and determine me to leave off immediately. The only Favour I fhall afk of my Readers in fuch a Cafe is, quickly to forget that ever any fuch Attempt was made,

All

ADVERTISEMENT

All Books of Note publish'd abroad,
which no Abstract is given, shall be exac
mention'd at the End of each Volume, w
whatever happens remarkable in the Univer
ties of Muscovy, Sweden, Denmark, G
many, Holland, Switzerland *and* France.

A Table of Contents, and an Index of
Authors cited, shall be printed with each V
lume.

My Correspondents are desired to fra
their Letters and direct them to the Rev
Mr. Droz *in* College-Green, *Dublin.*

TABLE

OF

ARTICLES.

ARTICLES.

ARTICLE VII.

A

A .

Literary Journal,

October, *November, December,* 1744.

ARTICLE I,

Hiſtoire *de* l'Academie Royale des Sciences, 1738. Avec les Memoires de Mathematique & de Phyſique, *pour la meme anneé, tirés des Re-*
gitres de cette Academie.

That is to ſay,

The Hiſtory *of the* Royal Academy of Sciences at *Paris, for the Year,* 1738. with the Mathematical and Phyſical Memoirs, for the ſame Year; taken out of the ſaid Academy's Regiſters, a large 12°.

THERE

(a) THERE are few Books of any Length which do not lose something of their Character as they encrease in Bulk. The Uniformity of the Subject, without any other Fault, disgusts the Mind, which requires Variety of Objects to amuse it, and flags without them in a Journey of some Continuance. Even the Choice of Objects is of less Importance to excite, or to keep up Attention, than their Variety. Be they what they will, as they succeed each other, they draw the Mind forward to examine them, and lead it on from one Enquiry to another. "One would think, " says the celebrated *Montaigne* (b) that " the Mind is afraid of losing itself in So- " litude, seeks something sensible to hold " by, and is ever in quest of new Objects " to lean, and to rest upon them". We are scarce acquainted with an Object, before we are sated with it, and from our natural Inconstancy, seek some where else the same Charm which recommended it at first,—its Novelty. " Our usual Gate, *says the same* " *Montaigne*, is an unsteady reeling from " right to left, forwards, backwards; up-hill, " down-hill, as the Wind blows and Objects " drive us. We scarce see a new Object,

" but

(a). Biblioth. raisonnée. Tom. xxviii. pag. 438.
(b) Essais de Montaigne, Liv. I. ch. 4. pag. 18. *Paris* 1725.

" but we will it. The Wish follows the
" Perception instantaneously almost, and as
" we seize with Greediness, we let go with
" equal haste. The *Cameleon* does not change
" its Colour with readier Obedience to the
" Objects which surround it, than we do
" our Inclinations. We determine solemnly
" this Moment. The next we have already
" chang'd our Mind—And in one Moment
" more come round again to our first
" Thought. Our Will is in perpetual Vi-
" brations, and we are ourselves Inconstancy;

Ducimur ut Nervis alienis mobile lignum.

(c) " We move not. We are carried down
" the Stream. And as the Current is either
" slow or rapid, we glide smoothly, or are
" hurried away with Violence."

Nonne videmus
Quid sibi quisque velit nescire & quærere
semper
Commutare Locum quasi Onus deponere
possit.

" Every Day has its own Whim, and the
" next brings a fresher one along with it.
" We fluctuate from one Caprice to another,
" and will nothing heartily, nothing tho-
" roughly, nothing constantly."

PART I.   b   Man

(c) Montaigne, ibid.

Man therefore, *concludes the French J*
nalift, (*d*) feeks always for fomething n
and this he always finds in the Works
the Academy of Sciences, with this a
tional Advantage, that he may exercife
Inconftancy upon Objects agreeable and
ful, as well as new.

The Gentlemen who furnifh the M
rials of this Work have chofe fo wide a Fi
that they can never want Employment,
the Beauties of Nature, and the Impro
ments of Art, are equally exhaufted :
there is nothing new to be confidered ur
Heaven, and no new Method left of c
fidering old Objects : Till every thing
been examined, and under every Light.

I intend to give at prefent an Abftrac
one Volume, and for the future, of e
Volume, when publifhed.

The Memoirs for the Year, 1738.
very curious. I fhall confine this Abft
to the following (*e*).

F

(*d*) The Author of *La Biblioth. raif.*
(*e*) There is a curious Memoir prefented to the Acade
by Mr. *Geoffroy*, on Pewter, efpecially what is Eng
But as this Subject muft be better underftood at home
by Foreigners, I thought proper to omit it.

How to make Timber for Service, strong and durable.

THIS Memoir was prefented by Mr. *Buffon*, in which he propofes *an eafy way to improve the Solidity, Strength, and Duration of Timber for Service.* The Expedient confifts in barking the Tree from top to bottom, in the rife of the Sap, and in letting it dry ftanding. What *Vitruvius* and *Evelyn* tell us on this Subject deferves fome Attention. The firft fays in his *Architecture*, " that before Trees are felled they ought to " be tapp'd at the Root, to the very Heart, " and left to dry ftanding, after which they " are much better for Service, and may be " made ufe of immediately.

The fecond relates in his *Natural Hiftory*, " that about *Stafford* in *England*, they bark " the large Trees ftanding, at the time of " the rifing of the Sap, let them dry till the " Winter following, and then cut them " down ; that the Trees ftill live without the " Bark ; that the Timber is much the hard- " er for it, and that they make as much ufe " of the Sappy part, as of the Heart *(f)*.

b 2   This

(f) This Part is call'd in French *Aubier*, and is the outermoft Ring of the Timber next the Bark. Tis weaker than the Heart.

This great Diſcovery deſerved the Attention of Naturaliſts and Architects, but they have neglected it.   Mr. *Buffon* made the following Experiments, on Timber, barked, and not barked.

A Joyſt taken out of the Body of a barked Tree weigh'd 242 Pounds; it broke under 7 thouſand 940.   The Joyſt of a Tree with its Bark, of equal Size, weigh'd 234 Pounds; it broke under 7 thouſand 320.

The Beam of a ſecond barked Tree weigh'd 249 Pounds; it yielded more than the firſt, and broke under the Load of 8 thouſand 362 Pounds.   The Beam of a Tree not barked, of equal Size, weigh'd 236; it broke under 7 thouſand 385.

The Beam of a Tree barked and expoſed to the Injuries of the Weather, weigh'd 258 Pounds; it yielded more than the ſecond, and broke under 8 thouſand 926.   The Beam of a Tree with it's Bark, of equal Size, weighed 239 Pounds, and broke under 7 thouſand 420:

The Beam of a *light-headed* Tree, which Mr. *Buffon* always judged to be the beſt, was found to weigh 263 Pounds, and broke only under the Load of 9 thouſand 46. The Tree of equal Size, weighed 238 Pounds, and broke under 7 thouſand 500.

Another

Another Experiment, much in favour of barked Timber, proves that the Timber of the Branches of a barked Tree, even with confiderable Defects, is heavier and ftronger than the Timber taken in the Trunk of a Tree juft above the Root, which was not barked, and which had no Defects.—But what follows is yet more favourable.—They took out of the fappy Part of a barked Tree, many fmall Pieces of three Feet long and one Inch Square, among which they chofe five of the beft, to break. The firft weighed 23 Ounces $\frac{5}{32}$ and broke under 287 Pound. The fecond weighed 23 Ounces $\frac{6}{32}$ and broke under 291 $\frac{1}{2}$ Pounds. The third weighed 23 Ounces $\frac{4}{32}$ and broke under 275 Pounds. The fourth weighed 23 Ounces $\frac{28}{32}$, and broke under 291 Pounds. The fifth weigh'd 23 Ounces $\frac{14}{32}$, and broke under 291 $\frac{1}{2}$ Pounds. The middling Weight is of about 23 Ounces $\frac{11}{32}$, and the middling Load of about 287 Pounds. Having made the fame Tryal with many Pieces of the Sap of an Oak with its Bark, the middling Weight was found to be of 23 Ounces $\frac{2}{32}$, and the middling Load of 248 Pounds; and having alfo done the fame thing with many Pieces of the Heart of the fame Oak not barked; the middling Weight was found to be of 25 Ounces $\frac{10}{32}$, and the middling Load of 256 Pounds.

All

All this proves, that the fappy Part of
barked Tree, is not only ftronger than
common fappy part, but even more fo th
the Heart of the Oak, though it wei
lefs than the latter. Thefe Experiments,
many others to be found in the Book, le
no Room to doubt the truth of the Fa
viz. that the Timber of Trees barked
dryed ftanding, is harder, more folid, heav
and ftronger than the Timber of Trees
down with their Bark, and confequen
more durable.

What is the phyfical Caufe of the Solid
and Strength of the Tree barked and fta
ing? It is eafy to guefs. We know t
Trees grow large by additional Stratas
new Wood, which are form'd at every R
of the Sap, between the Bark and the
Tree. Barked Trees do not form thefe n
Stratas, and though they live after they
barked, they cannot enlarge; the Subfta
defigned to form the new Wood is ftop
and muft fix in all the void Places of
fappy Part, and of the Heart itfelf, wh
neceffarily encreafes the Tree's Solidity,
confequently its Strength, fince, according
our Author, the weightieft Timber is
ftrongeft. This Explanation does not requ
to be more inlarged upon.

*Of the Cortex Peruvianus, common-
ly called, Jefuit's Bark.*

Mr. *La Condamine*, who had the Courage
to undertake a Voyage to *Peru*, with other
Members, has fent to the Academy the
Hiftory and Defcription of the Tree produce-
ing this excellent Remedy. This Relation
is much to be depended upon. Mr. *La Condamine* went to the Place where it naturally
grows, and from which it is tranfported into moft Parts of the World. Going in 1737
from *Quito* to *Lima*, he went out of his
Way to *Loxa*, to obferve this Tree.

Loxa, or *Loja*, is a fmall Town founded
in 1546 by *Mercadillo*, one of *Gonçales Pi-
zarro*'s Captains; in an agreeable Valley, on
the River *Catamayo*. The two Meridian
Heights of the Sun, which Mr. *La Condamine* obferved there, the 3d and 4th of *February* 1737, confpire to place it in the 4th
Degree and almoft one Minute of Southern
Latitude; that is to fay, neaf 70 Leagues
more to the South than *Quito*;—nearly under
the fame Meridian with it,—and about 80
Leagues from the Coaft of *Peru*. The
Elevation of its Soil is a Mean between
that of the higheft Mountains, which form
the great Girdle of the *Andes*, and that of
the Vallies on the Coaft. The Mercury
which

which ftood at about 28 Inches on the Level of the Sea at *Panama*, 8 Degrees of North Latitude, at *Manta* which lies one Degree, and at *Callao*, the Port of *Lima*, which lies 12 Degrees South Latitude, and which ftood on the higheft acceffible Mountains in the Neighbourhood of *Quito*, at 15 Inches, ftood at *Loxa* the third of *February* 1737, at 21 Inches 8 Lines; from which we may conclude, by the Comparifon of the feveral Experiments made at known Elevations, that the Level of *Loxa* above the Sea, is of about 800 Fathoms. The Climate is very pleafant, for tho' the Heats are great, they are not exceffive.

It is in the adjacent Parts of this Town that the Bark is gathered. The beft, at leaft the moft reputed, grows on the Mountain of *Cajanuma*, about two Leagues and a half from *Loxa*. From thence was taken the firft that was brought into *Europe*. Fifteen Years ago the Traders provided themfelves with a Certificate before a Notary, to fhew that the Bark they bought was of *Cajanuma*. Mr. *La Condamine* went up this Mountain the third of *February*, and fpent the Night on the top of it, in the Houfe of a Man who refides there, to have thefe Trees near at hand, their Bark making his common Occupation, and his only Trade. In his Way, on the top, and at his Return, he had the Opportunity of examining many of thofe Trees,

and

and making on the place the firft Draught of a Branch with the Leaves, the Flower, and the Seeds, which are found altogether at every Seafon of the Year. The next Day he brought with him to *Loxa*, many Branches in Bloffom, which ferved him to finifh his Draught, and to colour it naturally, fuch as it is in his Memoir.

They commonly diftinguifh three Sorts of Bark-Trees, white, yellow, and red. The yellow and red have no remarkable Difference in the Bloffom, the Leaf, the Fruit, or even in the external Bark; but in cutting, the yellow is known by its Bark, not fo high coloured and more tender. Thefe two kinds grow by one another, and their Bark is us'd indifferently. The outfide of either is equally brown, and this paffes for the fureft Mark of the Bark's Goodnefs; it is required alfo, that the outfide fhould be rough, crack'd, and brittle.

The white has a Leaf fomewhat rough, rounder, and lefs fmooth than that of the others. Its Bloffom is alfo whiter, its Seed larger, and the outfide of the Bark is whitifh. It commonly grows on the top of the Mountain, and is never found with the yellow or the red, which moft commonly grow at mid Hill, in the Hollows,

and moſt ſheltered Places. This Tree is
never found in the Plains; it grows ſtrait,
and riſes above the Trees it is ſurrounded
with, there are ſome larger than a Man's
Body; the middling ones are eight or nine
Inches in Diameter.

To ſtrip the Bark off the Tree, they
make uſe of a common Knife, the Blade of
which is held by both Hands; the Workman makes the firſt Cut, as high as he can
reach; and bearing upon it, he brings it as
low as he can. The great Conſumption
that was made of theſe Trees is the Reaſon,
why there are hardly any found now but
young ones, thick as one's Arm, and about
twelve or fifteen Feet high. All the large
Trees that were ſtripp'd died; this Opera-
tion deſtroys alſo ſome of the young ones,
but not many.

Formerly the thick Bark was moſt valued,
but at preſent the thin. The Difficulty
there is in drying the thick Bark well, is probably what has diſcredited it. The Tree
muſt be ſtripp'd of its Bark in dry Weather,
the Bark taken off, expoſed to the Sun
many Days, and not pack'd up until it is
perfectly dry.

The Leaves of this Tree are ſmooth and
of a fine green; their Circumference is
even, and in the Form of the Head of a
Spear, rounded at the lower part, and end-

ing

ing in a Point.   Their middling Meafure is
an Inch and a half or two Inches broad, and
two and a half or three Inches long, they
have a Stalk which runs up through the
middle of the Leaf, it is rounded at the
Bottom, of a deep and bright red, efpecially
the lower half, which Colour is often
communicated to the whole Leaf in its
Maturity.   Each Branch at the top of the
Tree terminates in one or many Bunches
of Bloffoms, which refemble, before they
are blown, by their Figure, and blue and
afh Colour, the Flowers of Lavender. When
the Buds open they alter their Colour, the
Flower is much of the fame Bignefs and
Form as the Hyacinth.   When the Bloffom drops, the Calix fwells in the Form
of an Olive, and as it grows changes into
a Fruit with two Cells; while it dries it
fhortens and becomes more round, and
parts at laft from top to bottom into two
Semi-Shells feparated by a Partition, and
lined with a yellowifh, fmooth, and thin
Skin; out of which fall reddifh, flat, and
in a manner leavy Seeds, many of which
have not half a Line Diameter.   Thefe
Seeds refemble in Shape, but are lefs than
thofe of the Elm.   The Author's Memoir gives a very ample Defcription of the
Leaves, Bloffoms, Fruit, and Seeds of this
Tree.

The

The Virtues of the Bark, tho' acknowledged and experienced in the whole Can-
ton of *Loxa*, were long unknown to the
reft of the World.　The Difcovery of 'this
Remedy was occafioned by an obftinate ter-
tian Ague, of which the Countefs of *Chinchon* could not be cured for many Months.
It was in 1638.　The *Corregidor* of ˎ*Loxa*
came to *Lima*, prepared the Bark, and after
fome Experiments made on other fick Perfons, the Countefs took the Remedy and
was cured.　She immediately ordered a great
Quantity of the fame Bark to be brought to
her from *Loxa*.　She diftributed it to all
thofe that wanted it, and it was known
then under the Name of the *Countefs's Powder*.　Some Months after fhe left that Care
to the Jefuits, who continued to diftribute
it *gratis*, and it was then called, *Jefuits
Powder*.　They fent fome to Cardinal *Lugo*
at *Rome*; at whofe Palace it was diftributed
gratis, and afterwards at the Apothecary's
Shop of the *Roman* College, where it was
given *gratis* to the Poor, and fold at a high
Price to others.　They affure us, that the
head Jefuit of *Peru*, going to *Rome* through
France, cured the then Dauphin, afterwards
Lewis XIV. of an Ague, with the Bark.

In 1640. the Count and Countefs of
Chinchon being returned to *Spain*, *Juan
de Vega* their Phyfician, who had brought
　　　　　　　　　　　　　　　　with

with him a Provision of Bark, fold it at *Seville*, at the Rate of a hundred Reals the pound. This remedy loft much of its Reputation. The Inhabitants of *Loxa*, not able to furnish the great Quantities demanded, mixed other Barks in the Bales they fent to the Fairs of *Panama*, for the *Galleons*. Merchants would hardly then give half a Piafter the pound, inftead of Four and Six, it was formerly fold for at *Panama*, and Twelve at *Seville*. In 1690. many thoufand Weight of it remained at *Picera* on the Quay of *Payta*, the neareft Port to *Loxa*, no body willing to fhip it. This begun the Ruin of *Loxa*, which is now as poor as it was wealthy when it's Commerce flourifhed.

The Barks mixed with the Jefuit's, to encreafe it's Weight and Bulk, are the *Alizier* and the *Cucharilla*. The firft has a more ftiptick Tafte, and the Colour more red in the Infide, and more white at the Outfide. The fecond comes from a Tree very common in that Country, which no other way refembles that of the Jefuits but by the Bark. To prevent this Fraud, they now vifit every Bale at *Payta*, where the greateft part of Jefuits Bark, defigned for *Europe*, is fhip'd for *Panama*. Mr. *La Condamine* was Witnefs to this; yet it does not prevent the Buyers from being cheated.

Loxa

Loxa is not the only Place wh
Bark is found; there is fome at A
near *Rio Bamba*, near *Cuença*, and
Mountains of *Jaen*. This laft
efteem'd, and is thought of the Whi
mentioned above.

The Name of *Quinquina* is An
but the Bark is only known there un
Name of *Corteza*, or *Caxara de L*
more commonly *Cafcarilla*. There
ther Tree very famous, and known i
ral Provinces of Southern *America*,
the Name of *Quina-Quina*, and in th
vince of *Mayna*, on the *Maranon*, und
Name of *Tatche*. They make ufe
Seeds, named by the Spaniards *Pepi*
Quina, to make Fumigations, which
pretend to be Salutary and Strength
The Root of this Tree, always called *S*
Quina by the Natives, and by the
Name afterwards by the *Spaniards*,
for an excellent Febrifuge, before
Difcovery of the Tree of *Loxa*.
Jefuits of *Pez*, or *Chuquiabo*, ufed tc
it to *Rome*, under it's true Name of *Q*
Quina, where it was prefcribed for inte
ing Fevers. The Bark of *Loxa* comir
Rome through the fame Channel, the
Febrifuge was confounded with the
and that of *Loxa* having prevailed, it
tain'd the Name of the firft, now al
int

intirely forgot. *Badus (k)* confounded thefe two Trees, not knowing the old. Mr. *La Condamine* took the moft part of the fore-going Hiftorical hints, from a Manufcript kept in the Library of the College of the *Jefuits* at *Lima*, and wrote by *Don Diego de Herrera*, who died in 1712, aged near 100 Years. As he had run over the whole Kingdom of *Peru*, he may be efteem'd an Eye Witnefs of the Facts he relates. The Title of the Work is; *De cortice Quinæ-Quinæ & de Loxa, etfi diverfarum arborum uniformis virtutis.* This MSS. is but a Part of a larger Work, with this Title, *Circa Materias Peruanas, fcilicet de Thermis, de aquis, de Morbis endemiis, regionalibus,* &c.

Of Monfters.

EVer fince it has been difcovered that all Animals are produced by Eggs, and that all their Parts being contained in their Cover, want only a proper Manifeftation to appear in their natural Form, the Syftems about Monfters, have been reduced to Two, which include at once all the poffible Caufes and Differences of that Formation. The Firft Syftem is this: There are Sperms effentially monftrous, or that are original-

B 4

ly

(k) Bad. Anaft. Cort. Per. Cap. 1.

ly formed fuch, and, as well as the Natural ones, only want a proper Agent to unfold them. In the fecond Syftem, the Formation of Monfters is imputed to accidental Caufes. There is but one kind of Eggs, all the Parts they contain are originally in a natural Order, they become Monfters only by a kind of Chance, that is to fay, by the fortuitous Concourfe of accidental Caufes, which act the more eafily on the Sperm of the Egg, as it is but a kind of ropy Matter, whofe Parts, being foft, delicate, and fupple, quickly receive all extraordinary Impreffions.

Mr. *Du Verney* a Favourer of the firft Syftem, gave a Memoir in 1706. with the Defcription of a Monfter compofed of two Male Children joined together at the lower Part of the Belly, called the *Hypogaftric* Region. All the other Parts, both external and internal, were like thofe of other Children, from the Head to the Place of Junction, where they were furprifingly monftrous. Mr. *Du Verney* concludes from his Examination of thefe Parts, that they are not the Work of Chance, but the Effect of a Defign form'd and executed by a free and all-powerful Intelligence. He pretends, that the Infpection of this Monfter fhews the Creator's infinite fkill in Mechanicks.

Mr. *Lemery* declares himfelf for the fecond Syftem. He now gives a Memoir againft Mr. *Du Verney.* He pretends, that fince

the

the Monſter, deſcribed by the ſaid Author, is formed of two very diſtinct Children, there is Reaſon to think that the two Sperms, naturally ſeparated, met in the Womb, and were united in conſequence of the Softneſs and Flexibility of their Parts, which mutually penetrated one another, and were mixed. What is often taken Notice of in Vegetables, corroborates Mr. *Lemery*'s reaſoning : two Apples, two Pears, two Cherries joyn'd together, are Monſters. Are we to believe theſe Fruits were ſuch in their Origin, or that they were diſtinct at firſt? Have we not Reaſon to think, that the Proximity and mutual Contact united them? the Grafts ſeem to prove it ; they unite themſelves to the Tree they are grafted in, and make together but one ſingle Tree.

Examples of ſuch Junctions are ſeen every Day, there is in the Foreſt of *Bologne* ſuch an intimate Union between two Oaks, that the Name of Marriage has been given to it. This Union was made by a Branch from each Tree, which met and penetrated one another ſo, that they are now perfectly joyned ; why ſhould not ſuch Unions be made between the Parts of the two Fœtuſes, eſpecially when they are yet but Sperms, lately fallen in the Womb.

But what proves the Union of the two Fœtuſes in the above mentioned Monſter, to be the Effect of Chance, is this ; at the

Place

Place of their Junction, Mr. *Du Ver*.
tinctly perceiv'd a Scar, which he ca
inserted in the first Figure of his M
and by which he declared that the
seemed to be joyn'd together ; does n
Cicatrice suppose a *Solution of Cont*
and afterwards a Reunion by the nou
Juices at the Extremity of the cut Pa

Another Reason ; the Place of th
Fœtuses Junction is the only one tha
tains monstrous parts ; every where ell
are in their natural Condition. Ar
reason of it is, because the Place c
Junction is the only one that was e:
to the Stress of the Pressure.

Add to this, that in the above M
nothing is to be seen but Disorder and
fusion, every thing is overturned ; ar
Mr. *Lemery* explains very well by the
sideration of the Monstrous Parts. M
this be imputed to the Author of N
and is it not better to ascribe it to th
tuitous and immediate Action of some
dental Cause. Mr. *Lemery* inlarges
this in a second Memoir, but as he i
to give two more, and as Mr. *Winslow*
appear in the Defence of Mr. *Du V*
System, it is proper to wait for those I
which I shall give an Account of, as
as they come over.

Of the Action of a Musket-Ball, which may run through a solid Body, without moving it Sensibly.

MR. *Camus* propofes and examines in his Academical Memoirs, the following Phænomenon. *A Door which you may eafily move on its Hinges by pufhing it with the Finger's-end, does not appear to be moved by a Musket-Ball, which ftrikes it with a fufficient Force to pierce it through : It even happens that the greater the Swiftnefs of the Ball is, the lefs is communicated to the Door.* Mr. *Camus* explains this Problem by an Algebraic and Analytic Calculation, and Mr. *Fontenelle*, to make the Solution the more intelligible, confiders it phyfically. Natural Philofophy fays he, *fhews why and how a thing is ; Calculation how far it is fo, and what may be its Variations.*

" It appears to us, fays Mr. *Fontenelle*,
" that the Solution of the prefent Queftion
" depends on a Principle fomewhat Paradoxi
" cal, but receiv'd in the *Elements of Geo
" metry de Infinito* ; which is, that no Im
" pulfion, let it appear ever fo fhort and in
" ftantaneous, is to be made in a Time infi
" nitely fhort ; every Effect requires a Finite
" Time. A limited Time, tho' ever fo
" fhort, is therefore requifite to pufh the
" Door

" Door with the Hand: Since that
" is limited, another Time may be t
" and this would not be long eno
" push the Door. The Time during
" a Ball, whose Swiftness enables
" run through the Door, shall move,
" will, a Line, is prodigiously shor
" may very easily be shorter than the
" necessary to push the Door, the
" length ; consequently the Ball, t
" of its great Swiftness, will not put
" Door, and, because of that same
" ness, will pierce it.

When the Ball has in the least pene
the Thickness of the Door, it loses so
it's Celerity in the Action of Piercing
it may lose it so, that having no more
a certain Degree of it, it shall only
If this happens precisely when the Do
been pierced through, the Ball, whic
then has been piercing, pushes in tha
Moment, and it will be the same Ca
if a Ball, moved with a certain deter
Swiftness, had struck a quiet Body
certain Mass. The Effect will follo
Laws of Motion in the Percussion of B
perfectly hard and without Elasticity.

If the Ball has not the Strength
through the whole thickness of the D
pushes whilst it ceases to pierce, and p
so much the more, as it retains the
of it's original Celerity, for tho'

in the Action of piercing, it moves yet because it follows the Door push'd, which yields to it. It is plain that if the Ball goes through the whole Thickness and further, it does not push, and is the further from being able to do it, in as much as it had originally a greater Celerity.

Mr. *Camus* joins to this Fact, two common Experiments, 1. If you put a Card on the End of your Finger, and a Crown on the Card, in such a Manner that the End of the Finger answers exactly the middle of the Crown; in striking the Edge of the Card with a Fillip, the Card will slip between the Crown and the Finger, and the Crown will remain on the Finger's end. 2. If you put a Napkin well roll'd up in a Glass, and a Piece of Money on the Top of the Napkin, you may by a dextrous sudden Stroke, throw the Napkin out of the Glass without overturning it; it will slip from under the Piece, and the Piece will fall into the Glass. You see in this last Experiment, that the Stick makes the Napkin bend in the middle, that the two Ends of it draw near each other, that the lower End rises and comes out of the Glass, that the upper End sinks, and that all this is effected before the two Ends can be horizontally carried away. The two Ends of the Napkin draw near one another in obedience to its bending, which is the first Effect of the Percussion,

Percuffion, which cannot give at once to the whole Napkin as great a Swiftnefs as that which it gives to its middle Part, and it is in this that the Experiment has fome Relation to the Ball which pierces a Door thro' and thro', without communicating to it any fenfible Degree of Motion.

ARTICLE II.

The Hiftory of the Royal Academy for the Year 1739. a large 12°.

(a) AMONGST the many curious Subjects contained in this Volume, I fhall, for the Prefent, mention only the two following.

The firft concerns an extraordinary Sleepynefs of a Woman 27 Years old. The Phænomenon is furprizing, tho' not without Example. This Woman, married the 22d of *April*, 1738, a Man of 60, lived with him, without any Indifpofition, to the 22d of *June* the fame Year; fhe then flept for three Days without awaking, or a Poffibility of being awaked; fhe at laft awaked naturally, called immediately for fome Bread, and, whilft fhe was eating it, fell afleep again in about five or fix Minutes. This fecond Sleep lafted thirteen whole Days, during which

(a) See Bib. raif. Tom. 31. pag. 172.

which time fhe neither eat nor drank, nor had any other Evacuation but her monthly ones which were perfectly regular. She continued waking at this time near as long as the former; eat Bread again, anfwered natural Calls, and fell afleep again, but only for nine Days; for it was thought the Sleep would be every time longer. During the Remainder of the Year 1738, her Life was but a continual odd Alternative of Sleeps exceffively long, and of fhort and much difproportioned Wakings. The fhorteft Sleep was of three Days, and the longeft of thirteen: her longeft Wakings lafted half an Hour, at one time indeed fhe was awake for three Hours, and at another twenty four; but this happen'd after her having taking an Emetic, and being bled in the Arm, and in the Foot.

This Woman's Sleep was fuch a dead one, that fhe could not be rouzed out of it, even by warming her Fingers, till they were almoft burnt. As to the reft, it was extremely eafy and natural, no Agitation, no extraordinary Heat, the Refpiration very free, the Pulfe in good Order, and even fomewhat ftrong, the Colour of her Face not at all altered, and a gentle Perfpiration, as in a State of Health.

Tho', as I have faid, we have Inftances of fuch extraordinary Sleeps, thefe Cafes are not lefs aftonifhing and difficult to be accounted for. It is a Pity the Academy's

Hiftorian

Hiftorian could not give us the Sequel of this Event.

Here is another Fact no lefs fingular, but more eafy to conceive. A Woman, happily delivered of her fixth Child, felt a few Days after her Lying-in, a Pain, but very tolerable, in the hypogaftric Region of the left Side. Her Belly began to grow by Degrees larger, the Pain that had been fixed to the left Side, became general in the whole Cavity of the Belly, and more violent. Having for five Years received no Relief, either from Phyficians or Empyrics, fhe gave herfelf up to her growing Pain. The Swelling increafed to fuch a Degree, in the two following Years, that the Patient could not lie in her Bed but on her Knees, fupported on her Elbows, her Face againft the Bolfter, becaufe her Belly was to be lodged in a large empty Space funk into the Middle of the Bed. She did not come out of it the three laft Months of her Sicknefs; till then fhe had been ftill ftirring in her Houfe, and performed her natural Functions, as ufual. The courfe of her Menftrua had been pretty well the three firft Years, but the three laft was entirely ftop'd.

After fhe was dead, they took out of her Body by Punction, forty-two Pints of a Water, refembling Coffee in Confiftence and Colour, and without any Smell. At the opening of the Body they faw a large Cyfte, or Bag,

out

out of which this prodigious Quantity of
Water issued, that fill'd almost the whole
Capacity of the Belly, so that it had reduced
all the Intestines to the third Part of their
natural Size; and that at the first sight they
were surprised, not seeing the Bowels of the
lower Belly. The Liver, grown skirrous,
had been drove against the Diaphragm, and
the Diaphragm along with it to the Middle
of the Thorax; the Spleen and the Gall
Bladder were quite disfigured. It is easy to
account for all these Disorders caused by the
Extension of the Cyste; but what is this
Cyste, or what was the Part that had been
so enormously extended? The Surgeon that
made the Dissection thinks it was the left
Ovarium.

Every Physician, every Surgeon, that will
reflect on the Circumstances of this dreadful
Disorder, may thereby learn to judge, with
more Certainty, of its Nature, of its Progress, of its Effects, when a like Case shall
offer; and for ought I know it may have
been seen many times, without any body's
being able to guess what it was.

In this Memoir is contained an Instance of
the Efficacy of Mrs. *Stephens*'s Remedy to
cure the Stone. Messieurs *Geoffroy* and *Morand* communicated to the Academy the following Experiment. A Man of about 55
Years of Age, who had long labour'd under
all the Symptoms of the Stone, and the

PART I.　　　　C　　　　most

moſt painful ones, was perfectly cured in three Months. The two above named Gentlemen were Witneſſes of the Fact, and are good Judges. It is true, the Man was not probed after the Cure, to be certain that there remained no Sone in the Bladder, conſequently this Experiment cannot be intirely relied upon. It may be ſaid ſtill that the Patient might have received ſome Relief, and that the Stone, without been diſſolved, may have ceaſed for a while to cauſe Pain. Have not Stones of a conſiderable ſize been found in the Bladders of People, who during the whole Courſe of their Lives had never felt the cruel Pains commonly attending this Diſorder? *We ſhall not be any more in Doubt,* ſays Mr. Fontenelle, *when Patients well cured, to all Appearances, and who were found by the Probe to have the Stone before the Uſe of the Remedy, ſhall be probed again after the Cure, or opened when dead of ſome other Diſorder, and no Stone found in them.*

It remains to know if the Probe is always a ſure Means of diſcovering whether a Patient really has the Stone; ſome People think not. However, it muſt be own'd it is the one leaſt liable to Error; ſo the whole Certainty of the Remedy's Efficacy depends on a great Number of well *certified, well averred Experiments made by ſkilful Perſons.*

ARTICLE

ARTICLE III.

Hans Egede ...... Nachricht von .... der Groenlandischen Mission.

That is to say,

A Relation of the Mission of Groenland *by* John Egede *Missionary,* &c. Hamburg, 1740. 2. *Tom.* 4°. *Tom.* I. *pag.* 288. *Tom.* II. *pag.* 131. *besides the Prefaces,* 11 *Cuts and* 1 *Geographical Map.*

AS there is already an Abstract of this Book in the *London Magazine* for *December*, and continued in *January, (a)* translated from the *French* of *La Bibliotheque Raisonnée (b)*, I shall confine my self to the essential Articles contained in it, correct two Mistakes of the *English* Translator, and add a few Reflections on the *Groenlanders*, and some thoughts on Missions in general. " *(c)* Ancient *Groenland* is a vast Tract of the Continent of *America*, to which it belongs, rather than to *Europe*, as it lies on

C 2 the

(a) The Dublin Edit:
(b) Biblioth. raif. Tom. 31. pag. 37.
(c) What is contained between these two " is almost entirely given in the Words of the Magazine, and that for the sake of those of my Readers that have not that Book. This is given above the fourteen Sheets promised in the Advertisement.

the other fide of the firft Meridian, from 325 to 340 Degrees of Longitude. It is joined to the Continent of *America*, above the 78 Degree of Latitude where it forms what the *Englifh* call *Baffin's-Bay.* -|- On the other Side, it is fuppofed, but without certainty, to be joined to the Continent of *Spitzberg.*

It runs Southward terminating in a Point almoft like *Afric*, and ends at 59 Degrees, 50 Min. by Cape *Farewell.* By a Voyage which the Author undertook, and by the unanimous Report of all the Natives of the Country, he was convinced, that this vaft Promontory is not cut thro' by Streights, and that *Forbifher's* Streights are no other than a Bay, which does not communicate with the Weftern and Eaftern Seas. This is a confiderable Correction to be made in Mr. *de l'Ifle's* and Mr. *Moll's* Maps.

According to this Pofition, *Groenland* has two long Coafts, which join to the South. Mr. *Egede* travelled on the Weftern Coaft, from 60 to 65 Deg. and his Son was beyond 69 Deg. where he now refides in Quality of a Miffionary. The Seas which wafh it to to South, are called *Davis's* Streights, and more to the North lies *Baffin's-Bay.*

But the Eaftern Coaft, tho' nigher to *Iceland*, from which it is but about forty Miles diftant, is almoft entirely unknown. Frightful Shoals of Ice render it inacceffible to

European

European Veffels; the ufual Accefs to it is by Land, and that from the Weftern Coaft. The *Groenlanders*, however, attempt the Paffage at the Hazard of their Lives, fometimes by Sea in their Canoes, and fometimes even on the Ice.

Settlements in *Groenland* have been attempted feveral Times, and Colonies fubfifted there for feveral Years, but afterwards perifhed by the Severity of the Climate, fo that it may truly be faid that *Groenland* was not known till 1721. and that the Merit of the Difcovery is entirely to be afcribed to Mr. *Egede*.

As to the Product of this Country, the Trees are low Birch, feldom above twelve Feet high, Alders and Willows; their Plants are Scurvy-grafs, Honey-dew, which is a kind of Manna, and an infallible Cure for the Scurvy; Angelica, Tormentil, and half a Dozen other Plants, which are not found beyond 65 Deg. for farther North, even Grafs is a foreign Commodity. Corn never comes to Perfection under the 64th Deg. only Coleworts and Radifhes will anfwer, as in this Country no Plants will do, but fuch whofe feed ripens in two Months at fartheft after fowing, and fuch as in this fhort Summer, can ftand out againft very nipping Winds, and very piercing Colds,

C 3

Upon

Upon what can a Man live in a Country, wherein nothing grows, and that has no Trade? Whales Flesh, Fish, a kind of Bacon made of Sea-Calves, and Legs of Rein-deer, which last are reckoned delicious though tough. This is what the *Groenlanders* feed upon, they know nothing of Bread, Pulse, Fruits, Milk, or even Salt.

It is not uncommon to find in this extreme Part of the North hot Mineral Waters: They have such in *Iceland,* and even a Volcano. There is also Verdegris, Lead-Ore, Iron, Cryftals, and Afbeftus.

The Heavens are not more favourable here than the Earth. Their Summers are expofed to dreadful Tempefts ; and the Mountains of Ice, with which the inland Country is entirely covered, render the Nights very cold, even when the Sun has it's greatest Power. Then imagine what their Winters are. They begin in *August,* and are not over till *May.* The Intenfity of the Cold is exceffive ; in 68 Deg. Spirits of Wine freeze. There is not even Snow to cover the Ground, it being nothing but Ice, which fometimes looks beautiful. There are Rocks of white Ice, as alfo of blue, which is produced from fresh Water, and there is Ice perfectly green, which is produced from falt Water. Mr. *Egede* upon diffolving it, found that the Colour

difap-

difappeared, not becaufe that Colour, as he thinks, confifts in a volatile Sulphur. The perpetual Ice in the Ice-houfe of *Switzer-land* is of a beautiful azure Colour; diffolve it, and it becomes clear Water; but do not diffolve it, and a fmall piece will appear no other than common Ice, for Ice muft be of a great thicknefs to have any Colour, and the Water of which it is formed, does not appear blue, but when the Bottom is not feen.

The Fogs in this Country are almoft un-interrupted and very inconvenient, as they hinder the Inhabitants from Fifhing, without which they have no other means of fubfifting.

As to the *Aurora borealis*, 'tis thither one muft go to fee it in Perfection. It appears regularly after new Moon, and fhines fo bright that one may read by it's Light. It is a Fire which diffufes itfelf with aftonifhing Swiftnefs all over the Horizon."

Mr. *Egede* fays, that in Groenland, *the Tides are very high and very ftrong after the new and full Moon*; and adds this particular Re-mark, *that at the Flow of thefe Tides there appear a great many Springs not obferved before, and which fubfide when they Ebb.* The Tranflator fays (d) that this *Phænomenon is*

C 4   *well*

(d) Lond. Magaz.

Z.

well attested; and on the contrary the Author of the *French* Abstract argues by way of supposition; *if this Phænomenon was well averred, it would please those Naturalists who derive the Origin of Springs from the Sea,* &c. Then the Fact is not sufficiently attested. It is to be wish'd, that Mr. *Egede* would give an Answer to this Paragraph of *La Bibliotheque raisonnée,* and more fully evidence the Fact in Question; which, if true, is certainly a strong presumption in favour of the System that subterraneous Canals do convey Water from the Sea to the Mountains. Till then we must suspend our Judgment.

" In so barren a Country, Animals cannot but be scarce : Rein-deer live here, who by a natural Instinct break through the Snow with their Feet, in order to come at a kind of Moss which they feed upon. Here are likewise white or grey Roe-bucks, white Hares, and Dogs, like those of *Osbia,* as indolent and stupid in their kind, as their Masters. But Cows, Horses and Sheep cannot live here; whereas there is plenty of them in *Iceland.*

There is abundance of Birds, some have a very charming Note. And this is a peculiar Privilege of the *North*; for under the torrid Zone the Birds are very beautiful, but their Note is disagreeable.

The

The Sea is better peopled than the Land. Here are Whales of different forts, as Nar-whals and Cachillots, several kinds of Sea-Calves, and Salmon. 'Tis the Sea, not the Earth, which fupports the Natives.

As indifferent as the *Groenlanders* are, they do not want Induftry to avail them-felves of the Plenty of their Seas. They boldly attack the Whales, and kill them with Harping-hooks, and Spears; they have no other Veffels than Canoes; fome of thefe are made of the fmalleft Skins; they are work'd by Men, who never row in large ones; thefe they leave to the Care of Women as there is no great Danger, nor Dexterity requifite in managing of them. A *Groenlander* enters one of the fmalleft, blows it, fets out upon the Waves, not minding their Rage; they exert their utmoft to overfet this piti-ful Veffel, and he with a ftroke of the Oar brings it to an Equilibrium again. They make thefe fmall Canoes fcour very fwift, fo as to go twelve (e) *German* Miles a Day. In thefe they go from Time to Time, in fearch of Sea-Calves. They have befides other methods of taking them; fometimes they
crawl

(e) A *German* Mile is two *French* Leagues, or near fix of our *Englifh* Miles.

crawl along the Ground to furprife them in Holes in the Ice ; fometimes they furround them in little Lakes, where they catch them with Nets, and kill them upon the Ice ; at other times they drive forwards upon a fort of moveable Trivet, that they may not make a Noife, being fure of their Aim, as foon as the Animal fhows his Snout.

The Houfes in *Greenland* are not ill contrived ; for they are very long, and one of them is fufficient for feven or eight Families: They are built of Stone or Turf, about 10 or 11 Feet high ; on one Side are Windows made of the Guts of Sea Calves ; on the other Side are kinds of Beds, made of Boards which reft upon Pofts, and are covered with Skins of thefe Animals. The Roof is flat, and the whole Houfe is covered with old Hides which have been ufed for the little Canoes already mentioned. The Doors are very low, fo that they creep in ; as a greater opening would too freely admit Air. The Boards ferve alfo for Tables and Chairs. The Women work upon them on one fide, and the Men on the other. For here, as among the *Hottentots,* the Women are not fuffered to come into the Men's Company, they dare not eat before them, and they do all the Work of the Houfe. The fame thing is obfervable in the Accounts given us of the Caraïbes ; and generally the more ftupid and

barbarous

barbarous a People are, the more Women are ill ufed.

To return to their Huts. In thefe is kept up a conftant Fire, but their Hearths are only large Lumps of Stone, in which they burn the Fat of Whales; for they have fcarce any Wood, as not a Tree grows towards the North. They drefs their Victuals at thefe Fires or Lamps in Marble or Brafs Kettles. They have befides feven or eight other fmaller Lamps, conftantly burning in the fame Apartment, which yield fo much Heat as obliges all within the Houfe to go almoft naked. What is moft difagreeable to Europeans is the Stench, but the Groenlanders like it. In Summer they quit their Huts and range up and down to fifh and hunt. They ufe then a fort of oblique Tents, like thofe of the Tartars, near the Cafpian Sea. This Exercife is very difficult and dangerous, for they are obliged to hunt the Rein-deer amidft Rocks covered with Ice, and purfue the Fifh upon a Sea always half frozen, and very tempeftuous.

The Groenlanders are generally of low Stature, their Nofe large and flat, of a brown Complexion, and have weakly Eyes; which is occafioned by the fharpnefs of the Winds. They are heedlefs, difpaffionate, timorous; but fo hofpitable, that they chearfully give part of what they have to eat, to any Stranger, without expecting either Entreaties or Thanks.

Thanks. Their Dreſs is ſuitable to the Climate; it is compoſed of Sea-calves Guts and Skins, made ſo as to keep them up in the Water, by means of the Air which it takes in; it is like a Bowl put into Water. By Help of this they launch without any Fear into the Sea, and bear themſelves up like Water Fowls near a Whale, when they are cutting out it's fat.

The Women's Dreſs is very near the ſame, but they keep themſelves neater. They put on Laces or Borders made of their prettieſt Skins; they are fond of Coral Bracelets, and love Variety of Colours; their Deſire of pleaſe-ing induces the Belles of *Groenland* to em-broider even their Faces, which they do with the Point of a Needle: An odd Way of De-coration much practiſed in *America*.

Polygamy is not prohibited, yet is rare; for a Man muſt be rich to have two or three Wives, which Number they rarely exceed, and moſt of them have but one. When a Man has more than one, the firſt married has the Precedence: This is very well judged, as it is a kind of Comfort to her when the Huſband takes a new Wife. Theſe Wives live together without any Jealouſy; for they are happy enough in this Country, not to know that delicate Paſſion: Yet the *Groen-landers* are not unpractiſed in Gallantry, even when criminal. Before the Arrival of the *Danes*, they frequently had very undecent

Feaſts;

Feafts; they even ufed to pay their Magici-
ans, for what is reckoned the greateft Af-
front among other People. But the *Danes*
have now much reformed them. The young
Women never come to thefe Feafts; they
have always fhewn a great Referve, and they
are feldom marry'd againft their Liking.
Even after they are lawfully married, whether from Fafhion or Modefty, they are not
feen for fome time.

Their Marriages are not very ftrict, for
the Hufband divorces his Wife without Ceremony, if fhe is difagreeable or barren;
which, as among the *Jews*, is reckoned a
Difgrace. But thefe Divorces are rare.

The Women accuftomed to work for the
Men, feel fcarce any Pain in Child-bearing,
but immediately return to their Work: The
Child is not more tender, for his firft Food
is Whale-Oil.

Mankind is the fame every where; even
the *Groenlanders* have their Pleafures, Diver-
fions, Balls, and Exercifes. The next Neighbours meet, for there are no Villages, nor
Hamlets among thefe wandering People.
They eat heartily, beat on the Tabor and
dance to it: they wreftle in different Manners, they hang themfelves by the Feet,
fwing upon Ropes, or play at Foot-ball.

But there is another Exercife, which the
Reader will fcarce expect in *Groenland*, it is
Poetry; and what is more, Satire. Two
Wits

Wits fend each other a Challenge in form ; both fides prepare for the Conteſt, each compoſes Invectives againſt his Antagoniſt. The day appointed, the Aggreſſor begins firſt, and chants his Satire to the Beat of a Tabor ; when he has done, his Antagoniſt riſes, and returns, in Tune, the ſharpeſt Reproaches. The other replies, and ſo on alternately, till one of them has exhauſted both his Spleen and his Poetry, he who is firſt ſilenced is vanquiſhed and ſubmits. The *Icelanders* have the ſame Cuſtom, and they compoſe Satires ſo virulent as to cauſe their Antagoniſts to hang themſelves." Would not a *Groenlander*, think we, judge much in the ſame manner of Wit and Humour, ſhould he chance to ſee what paſſes in the Univerſities of *Europe*, not to mention the Manner in which the moſt part of learned Diſputes are carried on in our Writings ?

The *Groenlanders* profeſs a kind of Religion, (if it deſerves the Title) which conſiſts chiefly in the Belief of the Immortality of the Soul, and a double reſidence for it ; the one in Heaven, known only to them by Tempeſts and frightful Meteors, and therefore deſigned for undeſerving Men ; the other under Earth, where they have plenty of Proviſion, and their God reſides with his ſuppoſed Mother, reſerved for Women who die in Child-bed, and Men drowned in Fiſhing.

Theſe

Thefe are their Heroes. *(f)* The Tranflator
adds *a fign of their good Underflanding!* It
feems he did not rightly apprehend the meaning of his Original; the *French* Author inftead of ridiculing the poor *Groenlanders* for
their Notions of *Heroifm*, compares them to
ours, and gives the Preference to the former. *Are they,* fays he, *lefs rational than
we who give the Name of Heroes to the De-
ftroyers of Mankind?* Surely no great Name
was ever fo proftituted. *Alexander, Cæfar, &c.*
have been celebrated as Heroes for their
numberlefs Barbarities. What did not the
beft among the *French* Poets, *Boileau, Ra-
cine, Pavillon,* &c. fay in praife of their
Lewis the XIVth? and what are thefe pretended Heroes but horrid Monfters? A true
notion of Heroifm muft be relative to the
Faculties and Power of the Hero, confidered as to his Situation in Life. Our beft
Actions if applied to an Angel would hardly
deferve the leaft Attention, and fome general proofs of good Nature, Humanity, Firm-
nefs, true Courage, and the like Virtues,
which we are fo well pleafed with in a Sa-
vage, muft be carried to a fuperior degree
by a politer *European*, to draw our Admiration. If this Notion of *Heroifm* be juft,
a *Groenlander*, who to provide his Family,
his Neighbours, his Friends, with the Neceffaries

cessaries of Life exposes his own, is really a Hero.

Mr. *Egede* tells us, that the Small-pox brought from *Denmark* to *Groenland* is so fatal to it's Inhabitants; that of many thou-sands infected with it, scarce one recovers. This cannot be imputed to any known Cause, but their being deprived of Remedies and Physicians to apply them properly. This is a convincing proof of the usefulness of Phy-sic. If without it's help, the small-Pox alone is so fatal, what Destruction would it make in these Regions, where hardly one in ten escapes it, were we equally destitute of that same help? If the hardy Constitution of a *Groenlander*, inured to Labour and Fatigue, cannot resist one single Disorder, what would become of the delicate and weakened *Europeans* exposed to so many, if deprived of proper Remedies?

The peaceable Disposition of the *Groenlanders* is very remarkable. They have not even a word for War. They express the utmost Surprise and Concern when they see any severity used to a Soldier, or a Slave. Is he a Dog? say they. This, I apprehend, may be judged as a peremptory Answer to the famous Mr. *Hobbes*'s Principle, that *Men are naturally in a state of War.* The *Groenlanders* demonstrate innate Benevolence and generous Affections.— What they do proceeds from uncultivated Nature.—They live cor-
dially

dially together.— Numerous Families never
part.— They have no Weapons but thofe
requifite to protect them againft wild Beafts,
or procure them Subfiftence. How happy
would politer Nations be, if with their
Knowledge they had preferved their natural
Innocency, and focial Affections!

(g) There is an Obfervation in *la Biblio-
theque raifonnée*, which deferves Infertion.
The Journalift obferves the Indifference of
Proteftants as to the Converfion of Infidels,
often objected to them by the Church of
Rome, and urged as a proof of their want
of proper Zeal; but then affigns fuch reafons, as demonftrate how they have great
Advantages in this point, no way arifing from
a larger fund of Zeal, but more favourable
Circumftances. — They have an infinite
Number of Ecclefiaftics under the abfolute
Command of their Head.— They have nothing to lofe; nor dare they, if they had a
mind, refufe a blind Obedience to their Superior's Orders. The Church's Doctrine
about that kind of good Work's,—it's Ca-
nonization,—the Power the Miffionaries obtain over their Converts,—the Hopes of re-
covering by their Miffion part of that dear
Liberty, which in general they have unwil-
lingly facrificed to their Convents, and which
ought to be purchafed at any rate,— a kind

PART I.　　　D　　　　of

of Empire in the *Indies*,—and in Cafe of Misfortunes, a diftinguifhed Place in Heaven. Thefe are fufficient Springs to raife a Zeal for Converfions. The over-grown Power of the Church greatly facilitates thefe Undertake-ings. She can procure powerful recom-mendations, free and open Accefs every where, Treafures, fecret Agents; nothing is wanting. And yet, with all thefe helps, what kind of Chriftians do they make.— Four Popes fuc-ceffively blufhed at the Converfions in *China* ; and the moft artful Society in the World could not hinder them from publicly own-ing that it is impoffible to be a Chriftian, and at the fame time adore Anceftors who died in Paganifm.—Is it edifying to fee Fa-ther *Quechelli* (*h*) driving his Flock to Church, with a Cudgel in his Hand ; or to fee Monks founding a Monarchy in *Paraguay* ?—What Neophytes are thofe *Chinefe* who never heard Chrift's Paffion preached ? Or thofe *Ame-ricans* who without referve prefer his Mo-ther to him; *She is always good, and he al-ways ready to punifh.* (*i*)

Proteftants have in proportion a fmall number of Ecclefiaftics, who for the moft part marry, (without Sin I hope, fince the Apoftles themfelves were married,) and yet
this

(*h*) Relation *du Congo*. Viérne, 1713.
(*i*) See the foolifh Prayer of the Neophyte Huron *in the Voyage of le Beau.*

this is a confiderable hindrance; it ties them to their Country, and makes the Dangers of the Undertaking more dreadful.

The Proteftant Religion encourages not the Man, who, in order to fave his Soul, is determined to do any thing but live virtuoufly. It does not promife Heaven to the being Baptized, to the Adoration of the Crofs, to the paying well the Prieft, to a dread of the Torments of Hell, (k) to an implicit faith in a fet of Men, or to fruitlefs Endeavours to believe what is not to be conceived. It requires a Faith of a quite different Nature, a Faith grounded on Knowledge, a Faith confidered as the principle of Virtue. It requires an inward Purity, and declares, that *without it no one fhall fee the Lord.* Confequently a *Proteftant* has no other Motive to become a *Miffionary*, but the defire of doing good, a defire ftrong enough to make him encounter Difficulties of all kinds; and it is plain that one fingle Convert of a *Miffionary*, acting upon that Principle, is worth all thofe fo much boafted of by the Monks.—— Mr. *Egede* is that truly *Proteftant-Miffionary.* He gives up his Living; he abandons his Country, he advances what little Money he has for a Miffion to a Land unknown, fright-

ful

(k) What is called *Attrition* is thought, by the greateft part of the Church of *Rome*, fufficient to Salvation: Thofe that require *Contrition* hardly dare to print their Thoughts. They are ufed as *Janfenifts.*

ful without Riches, affording no Pleafures, and almoft entirely deftitute of Neceffaries. He relies upon the Almighty's Protection, and chearfully goes to inftruct the ignorant, the helplefs *Groenlanders*.

Though what has been faid excufes the Proteftants, when compared in this refpect to Roman-Catholics, yet it is not a fufficient Juftification, if the Cafe be confidered in it felf, and without reference to others.— Would not Seminaries, defigned for fo pious and ufeful a Study, deferve the Countenance and Protection of Proteftant Princes. This would be a noble Adddition to the Plan of the worthy Society *de propaganda Fide*. In hopes that fuch an Eftablifhment may be formed in time, I will venture fome hints concerning the manner of rendering it ufeful.

I. There would be hardly any hopes of fuccefs from fuch a Miffion to Infidels, who have been formerly fubdued, and ill ufed, by Conquerors that bore the Name of Chriftians. The Cruelties practifed againft thofe innocent Fellow-creatures, the Breach of folemn Treaties, which fome *European* Nations have been guilty of, the horrid Trade of Slaves, the rapacious Avarice of fome, the fhameful Intemperance of others; in fhort, that unaccountable Corruption, which, to our fhame, they have been Witneffes of, muft have impreffed on the minds of thofe

poor

poor Nations a ftrong Prejudice againft us.
It would therefore be advifeable to vifit
chiefly thofe who are not prepoffeffed with
an ill Opinion of our Religion, and probably
they would foon be prevailed upon to prefer it to their fuperftitious and troublefome
Idolatry.

II. When we talk of Seminaries in which
fuch Perfons fhould be educated, it is not
to be expected that all, nor the greateft Part,
of them, would really become Miffionaries.
That fhould be left intirely to their free
Choice, and no other means ufed but Arguments and Perfuafion.   Violence is warran-
table in no Cafe, much lefs in religious Affairs; we fee the ill Effects of it in the
Church of *Rome.*   A willing Man, like Mr.
Egede, is the only proper one to fucceed in
fo difficult an Attempt.   What is not done
chearfully, is always ill done.   But it is to
be fuppofed, that among a Number of Men,
train'd up from their Youth in a right way of
thinking, fome few will freely, and of their
own accord, offer themfelves to affift in a
Work fo glorious and truly Apoftolical.

III. All the Care poffible muft be taken
of the Morals of the Miffionaries.   Even a-
mong us, good Examples influence more than
the beft Difcourfes.   How much more muft
this prove true among People unable to make
proper Allowances? *Practife what they fay,
and be not Imitators of what they do,* is too

D 3   nice

nice a diftinction ; and tho' every one's in-
tereft makes it his indifpenfible Duty, yet as
that Duty is attended with Difficulty, a
fteady Purfuit of it requires more Reafon
than is to be found in the generality of Men.
What Succefs can be expected from an Ex-
hortation againft Crimes, the Preacher is no-
torioufly guilty of? The Contraft is too glare-
ing ; and if the Hearers reform, it muft be
owing to their prudent Reflection, not his
Perfuafion. Can Infidels admire the Man
who confutes his belief by his practice. To
make Chriftians, Chriftianity muft appear in
all it's Beauty, Lovelinefs, and Charms ; it
muft be reprefented as enforcing all the focial Virtues. A Behaviour fuitable to our
Inftructions is the beft proof that we are in
earneft, and the moft perfuafive Eloquence.

IV. The laft Precaution, I fhall mention,
concerns the Principles which the Miffionaries are to lay down as the Bafis of their Inftructions. Natural Religion is the Foundation of Revealed, fo far is it from being
deftroyed by it. This laft is defigned
to fupply the Deficiency of the former,
not to abolifh it. Any kind of Oppofiti-
on between Faith and Reafon ferves only to perplex the Underftanding of the
Multitude, and never fails of diffatisfying
thofe, who think they have a Soul capable
of reafoning, given to them for that Purpofe.

pose. The Generality of Mankind, it is true, always was, and still is, fond of *Mysteries*; they guess there is a peculiar Excellency in what they do not understand; this is very difficult to account for; yet the Fact is undeniable; but certainly no use can arise from the pretended Belief of *Mysteries* considered in the full Extent of the term; it may be very easy to make Christians, in the Sense given to that Name by the greatest part of those, that glory in it, that is to say, *Men who think they believe what they have no Notion of.* The Roman-Catholics have effected a prodigious Number of such Conversions, and that without much Trouble; for this Requisite of theirs is perfectly consistent with the most profound Ignorance: The less Knowledge and Understanding they find, the sooner the Conversion is made. But these are not Christians in Reality, and there is no need of going so far to have the Pleasure of giving a Name, or producing a Sound without Meaning.—We are surprised Providence did not long ago interpose in favour of that prodigious Number of People, who never heard of God having sent his only Son into the World.—But, without presuming to found the deep Ways of the Almighty, we know that, according to the Methods he always pursued (and we must own they are the best), in order to instruct the ignorant, some body must be sent

to

to them. And where is the Meſſenger fit
for that Taſk? Was there any of the former Chriſtians, ſince the Apoſtolical Age,
or is there any now, free from conſiderable
Prejudices? If not, they would propagate
thoſe as well as the uſeful Truths they are
acquainted with, and probably with incomparably more Zeal and Succeſs. The Reformation, no doubt, has delivered us, from
numberleſs *Abſurdities,* and *Incumbrances,*
too heavy to be borne by a reaſonable Creature; but the good Work is not yet finiſhed, it is but begun. We talk much of
Perfection, but proceed ſlowly towards it.
Men, it is to be hoped, will grow better
and wiſer, and who knows if our common
good Father does not wait for thoſe better
times, to bring to his Knowledge all the
idolatrous Nations, to avoid their being expoſed to what his Church has undergone almoſt ever ſince it was founded. If ever we
ſee Chriſtians leave off their old Fondneſs of
walking in the dark, and become *Children
of Light*; if ever their Religion, as yet
incumbered with Articles of human Invention, and deform'd by Tenets ſuperadded
by Sects and Parties, ſhould be reſtored to
it's primitive Simplicity, Purity, and Amia-
bleneſs, then we may hope that the time
draws near, when all ſhall *know the only
true God, and Jeſus Chriſt, whom he has
ſent.* Miſſionaries formed on ſuch Princi-

ples may do more Good in a few Years,
than could have been otherwise done thefe
fixteen Ages paft.

ARTICLE IV.

Johan Georg Keyflers Mitglieds der K. Gros-
Britannifchen Societaet Neuefte Reife durch
Teutfchland, Böhmen, Vngarn, die Schwe-
itz, Italien und Lothringen, worinn das
merkwurdigfte diefer Lander . . . durch
die naturliche, Gelehrte, und Politifche
Gefchichte, Mechanic, Mahler, Bau,
und Bildauerkunft, Muntzen und Alter-
thümer erlaütert wird.

That is to fay,

A new Voyage *through Germany, Bohemia,*
Hungary, Switzerland, Italy, and Lorrain ;
where the moft remarkable things in thofe
different Countries are illuftrated by the
natural, Literary, and Civil Hiftory, the
mechanical Arts, Painting, Architec-
ture, Sculpture, Medals and Antiqui-
ties. By John George Keyflers, *Member*
of the Royal Society of Great-Britain.
Hanover, 1740, and 1741, 2 Tom. 4°.
Tom. I. pag. 810, befides the Tables.—
Tom. II. pag. 1450. with Cuts.

THE

(a) THE Travels of Gentlemen are for
the moſt Part undertaken, without any View to the Public Utility, and
attended with certain Diſadvantages to
themſelves, being unable to make Obſervations, deſtitute of the Knowledge of
thoſe different Arts, which they go to
ſee the moſt perfect Models of; very
ſeldom fit or in a Condition to appear at
Courts, they ſee but the bare Surface of
Things. Mr. *Muralt*, ſpeaking of the Generality of Travellers, ſays pleaſantly, that
they run over the World, juſt as Children
over a Book, to look at the Cuts.

Our Author is of a quite different Character, he has ſeen the World in the beſt
Point of View. He carried from home a
formed Taſte for the liberal Arts and a juſt
Notion of the *Beau Monde*; he knew how
to make uſe of his Eyes uſefully for himſelf
and for thoſe that ſhall read his Work.

He travelled as Governor to the two
young Barons of *Bernſtorff* and *Gertau*, a
Family well known in *England*. The eld-
eſt is Counſellor of War for the Dutchy of
Zell; the youngeſt is in the King of *Denmark's* Service, and was his Miniſter Plenipotentiary to the Diet of the Empire, at
the preſent Emperor's Election.

Mr.

(a) Bib. raiſ. Tom. 28. pag. 399, and Tom. 29. pag. 36.

Mr. *Keisler* with his Pupils left the Univerfity of *Tubingen* in 1729, It appears by the Book that they were abundantly provided with necefſary Recommendations to appear with Dignity at all Courts, and where-ever it was convenient.

Mr. *Keisler*'s Object is whatever deferves the Attention of a Traveller, the State of Nations; the Courts of Kings and Princes; their particular Characters, which he illuftrates with an agreeable Variety of curious Facts; the Produce of their Countries; the Palaces, the Clofets of Curiofities of all Kinds, the Infcriptions, and the moft material Things which the natural Hiftory of each Country affords.

The firft Volume contains the Defcription of *Suabia*, *Bavaria*, the *Tirolefe*, *Switzerland*, and part of *Italy*. This laft is the chief Object of his Attention. Meffieurs *Burnet*, *Miſſon*, *Addifon*, and *Blainville* did not exhauft this fine Country. Each of them had a different View and ftuck to it, yet none of them made the political Hiftory of that Country which is the moft univerfally ufeful, his chief Object. Befides they almoft entirely neglected the Court of Savoy, which now acts fo confiderable a Part amongft the Powers of *Europe*. Mr. *Keisler* gave it a particular Attention, and it is chiefly this Part of his Work I am going to abftract.

Our

Our Author begins with the Character of the late King *Victor Amadeus*. He reprefents him with that Air of Refervednefs, and Secrecy fo common at his Court, and which it has preferved under the prefent King, both in its Manners and Negociations. He gives fome Inftances of that Prince's great Oeconomy. He ufed to gather together all Sorts of Tradefmen to be inform'd of the loweft Price of each Commodity, and he did not fail to make ufe of his Difcoveries, either to reduce the Penfions of his Officers to the very Neceffaries of Life, or to leffen the Grants made to the Gentlemen of his Court, or to raife the Revenues. One Day, he ordered all the Farmers of the Mills in his Dominions to meet, and that very Morning the Rents in that Article were raifed 300,000 Livres.

This Spirit of Oeconomy did not hinder that Prince from being generous as often as there was any Occafion to reward Virtue. Our Author proves it by many Inftances. Here is one of the nobleft. One Day that the Prince of *Piedmont* (who died before his Father) and his Brother, who now holds the Crown of *Sardinia*, were taking the Air in a Coach along the *Po*, the Horfes took a Flight ftrait towards the River. In this extreme Danger the Baron of *Valaife*, the Prince's Gentleman of the Horfe, took a Refolution equally noble and dangerous. He

clapp'd

clapp'd the Spurs to his Horfe, and drove it in the Middle of the furious Horfes, which were running away with the Princes. He had the Happinefs to ftop them, but he was dangeroufly wounded. The Court did not appear at firft deeply affected with fo noble an Action; and the Baron, after being cured with great Difficulty, thought himfelf fufficiently rewarded with the Glory of having faved the Life of his Sovereigns. The People did fecretly grumble at fuch a noted Piece of Ingratitude, when after fome time a Fief worth from about 80,000 to a 100,000 Livres was added to the Duke's Eftate. The Prince had fecretly defigned it for one who to fave the Lives of his two Sons had facrificed his own, and the Prince of *Piedmont* had the noble Affurance to reprefent to his Father, not to do Things by half, but that it was proper to furnifh the Houfe that was to be the Reward of fuch a faithful Subject. The Duke accomplifh'd his Son's Wifhes, and the Baron of *Valaife* was agreeably furprifed to be put, by the Prince himfelf, into the Poffeffion of that valuable Prefent.

The fuperior Knowledge of King *Victor* diffufed itfelf on his People, and even unblinded them about Things which the Policy of *Roman* Priefts artfully keeps in the dark. Dr. *Richa* had the Boldnefs to accufe of Impofture a miferable Wretch which two Jefuits wanted to make the People believe was poffeffed by the Devil, and he gave fuch
convincing

convincing Proofs of the Cheat, that the
Public itself was undeceived. Upon this
the King took from that too intriguing Order the Direction of Youth, which has been
the true Cause of their Grandeur, and he
kept the Clergy under to a Degree which
has no Example in the Catholic Party.

This Prince grew superstitious in his last
Days, and expelled part of the faithful *Vau-
dois* out of his Dominions. Yet we must
observe, that the Edict of Expulsion in 1733,
only reach'd those that had been baptised
by Catholic Priests, and which were artfully represented as a kind of Relapse. The
remaining Part of that Nation, so justly res-
pected for its Sufferings, and for its ancient
Possession of Truth, was not disturbed.

Victor Amadeus was far from being insensi-
ble to Love; our Author gives some remarkable Instances of it. The Duke carried
one Day his Weakness for a Mistress so far,
as to oblige the Dutchess to take off her
Neck a Jewel, to satisfy the unreasonable Desire of the Countess of *Verue* her Rival.
The Particulars of this Passion are curious.
The Countess was not faithful. One Evening the Duke went to her Apartment, without giving any Notice of his coming. He
found tête a tête with her a Lord, who did
not expect such a dangerous third one. The
generous Prince took his Rival with one
Hand,

Hand, and a Light in the other, and brought him out of the Room, telling him he might bragg of having been lighted to the Stairs by the Duke of *Savoy*; but he warned him not to expect such kind Usage a second time.

As to the King of *Sardinia*'s Revenues our Author computes them at twenty Millions of *Piedmontese* Livres, which make twenty four Millions of *French* Livres. The good Oeconomy still prevailing at that Court, the Improvement in the Trade of *Piedmontese* Silks, and the Acquisition of Part of the *Milanese*, must have encreased them since. The Silks, above all, are a very considerable Article. Many Peasants make up in a Year 100, or 125 Pounds of raw Silks, the best of which are sold for a *Louis d'Or* the Pound. Mr. *Keisler* enlarges much upon that profitable Manufacture.

He fixes the Number of regular Troops to 22000 Men in time of Peace, besides 6000 armed Militia. This Army is much more considerable now. Every Body knows, that the King of *Sardinia* has 30000 Men in the Field, besides his Garisons.

Victor reduced his Officers and Soldiers to the smallest Pay, and took from the first all those accidental Perquisites, which in other Services make a Capital Article. On the other hand, to encourage the Nobility to enter into the Army, he received at his
Court

Court no other of his Subjects but Gentlemen that had ſerved, and he honoured ſo much the loweſt military Degrees as to make them paſs for a Mark of Diſtinction, even for the firſt Lords of his Dominions.

Our Author ſhews afterwards by a great Number of memorable Examples, what Influence the Attention of a knowing Prince has over his Subjects. The *Piedmonteze,* hardly known a Century ago, and who had been beat by *Swiſs* Militia, have given Proofs of Intrepidity equal to thoſe the *Roman* Hiſtory affords. What a Peaſant, a Miner, did in the Siege of *Turin* is an Inſtance of it. As he was working under Ground, he perceived over his Head the *French* intrenching themſelves in a Gallery they had made. In an Inſtant he took the Reſolution to ſave the Place with the Loſs of his Life; he made his Comrades to withdraw, deſired 'em to recommend his Family to his Prince's Generoſity, and blew himſelf up with 200 *French* Grenadiers. (*b*) It is a Query, whether a *Decius* did as much as this Peaſant, who could withdraw without Shame, and who had not the ſame Intereſt as a *Roman* Conſul in the Welfare of his Country.

Mr. *Keiſler* ſpeaks much of the *Turin* Academy, where the Jeſuits have no Share, and

(*b*) We have a recent Example of the Bravery of the *Piedmonteze,* in the Defence of *Coni,* and in the whole Tranſactions of the laſt Campaign in *Italy.*

and gives many Examples to prove that a
Number of *Italian* Prelates and Virtuofos
have little or no Religion.

Father Sachieri's prodigious Memory is
a notable Phænomenon in the History of
the human Mind. He could play at Chefs
~~with three different Perfons, without look~~-
ing at one of the three Games; and to
chufe the Piece he was to move, he only
wanted to know what Motion his Antagonift had made. He could befides entertain
the Company very agreeably. He had alfo
the furprizing Faculty of refolving in a
Moment a Problem of Geometry.

The Author fhews in the 34th Chapter,
how much the Nobility is oppreffed. They
are taxed in Time of War to a fourth or
a fixth Part of their Income, and the Prince
has deprived the greateft Number of them
of Part of their Eftates, by re-uniting to
his Domains or Lands what formerly belong'd to them. They have been forbid to
ferve in foreign Armies, or even to travel
without Leave. If we add to this the Taxes
which the Subject, even to the very Shoe-
boys when Abroad are loaded with, every Body will be forced to own that Defpo-
tifm is one of the greateft Evils, tho' in the
Hands of a Prince that has many Virtues.
Victor, the wife *Victor* himfelf invented
all thefe new Ways of raifing Money. It
is true, he made in a manner Amends for

PART I.   E

it; if he loaded his People, he gave them wherewithal to bear that Load. He took all the Pains imaginable to put Trade and Manufactures in a flourishing Condition, especially the Silk-Manufacture.

ARTICLE V.

Memoires *de* Maximilien Emanuel *Duc de* Virtemberg, *Colonel d'un Regiment de Dragons au service de* fuede, contenant *plusieurs particularitez de la vie de* Charles XII. *Roi de fuede, depuis* 1703. *jusquen* 1709. *apres la Bataille de* Pultowa *par* M. F. P. 8°. 1740. p. 333. fans la Preface.

That is to fay.

Memoirs *of* Maximilian Emanuel *Duke of* Virtemberg, *Colonel of a Regiment of Dragoons in the Service of* Sweden, containing *many particulars of the life of* Charles *the* XII. *&c.*

(*a*) **T**HOSE that are acquainted with the several Histories of *Charles* the XII. will find little or nothing in these Memoirs but what

---

what they already know. They may serve
however to clear up some Articles variously
related by Messieurs *Adlerfeld*, *Nordberg*, and
Voltaire; and for this reason I thought proper just to mention this Book. The Duke
of *Virtemberg* was only 14 or 15 Years old,
when he went to meet the King of *Sweden*
near *Warsaw*, at the end of 1703. He
never left him since, and there was between
them the greatest Intimacy, form'd by a
sameness of Inclinations, and kept up on one
Side, or for ought I know, on both, by Admiration and Gratitude. For the young
Prince, besides the continual Proofs he gave of
a Bravery much like the King's, shared with
him all his Dangers, and had even the pleasure to save his Life. *Charles* also had a
great Concern for the Prince's Life, but as
great as his Love for him might be, he did
not give him any great Marks of his Generosity, *(b)* during six Years that he served
him as Volunteer. It was only in 1709. a
short time before the fatal Action of *Pultowa*,
that he gave him a Regiment of Dragoons,
with a present of Ten thousand Guilders.
He was made Prisoner at *Pultowa*, after
having given signal proofs of his Valour,
which procured him the Czar's Admiration

E 2   and

(b) Probably the Prince received nothing because he did
not ask; for I heard from People that knew *Charles* the
XIIth, that he had not the Art of resisting the Duns.
Remark of the French *Journal.*

and Efteem. A malignant Fever carried him off the 25th of *September* 1709. at the Age of 20 Years and 7 Months. *Charles* was greatly fhock'd at this untimely Death, and faid he had loft, *the beft of his Friends.*

Thefe Memoirs are partly taken out of feveral *German* Papers, wrote by People that followed the Prince in his Campaigns, and partly from a Relation of the Baron of *Sittman*, a *Pruffian* Officer fent by his Mafter to the King of *Sweden*, and who made many Campaigns with him. It was in his Coach *Charles* retired after his Defeat at *Pultowa.*

ARTICLE VI.

Obfervations of the Author of *La Bibliotheque raifonnée*, *(a)* on the Univerfal Hiftory, firft printed in *London*, and afterwards in *Dublin*, fol. and 8°

THE *Univerfal Hiftory* was tranflated into *French* a fhort Time after it had appeared in *England*. The foreign Journals gave an Account of it as foon as they conveniently could. The Authors of *La Bibliotheque*

(a) Bib. raif. Tom. XXIX. p. 111. & 389. Tom. XXX. Pag. 235. &c.

liotheque raisonnée were the forwardest, and as according to the Meaning of the Title of their Journal, they give reasoned Abstracts of the Books that fall in their Way, the Gentleman, to whose Share this Book fell, not only gave an accurate Account of each Volume as they came out, but also added some Objections against it. This incomparable Book is too well known to require my giving an Abstract of it. I shall therefore confine my self to the Observations of the *French* Journalist, and to some Remarks of my own upon them. I thought his Reflections deserved the Attention of the *English* Reader, and that they might be serviceable, either towards a further Illustration of the Subject they treat of, or to the Authors themselves of this excellent Work, in case they should find some Weight in them. These Gentlemen are of too superior a Merit to be displeased with Objections to their Way of thinking, or explaining some particular Places, and the Manner in which those Objections are proposed, has nothing but what must be agreeable to them. The Author is for ever cautious of giving Offence, and he expresses in the strongest Manner possible his high Opinion of this most useful Work. " What Pleasure " does it not afford a Journalist, *says he*, " when he is to give the Public an Account " of Works so important as this is; where-

" in

" in he meets every where with an agree-
" able Variety of Facts, curious, well par-
" ticularifed, explained with great Order,
" Clearnefs, Plainnefs, and at the fame
" Time attended with a great Num-
" ber of Obfervations, that caft a
" new Light on the Text, and lead the
" Reader through the dark and difficult
" Paths of antient Hiftory."—— He often
paffes fuch Encomiums; but as it is impoffible Men fhould all think the fame Way,
he now and then differs from them. I intend to relate his chief Remarks.

I don't reckon among thefe what he fays
about *Benedict de Spinoza,* on the Article
of the Creation of the World: He blames
this Affertion in the Univerfal Hiftory, *(b)*
that *Spinoza's Syftem has been fufficiently expofed and confuted even by the weakeft of its
Adverfaries.* He quotes Count *Boulainvil-
liers,* who had thoroughly examined that Syftem, and who fays " that he found it the
" moft dangerous that ever was invented
" againft Religion; .... that tho' he had
" read many Anfwers to it, yet he did not
" meet with one Satisfactory;—— that the
" Authors who undertook to confute him
" either were not in Earneft, or did not
" underftand what they were about;——
" and that he dares to reckon among the
latter

(b) Univ. Hift. vol. 1. pag. 91. *Dub.* Edit. 8°. 1745. &
pag. 9. Fol. Edit.

" latter the celebrated Monſieur *Bayle*."
But our Author forgets that *Boulainvil-*
liers is ſo far from being an impartial Wit-
neſs in this Cauſe, that he is one of the
greateſt Defenders of *Spinoza*, and a moſt
artful one ; for in the Book he gave out
under the Title of *Refutation de Spinoza*,
he ſets off his horrid Syſtem in the beſt
Manner he poſſibly can, and merely for the
ſake of doing ſomething that may agree
with his deceitful Title, he, at the End of
his Book brings in two or three ſham Con-
futations; and therefore if ever that Syſtem
was dangerous, he is the Man that has made
it ſo. Conſequently our Author ought to alledge ſome other Authority to prove that
Spinoza's Syſtem has not been yet utterly
deſtroy'd. Whatever ſome Philoſophers beyond Seas may think of this ſtrange Syſtem, it is to be hoped that none in theſe
Kingdoms will attempt to revive it, ſince
it is already quite overthrown by ſeveral
Tracts diſperſed here and there in our *En-*
gliſh Writings, (which the foreign Author of
the Abſtract is probably unacquainted with.)
The late ingenious Work intitled, *Matho*,
or *Theoria Puerilis*, tho' chiefly calculated
for the Inſtruction of young People, is abundantly ſufficient to convince any attentive
Reader of it's Abſurdity.

Our Author diſlikes alſo that the Authors
of the *Univerſal Hiſtory* ſhould make ſo lit-

tle

tle of *Cartesius*'s Syſtem, as to ſay, that
it is liable to Objections that abſol
ruin it. He pretends, that *l'Abbé de M*
(d) has wrote in Defence of that Syſte
a Manner that might have deſerve
Anſwer from ſome *Newtonian* Ph
pher; and that it were proper to do
fore one can juſtly claim the Victory ii
Manner they do. On this Occaſio
quotes theſe Words of Monſ. *Fontenell*

   " A great, and one of the moſt formi
   " Objections againſt the *Carteſian* Vor
   " is drawn from this, that we ſee C
   " moving againſt the Direction of
   " Vortexes Motion. Mr. *Caſſini* p
   " in 1730, by a Comet, which he obſe
   " that, they might, as well as Planets
   " pear ſometimes againſt the Vorte
   " be retrograde, without ever ceaſing
   " direct. By this *the Newtonian V*
   " *ſhould be exploded, and the* Carteſian Pl
   " *reſtored.*— Mr. *Caſſini* ſhew'd in
   " that the Rotation of the celeſtial
   " that are in Appearance ſo different
   " *Kepler*'s firſt Law, may be reduced
   " and he ſhews in the ſame Differ
   " the Agreement between *Kepler*'
   " Laws in an Article where their Oppo
   " ſeemed manifeſt before.—So, as far

                "

(t) *Univ. Hiſt.* Vol. 1. pag. 149. 8o.—and pag.
(d) See *hiſt. de l'Academ.* 1723. 1728. 1729.
(e) Hiſt. de l'Academ. 1736.

" may judge of a future Event, in
" which the Chances of Fortune have less
" Share than in any other, the End of
" the War might prove advantageous to
" this System ;"—I don't know whether
these Experiments of Mr. *Caffini*'s, and
Monfieur *Fontenelle*'s Obfervations upon it
have been as yet anfwered. In cafe they
have not, I thought proper to relate them,
that fome Philofopher of our Side, might,
if he pleafes, more narrowly inquire into
this Subject, weigh the Strength of the Objections, and force the *Cartefians* out of this
laft Intrenchment. Had I fufficient Abilities to fucceed in it, the Nature of an Abftract would not allow it. Befides I very
much fufpect that the Public is already out
of Conceit with this old Difpute..

The Authors of the *Univerfal Hiftory*
handle this Queftion. *(f) Whether all
Animals, that already have been, or hereafter
fhall be, were at firft actually created by
God; or whether he hath given to each Kind
of Animals fuch a Power of Generation, as
to prepare Matter, and produce new Individuals in their own Bodies.* They are for the
firft Hypothefis, and our Journalift agrees
with them, tho' he is not pleafed with fome
of the Proofs they alledge. " For Inftance,
" *fays be*, I fee no Inconveniency in grant-
" ing

(f) Univ. Hift. Vol. 1. pag. 164 8º.—and pag. 43. fol..

" ing to Animals the Faculty of *producing*
" *new Individuals*, provided it be suppofed
" they act in this only as fecondary Caufes,
" and that they receive this Faculty from
" God, — But, fay they, (g) *the forming*
" *or nourifhing of the Foetus is a Work of*
" *Art and Reafon, which brute Creatures*
" *are not endued withal,* I allow it.— Nei-
" ther Brutes, nor Man himfelf underftand
" any thing in this Myftery; but are not a
" thoufand Things performed in Animals
" by a Mechanifm which God is the Au-
" thor of. The Chicken underftands nothing
" of the Formation of Blood, yet Blood is
" formed in it's Body by the Help of
" Springs which God has put in it. There
" is no Man able to form one fingle Drop
" of Blood out of himfelf, yet this Blood
" is formed every Day in his Body, with-
" out his knowing, or his being able to un-
" derftand, how this Formation is effected.
" — Why is a Flower adorned with fo ma-
" ny different Colours ?— Why have diffe-
" rent Parts of the fame Plant different
" Smells, different Taftes ? Why is one of
" thefe Parts four while the other is fweet,
" and why does the one fo agreeably affect
" our fmelling, whilft the other fhocks it ?—
" Did the Plant, as it was forming itfelf,
" know what it was doing ? No certainly.
" — What is then the Caufe of that great
                                        " Variety

(g) Ibid.

" Variety of Colours, of that great differ-
" ence in the Taſte and Smell of the dif-
" ferent Parts of the ſame Plant ? The
" Organization alone, the very Mecha-
" niſm of that Plant.— But if the hu-
" man Body may be the efficient Cauſe
" of Blood and of other Humours, in
" conſequence of the particular Structure
" of its Parts, will you take upon you to
" affirm, that it cannot be alſo the effi-
" cient Cauſe of the Foetus, in conſe-
" quence of the Faculty which God has
" put in him to produce its Fellow.—
" Another Remark on this fine Queſtion of
" natural Philoſophy, a Remark which I
" make the more readily, as I believe our
" Authors might be in the Wrong,
" for want of having conſulted modern
" Naturaliſts. They alledge, and this with-
" out any Proof, *(b) that the Females of all*
" *the Viviparous Quadrupeds are brought*
" *forth with their Teſtes or Ovaria, and*
" *all Birds formed with their Ovary or*
" *Egg-Cluſter containing the Seeds of all*
" *the Eggs they ſhall ever lay.*—I readi-
" ly grant that all Females have Ovaria,
" that the Eggs are found wrapt up in
" theſe Ovaria, and that the Embryo it
" ſelf, or the Foetus, is folded in thoſe
" Eggs, the Membranes of which it af-
                              " terwards

(b) Univ. hiſt. Vol. 1. pag. 165. 8°.—and pag. 43.fol.

" terwards breaks, when it is become a
" perfect Animal. But I afk whether
" thefe Foetufes come from the Male, or
" from the Female;— whether they origi-
" nally are in the Egg, or in that Humour
" which is called the Male's Seed.— The
" celebrated *Malpighi* has demonftrated
" that in a Hen's Egg there is no Sign
" of a Foetus before the Copulation, and
" that it is conftantly found in it, when
" the Egg was duly made teeming by the
" Action of the Cock.— Befides, *Hartfoe-*
" *ker* and *Leuwenboek* have fhewed, that pro-
" bably the Offspring of each Man, and of
" each Animal, are, as it were, in minia-
" ture in the well conditioned Seed of each
" Man, and that in the Copulation of the
" two Sexes, thefe firft Rudiments of the
" human Race go and join one or many
" Eggs of the Woman, which they penetrate
" and go through its Membranes, to lodge
" themfelves in the Place where they are
" to be folded and to grow."— According
to this Hypothefis, the Foetus originally
refides in the Male's Seed, and not in the
Female's Egg.

. The Journalift affirms, that the Authors
of the *Univerfal Hiftory* fall into a Contradiction on this fame Subject. Talking of
the Formation of Man, they fay, *(i)* that
the

(i) *Univ. Hiß.* Vol. 1. pag. 171. 8°.

the parent *Animal* cannot be the *Agent*, or
efficient in the Generation, or *forming*, or
nourishing of the *Foetus*; and yet five or
fix Pages after they make this Diftinction;
(k) that *it is more reafonable to believe that
tho' God has committed the Formation of our
Bodies to the Agency of fecond Caufes, yet he
has referved the Production of our Souls to
himfelf*, &c. Thefe two Places, *fays he*, include a manifeft Contradiction; in the firft
Animals are not, and in the other they are
the *efficient Caufe of the Formation of the
Foetus*; and by faying that *God referved the
Formation of our Souls to himfelf*, they give to
underftand that he is not the Author of the
Production of our Bodies.— Thus the Journalift.—It feems to me that in this Place he
did not rightly take the meaning of the Authors of the Hiftory. I fee no Contradiction in what he quotes from them. And
probably he would have feen no fuch thing
if he had confidered that by *efficient Caufe*,
they mean one thing, and by *fecondary Caufe*,
another thing. When they fay that the *parent Animal cannot be an efficient Caufe*, they
do plainly mean that Animals are not the
primary or immediate Caufe, &c. whereas
they apply that Notion to the Soul, and tell
us accordingly, that *tho' God has committed
the Formation of our Bodies to the Agency of
fecond*

_____

(k) Ibid.

second Causes, he did however *reserve to himself the Production of our Souls*; that is, he
thought fit to create them immediately, so
that he is in the strictest Sense the *efficient
Cause* of their Being, and makes use of no
secondary Causes to produce them.

Here is another Question, handled of old,
and renew'd by the Authors of the *Universal History (l)*. They ask whether the Souls
of all Men were created at once with
Adam's Soul, or whether they are created
successively, and as the Bodies they inhabit
require it. They seem to incline in Favour
of the last Opinion. *Why*, say they, *should
we imagine that God put forth all his crea-
tive Vigor at once in a Moment, ever afterwards remaining Spectator only of the con-
sequent Result, and permitting Nature alone
to do all, without any farther Interposition?
And how is it possible, that if our Souls were
ever in such a State of Pre-existence, we
should have so perfectly lost all Memory and
Consciousness of any thing?* I believe they
might have set aside this last Reason, for as
our Author remarks, a Child in his Mother's
Womb has a Soul, at least in the last Months
of her Pregnancy, and yet not one Man
can remember what Thoughts he had at
that Time. The greatest Number of modern Philosophers are of Opinion, that all
                                    our

_____

(l) Ibid. pag. 172. 8°.—and 46. fol.

our Ideas come to us by our Senses, and if
so, what could our Souls think of whilst
they are contained in the Semen, the Organs of which, if it has any, are probably
without any Action.— But I don't think our •
Author has the same Reason to find Fault
with the first Part of the above Proposition;
*viz. that we are not to imagine that God ex-
hausted in a Moment all his creating Power.*
" These Gentlemen, *says he,* seem to fear
" that God should be idle, were he not bu-
" sy in creating new Souls. But this Fear
" seems to me to be ill grounded. I would
" be glad to know what God was doing be-
" fore the Creation of the *Universe.* It can-
" not be said that he was then employed in
" creating. What did he do then ? Shall
" we say he was idle, as we should suppose
" it, if the Reason alledged by our Authors
" was grounded.— Besides, they give to un-
" derstand by this, that God wants Employ-
" ment in order to be happy; and this is a
" Thought we are not to entertain of a self-
" sufficient Being, who stands in no Need
" of his Creatures in order to be happy."
But I would willingly ask our Author what
he means by the Word *Universe.*— If he
means only our Globe, and those we perceive,
I may in my turn ask, who told him God
created none before. He formed Angels
before our Creation,— and why should we
not suppose that he has been creating from

all

all Eternity. I know that this is generally deemed impossible; but I profess I cannot feel the Strength of the Reasons alledged to prove that Impossibility. The Truth is, that we are lost in the Notion of *Eternity,* and for that very Reason, that we are very far from having a complete Idea of it, we cannot affirm that it is impossible an eternal Being should have been eternally doing something. Just as distinctly, and as much as we can conceive God existing from all Eternity, so we can conceive him eternally exerting his Power, his Wisdom and his Goodness. And therefore we may, without the least Absurdity, conceive millions of Beings as truly without a *Beginning,* as the Supreme. Tho' he is the Author, or Creator of all things, yet many things may be *Cotemporary* with him, (if I may thus express myself,) or have ever subsisted, being as it were, *eternal Emanations* from that eternal Source, or Spring, of the Universe. God's being during a whole Eternity doing nothing implies, I think, something shocking. So I would chuse to answer the Question proposed by our Author, in this manner;—before the Creation, (that is the one recorded in *Moses*'s History,) God was doing what he did at that time, what probably he has done since, what he will do for ever, he was creating Beings in order that they should be happy.—But *says our Author,* is not
God

God *Self-sufficient* ? I answer he is so, that
is to say, that it is constantly and invariably
in his Power to make himself infinitely happy,—and that one of the Means towards it,
and for ought I know, the chief one is,
the contributing to the Happiness of other
Beings.—If by *Self-sufficiency* you understand his being pleased with nothing else
but himself, independently on his Works,
then your Notion of God is not, cannot,
be true; you destroy his very Benevolence, that is to say, the chief of his Attributes.—It is not on this Occasion alone that
in subtilizing our Idea of God, we reduce it
to nothing; or what is yet worse, we represent him in such a manner that it is impossible for us to have those feelings of
Love and Gratitude, which a plainer and
more becoming Notion would infallibly
raise and improve in our Minds.—It might
be said that all this does not absolutely prove
that God did not at once make all our Souls,
because if he takes Pleasure in forming intelligent Beings, he may at all times form a
great many others, besides our Souls. It is
very true; but if my Reflection be right, I
humbly conceive it takes away all Proofs
from the other Side of the Question, and
it shews, that the Argument drawn from
the Expediency of God's doing at once all
the Good he was willing and had intended
to do, is not so consistent with the Notion

we muſt have of his Goodneſs, as the Belief that he continually delights in making
new Subjects for Happineſs.

(*m*) Our Author's next Remark concerns
this Place of the Book of *Joſhua,* wherein it
is ſaid that *(n) the Lord caſt down great Stones
from Heaven upon the* Caananites, and that
more died by Abnehabarad *Hailſtones, than
by the Sword of the Children of* Iſrael.

This Expreſſion made the *Septuagint,* and
after them (*o*) *Joſephus* and the Author of
Eccleſiaſticus, (*p*) think, that there fell only
Hail-ſtones, properly ſo called, but of an
extraordinary Size, which agrees well enough
with the Genius of the *Hebrew.* But on the
other hand, *ſay the Authors of the Univerſal Hiſtory,* (*q*) this is ſo far from being the
obvious Meaning of it, " that the word
Hail ſeems rather to be uſed here to expreſs
" the vaſt Quantity, Bigneſs, (*r*) Vehemency
" and Execution of thoſe Stones which fell ;
" and the Expreſſion of flying and
" falling as thick as Hail, is not only
" common to all the Ancients, but is
" likewiſe retained in moſt modern Lan-
" guages. For which Reaſon ſeveral learn-
" ed

(*m*) Univ. Hiſt. Vol. 1. fol. pag. 564.
(*n*) *Joſhua* Ch. x.
(*o*) Ant. Lib. V. Ch. 1.
(*p*) Eccleſ. XLVI. 6.
(*q*) *Univ. Hiſt.* Vol. 1. fᵒ. pag. 564. Rem. M.
(*r*) A Compariſon taken from Hail ſeems not fit to raiſe
our Notion of the bigneſs of the Stones. *Rem. of the Journ.*

" ed Men (s) have underftood it of a mi-
" raculous Shower of real Stones, as being
" the moft eafy and natural Meaning of the
" Text." . On the contrary, Mr. *Le Clerc*
thinks, that this is only a Hail-ftorm; he
gives the Name of Impofture to the Relations of Showers of Stones given by fome
Hiftorians, and the Name of Madnefs to
the Endeavours of many Authors to reconcile this Phænomenon with the known Effects of Nature.

To fhow that he is miftaken, the Authors
of the *Univerfal Hiftory* examine firft the
Teftimonies, Hiftory affords on this Subject, and afterwards the Arguments made
ufe of to prove the Poffibility of thofe E-
vents. As to the firft Article, they tell us,
that under the Reign of *Tullus Hoftilius*,
there fell Stones from Heaven on Mount
Albus (t), in the fame Manner as Hail falls
when it is driven by the Wind.— Another
Shower of Stones fell afterwards on the
fame Mountain, which lafted two whole
Days (u). The fame thing happen'd at
Rome, at *Capua*, and many other Places in
Italy (v). Thefe Stones were fometimes

F 2   hot,

(s) *Grotius Bonfret: Ger. Voffius, Jun. Munft.* and many
others.
(t) Tit. Liv. Lib. I. Dec. 1.
(u) Tit. Liv. Lib. XXV. XXX. XXXIV.
(v) Ibid. *de bell. Afric.* Cap. 47. Aman, *Bell Civil.* Li.
IV. Aug. de Civit. Li. III. C. 30. &c.

hot, fometimes cold, and fometimes like hard Lumps of Earth, and fometimes like Duft or Sand.— To thefe Inftances the fame Gentlemen add the following, which they look upon as an undeniable Fact, that Stones have been fufpended in the Air during a con-fiderable Time, and that they afterwards fell down very heavily.— Such is the Stone, which according to *Plutarch*'s Relation, (*x*) fell in *Thracia* in the River *Argos*; *Anaxagoras* thought it came from the (*y*) Sun; and the Author, from whom *Plutarch* borrow'd this Fact, certifies, that it was floating in the Air like a (*z*) luminous Cloud during 75 Days, in which Time many loofe Pieces came off of it, much in the fame Manner as what is called *Ignis fatuus*. The Stone itfelf was of fuch a prodigious Size, that *Pythagoras* never would (*a*) believe with *Ariftotle*, that it had been taken off a confiderable Rock, and drove up in the Air by a tempeftuous Wind, becaufe it would have been impoffible that it fhould have been fufpended in it fo long as *Damachus* affirm'd it had. *Pliny* certifies, that it was carefully preferved in his Time, and that it was of the Size of a four-wheel'd Carr (*magnitudine vehis*, and of a dark burnt Colour.—

(*x*) Vit. Lifand.
(*y*) See Diog. in *Anax.* & *not.* Menag. in *Laert.*
(*z*) Damachus *ap.* Plut. ubi fupra.
(*a*) Meterolog. L. 1. C. 7.

lour.— Such was also that Stone which fell in *Alsatia*, in the Middle of a Hail-Storm, the 29th of *November*, 1630. *(b)* This Stone, which is yet preserved in the Church of *Anxissem*, weighs near three hundred Pounds.— Such were the Stones which Count *Marcelline* affirms to have fallen in *Thrace*, the Year 1452 ; and many others which it would be unnecessary to mention.

This is not all. The same Authors relate Instances of some other stony Rains which are more natural than the foregoing, as they are caused by furious Hurricanes, by Earth-quakes, or by subterraneous Fires. Of the first Kind were those that fell on the *Persians* *(c)* when they went to plunder the Temple of *Delphos*, a Phænomenon which some Travellers assure to be very common in some Parts of *America* *(d)*.— Those that fell on the *Gauls* when they attempted the same Thing, are ascribed to a terrible Hurricane by *Pausanias*, *(e)* and by *Justin* to an Earth-quake. The last Kind is that which is caused by subterraneous Fires, of which the Authors of the *Universal History*, only relate the following Instance of a modern Date, *viz.* the Rain that preceded the wonderful Emersion of the Island *San-*

F 3   *torine*

(b) Gesner & Ans. de Boot. *Hist. Lapid. & Gem.*
(c) Diod. Sicul. Bibl. L. 11.——
(d) Voyages de Coreal, &c.——
(e) Pausan. L. i. Just. L. 24. towards the End.

torino in the *Archipelago*, in the Year 1707.
A terrible Noife like that of large Field-
pieces, or of Thunder, was heard for many
Days, during which they faw a prodigious
Quantity of Stones, rifing from the Sea,
like fo many Rockets, which fell at five Miles
diftance from the Place they came from.
During this time the Air was full of a thick
and fulphurous Smoke, mixed with Cinders
which fell in fuch a Quantity, that all the
Lands in the Neighbourhood were covered
with it.— Some fuch Thing happened in the
Year 1538, (*f*) in *Italy*, near the Village
Tripergola, whence, after feveral terrible
Shocks and Earthquakes, during which the
Sky was darkened, and the Ground was covered with Stones and Duft, which kept
pouring down from the Sky during the Space
of two Days, at the End of which, a Mountain was obferved to have reared itfelf in the
midft of the Lake *Lucrino*.

The Formation of thefe Stones in the Air
is thus accounted for by thofe Gentlemen.
(*g*) " That Duft, *fay they*, Sand, Earth,
" and other fuch Materials may be carried
" up a confiderable height in the Air by a
" ftrong Whirlwind, is no more than what
" is commonly obferved; here then we need
" but fuppofe that thefe mingling them-
" felves with other Exhalations, whether
" ful-

(*f*) Mountfaucon *in his Trav. to* Italy.
(*g*) *Univ. Hift.* Vol. 1. fol. pag. 566.

" fulphureous, bituminous, oily, vitrioline,
" and with the Moifture of the Clouds,
" are there conglomerated and hardened by
" their own Weight by the Preffure of the
" Air and Clouds, and thence fall down
" when they can be no longer fupported ;".
To give the more Colour to this Account,
they relate a Fact taken from an Author,
(*b*) which they think a very credible one ;
viz. that there fell in the Neighbourhood of
Abdone twelve hundred Stones, of a rufty
iron Colour, fome foft, fome hard, and in
every refpect much like thofe commonly
called Thunder-ftones. Thefe Stones fell
from the Middle of a Whirlwind, which
appeared like an Atmofphere of Fire, and
there were fome among them fo large, that
one weighed 60 Pounds, and another 120.
The Conclufion they draw from thefe Events,
and from the Poffibility of thofe Stones
being formed in the Air, is this, that there
is nothing in them but what is very natural, and might happen without a Miracle
to the *Canaanites*, and that if any Thing
was fupernatural in this Event, it was only the directing of that Storm to fall juft
at that Time and Place upon the flying
Canaanites.

Our Author makes many Objections a-
gainft this Hypothefis, which are in fubftance thus.   F 4   1. The

(*b*) Cardan *de variet.* Lib. XIV. Cap. 72.

1. The moft part of thofe Accounts of Stones, at leaft of thofe of a confiderable fize, muft be look'd upon as impoffible and contrary to the Laws of Gravitation ; for by them we know that a Body hard, heavy, and of a confiderable Size, cannot be long fufpended in the Air without falling again by its own Weight towards the Center of the Earth, where it is attracted, unlefs it be fuftain'd and ftop'd by an Obftacle able to refift that force which drives it continually downwards. Such is the Law of Gravitation, and this Law admits of no exception.

2. The Air, it is true, makes a certain refiftance to Bodies as they fall, and the more fo when they are of a larger Size. But this refiftance muft be very inconfiderable if compared to the Weight of fome of the Stones mentioned here. Porous Bodies, fuch as the Cork-Tree, for inftance, fall, I own, more flowly than other Bodies lefs porous, as Oak, becaufe thefe Bodies extreamly porous are of a larger Superficies, and have lefs Weight; yet they fall, in fpite of the great Number of their Pores. Pray now compare the fpecific Weight of the Cork-Tree, with the Weight of the moft part of the Stones fuppofed to have fallen with a Storm, and judge whether hard and maffy Stones could be not only kept up in the Air for a long time, but even fly about, and in a manner play in it, as

Birds

Birds do. For my part, I could as eafily
believe that *Elias* went up to Heaven without a Miracle, as that the Stone mention'd
by *Plutarch*, which was of the fize of a four
wheel'd Carr, fhould have been floating in
the Air during 75 Days.

3. That other Stone which fell in *Alfatia*,
affords another Phænomenon no lefs incredi-
ble.—Who faw it falling down?—Are they
to be credited?— It weigh'd three hundred
pounds, you fay.—Very well.—But for that
very reafon it cannot have been form'd in
the Air, without fuppofing at the fame Time
a prodigious refiftance in the Air, all the
Time of its Formation, to prevent it's falling down, and no Account is given whence
fuch refiftance could proceed.

4. The Journalift goes on : Will our
Authors fay, I am very incredulous.—*Duft,
Sand, Earth, and other Materials might be
tranfported in the Air by a Whirlwind; they
might be mixed in it with fulphureous Exhalations, and hardned*, &c. This I allow,
tho' for ought I know I may grant too
much. But however, I will not deprive
thefe Gentlemen of their beft Argument,
that it might not be faid they fought without Arms.

I have one fingle Queftion to put to them.
" What fize muft thefe Stones be of, to
" fall from the fuperior Part of the Atmof-
" phere, where you pretend they were
                                    " form'd

" form'd, and how long may
" pended in it?—If you fho
" that thefe Stones weigh'd
" Pounds; that they were fo
" inftant by the quick re-unior
" ticles they are compofed of, a
" fell that moment, this might
" poffible. But you don't ftop
" make the Fact abundantly mo
" ful; and of a Phænomenon,
" give for a Natural one, you
" of the moft furprifing Mira
" Stones which you produce as
" of a Monftrous fize. One is
" of a *four wheel'd Carr*; the oth
" near *three hundred Pounds,*
" play'd in the Air for the fpace of
" and the other fell in the mic
" Storm, without any Body know.
" ther it was fupported there for a

6. The fact of the Twelve hundr
fuppofed to have fallen in the Nei
hood of *Abdone*, is liable to the fan
culties. They weigh'd, one fixty, t
a hundred and twenty Pounds.
prevented their falling before they
that enormous fize?—Is the Air,
one Place of our Earth, able to ret
falling of a five or fix pound one,
fhould be fuppofed to be fufpended
and how came thefe to force the refi

of the Air only when they happened to be of such a prodigious Weight.

7. One single Fact well averred would do the Business effectually.—You'll say the Stone that fell in *Alsace* is to this Day preserved in a Church, any Body may see it,— and this is a fact attested by many Travellers,— " Softly, says our Author.—I grant " the Existence of that Stone. But what I " dispute is, that it was formed in the Air, " and that it fell from it,—This is the " Point."—

As our Author is of Opinion, that heavy Stones cannot be naturally form'd in the Air, he also contradicts the Authors of the *Universal History* in that Part of the Fact in Question, which they think miraculous; viz. *that the Storm should be so directed as to fall on the Canaanites*; and in this I think he loses the Advantage he had on the former Part of the Question. He pretends that the hurry the *Canaanites* were in, their Confusion, their Flight, might naturally occasion the breaking of that Storm : " Take " Notice, *says he*, of the time these Stones " or this Hail fell. It was when the *Canaanites* were routed, running away with " the greatest Precipitation. This Rout, " this precipitate Flight of a whole Army, " must have caused an extraordinary Agita-
" tion

(*i*) Rem. of the Journal.

" tion in the Air. The Cloud was then
" floating on the head of thofe Troops in
" Confufion: Moved and fhaken by the
" continual and violent impreffion it re-
" ceives from the inferior Air, it breaks, it
" divides itfelf, and being unfupported, it
" goes through the Air, where it meets with
" the lefs Refiftance, and impetuoufly falls
" on the *Canaanites*.

The Author, to maintain this Opinion
alledges two Facts related by Monfieur *Fon-*
tenelle in his Hiftory *(k)* of the Academy :
The firft is this.— " In the Month of *May*
" there fell in the Neighbourhood of *Iliers*,
" a prodigious Quantity of Hail of a mon-
" ftrous fize. The fmalleft was two Inches
" thick, the greateft as big as a Man's Fift,
" and weigh'd one Pound and a Quarter,
" and the middling was of the fize of a
" Hen-Egg, and in greater quantity. It
" was in many Places one foot high above
" Ground. The Corn in 30 Parifhes was
" laid down by it juft as if it had been cut
" with a Sickle. The Inhabitants of *Iliers*
" feeing this Storm, betook themfelves to
" their Bells, which they rung with fuch
" vigour, that the Cloud broke above their
" Parifh in two Parts, which went one on
" one fide, and t'other on the other, fo that
" in the middle of 30 Parifhes that were
                              " ruined

_____

(k) Hift. de l'Acad. An. 1703. p. 25.

" ruined, becaufe they had not fuch good
" Bells, this fingle Parifh received no con-
" fiderable Damage.

This Fact, tho' in appearance againft our
Author's Hypothefis, may be eafily reconciled to it; the following one taken from
the fame Book proves it.— " The Night be-
" tween the 14 and 15 *April,* 1718. there
" was at *Breft* a moft extraordinary Thun-
" der, of which Mr. *Deflandes* gave the
" Defcription to the Academy.— It was
" preceded by Storms and Rains, which
" had lafted for many Days, almoft with-
" out Interruption.— That whole Night
" there were brisk and almoft continual
" Lightnings. Sailors that had fail'd from
" *Landerneau* in a Boat, being dazled by
" thofe continual Fires and unable to direct
" it, left it to the Mercy of the Waves,
" which brought it to a Place of the Coaft
" which happily was very favourable for
" landing. At four in the Morning, they
" heard three claps of Thunder fo terrible,
" that the boldeft did fhiver. About the
" fame Hour, and on that Coaft that lieth
" between *Landerneau* and *St. Paul de Leon,*
" the Thunder fell on 24 Churches, and
" precifely on the Churches where they
" were ringing to drive it away. Some
" Neighbouring Churches, where they did
" not ring, were fpared. This the People
" imputed to its being Good-Friday, when

" it

" it is not allowed to ring Bells. Mr. *Def-*
" *landes* concludes from this, that the Bells,
" which may drive away a remote Thun-
" der, haften the fall of that which is near
" and almoft vertical, becaufe the Im-
" preffion they make on the Air, difpofes
" the Cloud to open itfelf."

From thefe two Obfervations our Author
concludes, that the Stones that deftroyed the
Canaanites, might have fuch a natural Origin. *Whilft they were running away,* fays
the Text, *the Lord caft down great Stones
from Heaven upon them ;* that is to fay, that
the Cloud broke and fell, the very inftant
the *Canaanites* were routed. " The fudden
" motion of an Army put to flight muft
" caufe a violent Agitation, and a kind of
" Undulation in the Air, which Waves fuc-
" ceeding each other carry the Confufion
" to a greater or a fmaller height in the
" Atmofphere, according to the greater or
" lefs Strength and Motion.   A little Stone
" gently thrown upon the Water, may give
" a clear Notion of what happens in the
" Air.   The Inftant of it's fall you fee in
" the Water, an infinite Number of Waves
" which regularly fucceed one another, and
" extend themfelves far from their Center.
" Thofe Waves are more eafily formed, and
" propagated in the Air, becaufe it makes
" lefs refiftance than Water.—What is there
" then;

" then, *says the Journalist*, fupernatural in
" the Cafe of the *Canaanites* ?

(*l*) I beg leave to put another Queftion :
Whether the fuppofition on which our Author's whole Syftem is grounded, may be
granted ; viz. *that the Motion of an Army
running away, caufes a great Revolution and .
Agitation in the Air* ; and whether one
fingle Bell does not ftrike it more fuddenly
and violently than the flight even of an Army
of a hundred thoufand Men ?—If fo, the falling of thofe Stones on the *Canaanites*, muft
be ftill look'd upon as very extraordinary, if
not miraculous.

(*l*) Rem. of the Journal.

ARTICLE

ARTICLE VII.

Traité *des* Sens *par Mr.* Le Cat, *Docteur en Medecine,* &c. 8ᵛ. Rouen 1740, & Amfterdam, 1743.

That is to fay,

A Treatife *concerning the* Senfes, *by Mr.* Le Cat, M. D. &c.

TO raife the Curiofity of the Public for this excellent Work, I need only fay that it is mentioned with Approbation in the *Philofophical Tranfactions* ; (*a*) by Dr. *James Parfons,* F. R. S.

(*b*) The Treatife concerning the Senfes is a Part only of a larger Work intended by the Author on *Phyfiology* in general. As this Piece is of the greateft Importance, and more adapted to the general Tafte than other Parts of Phyfic relative to the human Body, the Author thought he might pub- lifh it feparately. It is divided into five Parts, according to the Number of the Sen- fes ; viz. *Feeling, Tafte, Smelling, Hearing,* and

(*a*) *November* and *December,* 1742. Nᵒ. 466.
(*b*) See *Bibliotheque Francoife.* Tom. xxxvi. pag. 26. and *liotheque raifonnée.* Tom. xxxi. pag. 304.

and *Sight*. The Account given of the laft takes up about two thirds of the Book, becaufe it neceffarily introduces a difquifition upon Light and Colours.

Of FEELING.

THIS Senfe is the coarfeft, but at the fame time the fureft of all others. It is befides the moft univerfal. We fee and hear with fmall Portions only of our Body, but we feel with all. Nature has beftow'd that general Senfation where-ever there are Nerves, and they are every where, where there is Life. Were it otherwife, the Parts divefted of it might be deftroy'd even without our Knowledge. It feems that, upon this Account, Nature has provided that this Senfation fhould not require a particular Organifation. The Structure of the Nervous *papillæ* is not ftrictly neceffary to it. The Lips of a frefh Wound, the Periofteum, and the Tendons when uncovered, are extreamly fenfible without them. Thefe nervous Extremities ferve only to the Perfection of *Feeling*, and to diverfify Senfation.

Feeling is the Bafis of all other Senfations. All the Nervous Solids, while animated by their Fluids, have this general Senfation; but the *Papillæ* in the Skin, thofe of the Fingers in particular, have it in a more exquifite

PART I.   G   quifite

quifite Degree, fo perfectly, that they convey fome Notice of the Figure of the Bodies which they touch.

After this general Notion of *Feeling*, our Author fpeaks of it's Object. *The Object of Feeling*, fays he, *is every Body that has Confiftency or Solidity enough to move the Surface of our Skin.*—It was neceffary to perfect *Feeling*, that the Nerves fhould form fmall Eminences, becaufe they are more eafily moved by the Impreffion of Bodies, than an uniform Surface.

It is by the Means of this Structure that we are enabled, not only to diftinguifh the fize and figure of Bodies, their Hardnefs and Softnefs; but alfo their Heat and Cold.

Feeling is fo ufeful a Senfation, that it fupplies the Office of the Eyes, and in fome Senfe indemnifies us for their Lofs. A *Dutch* Organift grown blind, fucceeded well in his profeffion, and obtained the Habit of diftinguifhing by *Feeling* the different kinds of Money, and even Colours; fo that he became a formidable Player at Cards; for in handling them he knew what he dealt his Antagonift, as well as what he had himfelf.

Tickling is in refpect to *Feelings*, what an Hermaphrodite is in refpect to fexes. It partakes equally almoft of Pleafure and Pain. It makes one laugh, and it is at the fame time intolerable. Carried too far it becomes

ftrictly

strictly speaking a Disorder, and, if Historians may be credited, in some Cases a Mortal one.

In this Sensation the Organs of *Feeling* are affected with the light tremulous Motion, which occasions all voluptuous Sensations; but more lively in its Degree, and smarter, than that which usually attends on Pleasure : Too long continued, or too forcibly excited, it degenerates at last into nervous Tremblings, and convulsive Starts, which are the Source of Pain.

This Affection proceeds from that gentle Friction which is distinguish'd from all other Impressions on the Organs by the Name of *Titillation* ; which produces it almost without exception in all Persons, in those Parts at least of the Body where the nervous *papillæ* are most numerous, most susceptible of Motion, and best stored with animal Spirits. Such are the Edges of the Lips.—A Disposition in a low Degree inflammatory encreaseth the Sensibility of the *Papillæ*.—Hence *Itchings* which are universally attended with some Symptoms of Inflammation.—The Imagination has the same effect.— A declared Intention to tickle us, as it were alarms the Spirits, and awakens their Sensibility. We are tickled in some measure before we are touched. An accidental Impression, on the other hand, seldom produces

this

this Senſation; and it ſeems that the
of it is neceſſary to give the Nerves a
ſition to admit of it.

Of Taste.

TASTE in the Opinion of the *A*
is not confined to the Mouth
conſiders the Mouth, the Oeſophagı
Stomach as one continued Organ, anɗ
ſequently alſo *Taſte* and Hunger,
Liquids *Taſte* and Thirſt, as Modifiɛ
only of the ſame Senſation. The *I*
indeed taſtes in a more accurate degreɛ
however, different Flavours are impe
diſtinguiſh'd in their Paſſage throug
Oeſophagus, and even in the Stomaɕ
cite the Appetite in proportion to their ɕ
fulneſs.

Bodies are not the Object of *Taſte*, b
Juices with which thoſe Bodies are in
nated, or which are extracted from
Salts, either fixed or volatil, are the
principles which act upon the Organ;
ter ſerves only as a Vehicle, *(c)* and
tures of Oyl and Earth do no morɛ
modify the Impreſſions of the Salts.

(c) This does not agree with what the illuſtrious *Bo*
lays down in his *Med. Inſtitut.* wherein he ſays, that
one of the Objects of Taſte. Inſtit. Med. parag. 488. ɪ

The immenfe diverfity of Colours, all of them however reducible in their Original to *Seven*, are a pregnant inftance that a few primitive Senfations may be modified into fecondary ones of an unlimited Variety. It happens fo in Savours. Simple falts have each its own. By their feveral Combinations into compound Salts, they afford new Savours, as numerous as thofe very Combinations, which again are multiplied by their various mixture with Suphurs, Oyls, and Earths.

The Nervous *Papillæ* are the Organs by which we diftinguifh Savours. They are plac'd extreamly clofe, not only on the furface of the Tongue, but alfo in the Palate, the infide of the Cheeks, and in a word in the whole Mouth. This is proved by Experience. Mr. *Juffieu*, in *the Memoirs of the Royal Academy*, relates, that a Girl born without a Tongue, had her *Tafte* however.-- A Chirurgeon of *Saumur*, faw a Boy about eight Years old, whofe Tongue mortified in the fmall Pox, and fell off fo that no fign of it remained, who, however, could diftinguifh Savours. He had therefore other Organs for that purpofe than the *Papillæ* on the Tongue, tho' they are probably the moft Acute.

(d) The Author concludes from thence, that the whole Mouth is furnifhed with

G 3 thofe

(d) Obfervat. of the Author of *La Biblioth. raifonnée.*

thofe nervous Organs; but if he had not forgot his own Syftem, he fhould have concluded more, and difpenfed fome fhare of the *Papillæ* to the Oefophagus and to the Stomach. If they tafte they muft have Organs; and confequently their Surface muft be ftored with thefe little nervous Prominencies which are fo neceffary to Tafte. But the Truth is, there is nothing of this kind appears on the infpeftion of the Gullet or the Stomach; nor is there any Faft whatever to fupport the Author's Notion, and till he gives better Reafons to confirm it than he has yet alledged, the Reader may fafely reft on *Boerhaave (e)* and *Bellini's(f)* Notion, who confine the Organs of *Tafte*, and the Senfation alfo, entirely to the Mouth.

Imagination has a confiderable Influence on our *Tafte*, as well as on all other Senfations. " Why, *fays Mr. Le Cat*, did I at firft " difrelifh the bitternefs of Coffee which " now is my Delight ?—Why were Oyfters " odious as Phyfic once, which now to me " are a delicious Food ?— The Impreffion " of Coffee and of Oyfters on my Organs " are not altered; the Mechanifm of thefe " Organs is pretty near the fame. The " Alteration therefore muft be in the Mind, " which from the fame Impreffions forms " different Ideas." The Author concludes

from

(e) *Boerhaave.* ibid. 87. pag. 486. 487.
(f) Laurent. bellini. *Tractatus de Organo guftûs.*

from hence " that our Ideas are not connec-
" ted with the Impreffion made upon the
" Organ, not invariably at leaft, fince the
" Mind actually changeth them."

To this Action of the Mind he afcribes
the Influence of Mode and Fafhion on
the *Tafte*. The Mind refolves to like what
is recommended by the Mode, and fucceeds
at laft in reforming it's Senfations. Hence
we are reconciled in Time to the moft difagreeable Savours, and receive Pleafure from
the Objects of our Abhorrence.

Thus the Author. But is his Opinion
grounded, enquires the *French* Journalift,
which I tranflate. (g) " Have we not more
" reafon to think that the Mind has different
" Senfations, becaufe the Difpofition of the
" Organs is either altered, or differently af-
" fected ? Wine drinks delicioufly after
" Nuts or Cheefe. After Apples, Goofe-
" berries, or a Civil Orange, it is naufeons
" to my Palate.— I eat with Appetite to-
" Day, and relifh what is fet before me, I
" am well and my Organs are in order.
" The next Day every thing difgufts me,
" and the fame Food palls my Appetite
" which excited it the Day before. Has
" it loft its Relifh ? No. I am not well
" myfelf, and the Organs of Tafte are in-
" difpofed. This is certainly the Reafon of
" the different Senfations I experience, and
G 4 not

(g) Obfervat. of the Author of *La Biblioth. raifonnée.*

" not any Action of the Mind, by which it
" alters them. The Mind is absolutely paf-
" five in receiving the Impreffions of Ob-
" jects on its Organs; and it neceffarily feels
" as the Organs are affected.

(*b*) So far is well; and the Affertion that
the Mind is eternally paffive in Senfations,
is certainly a true one. But Mr. *Le Cat's*
Problem is not folv'd. 'Tis one thing to
fhew that his Solution cannot be admitted,
and another to affign the true one.— Independently of Sicknefs, of Age, of Accidents,
the Tafte alters by the mere Force of Habit; by Repetition only the fame Savour becomes pleafant, nay, bewitching, which in
the firft Tryals made of it was difagreeable
and even naufeous.— This remains to be accounted for upon the Suppofition that the
Mind is paffive. To fay that the Senfation
differs as the Organ is well or ill prepared
by prior Savours, or well or ill difpofed by
Health or Sicknefs, does certainly not reach
the Point.—

It may throw fome light upon this Subject to obferve, that all Senfations lofe
fomething of their Smartnefs by Repetition; That each Impreffion is fainter than
the former, and that the keeneft foften
by Degrees, into mild and gentle Feelings.

It may be added, that as far as we can
judge, there are no Savours effentially dif-
pleafing:

(*b*) Remark of the Journalift.

pleaſing: They become ſo by their Intenſe‐
neſs only. And as they remit of that, they
again become agreeable. There are no Per‐
ſons that we know of, who have a general
Diſguſt for ſweet, or ſour, or bitter. Some
Degrees of each may be too luſcious, too
ſharp, or too auſtere for them; but in a
lower Tone each of thoſe primitive and fun‐
damental Savours is to every Palate pleaſing.
And why not the ſeveral Combinations of
them under the ſame Reſtrictions?

Suppoſe this true, and the Phænomenon
is perfectly explained. I give it as a Con‐
jecture only which deſerves the Attention
of the Learned. I ſhall only add, that
ſhould it happen, by ſome peculiar Confor‐
mation of the Organs, that to any Indivi‐
dual any one Savour was in every Degree
of it diſtaſteful; that Individual, by the Hy‐
potheſis I go upon, could never be recon‐
ciled to it by Cuſtom. The Antipathy would
be unconquerable; and if any ſuch ſhould
be obſerved, as there is ſome Foundation in
Experience to ſuſpect there may, that An‐
tipathy itſelf would ſtrengthen the Hypothe‐
ſis. It would be an Exception which
would corroborate the Rule, and ſhew why
it generally held good, and why, in ſome
Particulars it fail'd.

To be continued.

A R‐

ARTICLE VIII.

Memoires *pour servir à* l'Histoire Na
  des Petrifications. Avec figures &c
  Indices.

•

That is to say,

Memoirs for the Natural History *of* F
cations in the four Parts of the V
4°. 270. pag

(a) MR. *Bourguet* Professor at
chatel in *Switzerland*, is th
thor of this Book. It is easy to judge
much Labour and Time it must have
him in examining the vast Number of
fied Animals he mentions; the greatest
of his Observations being grounded on
he has seen, and considered with a
Attention and Sagacity imaginable.

  The Work is divided into two
The first contains (besides the *Preface*
Epistle Dedicatory, and a *Dissertation*
Origin of Stones,) several Letters of
following Subjects. I. Letter. *On the C*
of Petrifications which resemble Marin
dies. II. Letter. *On a remarkable Pl*

•

1

(a) *Biblioth. rais.* Tom. XXX, pag. 127. and 267

meñon against the pretended Increase of the Bulk of the Earth. III. Letter. On the Petrification of small Sea-Crabbs on the Coast of Coromandel, and petrified Fishes found in Europe and in Asia. IV. Letter. On Fossils. V. On the Skeleton of a petrified Elephant VI. On Flints.

The second Part contains, I. The Method of settling, in their right Order, Fossils properly so called. II. An Index of many Authors who have treated of Petrifications. III. A second Index of several Places in the four Parts of the World where Petrifications are found. IV. A third Index for the Figures. V. Some Remarks to explain the Figures.

As I am necessitated to chuse among this great Variety of Subjects, I shall confine myself for the Present to one of the chief Articles, *viz.* the Letter on *Petrifications in general.*

This Letter was wrote by one of Mr. *Bourguet*'s Friends in the County of *Neufchatel.*

WHATEVER has been wrote on petrified Bodies may be reduced under the two following Heads. The first and most common Opinion is, that all those Fossils are mineral or terrestrial Bodies. The second, on the contrary, is, that all those thofe Stones are, without Exception, Plants, or Remains of Animals come from the Sea. Some among thofe who favoured the firft Opinion imagined, that thefe Foffils owe their Form and the Lineaments printed on them to meer Chance, and for that Reafon they call them *lufus naturæ.* Others have fuppofed that in the Bofom of the Earth there are Moulds, or Wombs, in which Part of the Matter of the Stratas took different Forms, without pretending to account *for the Formation* of thofe Moulds. Others thought that thefe Foffils originally came from a Sea-feminal matter, which they fuppofe was brought into the Bofom of the Earth, where it was unfolded and where it grew.

To put this Queftion in its full Light, our Author thought proper to take notice of three different States, in which thofe Bodies, and efpecially Shells, actually are. There are fome that feem to have fuffered no Alteration in the Ground, and which are ftill fo beautiful and complete, that they agree perfectly with thofe feen on the Sea-fhore. Such as thefe, fays Mr. *Woodward,* are found in *England.* There are fome alfo in *France,* near *Rheims* and elfewhere, without any Adhefion of Matter, either inwardly or outwardly; fome of which have preferved their brightnefs; others appear as if they had been calcined, without their Figure, or Lineaments. The fecond State of thefe Foffils is a real and fenfible Petrification. Such are the Shells which contain harden'd Marl, ftony, metalic and mineral Bodies, or the Matter of the Stratas in which they are buried, adhering to thefe Bodies, and which even penetrate into their Pores and their Subftance, without deftroying the Shell, which is ftill very diftinctly perceived.—— Befides, there are Bodies of Clay, Marl, petrified Sand, marble Flints, and other mineral and metallic Matters, moulded in the Shells, that have received their outward Impreffion from them, without retaining any thing of the Matter itfelf of the marine Body. Among thefe laft, there are fome whofe Surface was only applied to the Cavity of the Shell, and moulded in the interior Part, without affecting the Body itfelf. In others, the petrified or harden'd Matter has penetrated the Subftance of the Shell, as it was decaying, and has received the firft impreffion of the exterior Form of the marine Body. In others, the Matter of the *Stratum* which had gone through the Shell, taking the Place of what was confumed, fill'd the whole empty Space, and received the Impreffion, which the Shell had given to the furounding Matter.

Another effential Remark is, the great Refemblance there is between natural Shells, and thofe found in the Bofom of the Earth. 1. Thefe Shells confidered outwardly appear
                                    abfolutely

abfolutely the fame, if you obferve their Surface or Convexity, their Size, their Figure, their Circumference, their Divifions, their Lines and Lineaments, their Relievo's, their Knots, their Eminencies, their Sutures, and even the Points imperceptible by the Eyes. 2. This Refemblance is not lefs apparent in the internal Parts. The fame Subftance and Structure prevails thro' them all; the Matter that compofes them is the fame, it is difpofed and fettled in a fimilar Manner. The Direction of their Fibres and of the fpiral Lines obferved in them is alfo the fame, as well as the Compofition of the fmall thin Plates formed by the Fibres. Their Weight affords another Conformity, the fpecific Gravity of the foffil Shells is precifely the fame as that of their Species found on the Seafhore.— The Accidents common to Seafhells is another Proof of their Identity. Foffils are fometimes ty'd in the fame Manner to one another, the fmaller to the greater; they have their vermicular Paffages; Pearls, and fuch like Things are found in them. From thefe Obfervations, our Author fupports the following Syftem. Thefe originally marine Bodies cannot have been tranfported by any ordinary or natural Caufe, inafmuch as this Effect is greatly inferior to the Power of the higheft Tide, or the ftrongeft Tempeft, and muft therefore have been carried

ried by a general Inundation, or a displacing of the Surface of the whole Earth, even to a great Depth.

To give some Weight to this Assertion, the Author considers the Number of those Bodies, the State in which they are now to be seen, the Places where they are found, and their Situation there.—Their Number is prodigious; I assure my Readers, *says he,* " that having examined with some Care, " several Places in this Country, *(b)* I have " discovered in a small Compass of Land, " Shells by thousands. I have seen on a " Rock such an immense Number of great " Sea Muscles and other Shells, that at the " bottom of the Rock many Carts could be " loaded with the broken Pieces.—There are " in another Place on Mount *Jura* as many " Heads of Sea *Hedge-Hogs,* and small *Oy-* " *ster-Shells* as there may be *Emmets* in the " whole Country round about. I found as " great a Quantity of the same Heads of " *Hedge-Hogs* in a Pasture-Land.— And I " have reckoned near our City of *Neufcha-* " *tel,* in a smaller Extent of Land than may " be walk'd round in a Quarter of an Hour, " about four hundred thousand Sea *Hedge-* " *Hogs,* of the Kind called *Spatagi,* be- " sides a numberless Quantity of intermix- " ed Cockles, Muscles, *&c.*" If we observe that this unaccountable Quantity of petrified

Sea-

(b) The County of *Neufchatel* in *Switzerland.*

Sea-Animals lies on the Mountains of *Switzerland*, at about 80 Leagues from the *Mediterranean*, and 150 from the neareſt Shore on the Ocean, we ſhall be forced to agree with our Author, that this prodigious Quantity of Foſſils of ſo many kinds, was not brought and lodged there, either by Men inhabiting the Sea-Coaſts, by Birds of Prey, by high Tides, or by any ſuch other Cauſe whatſoever.

As the Author aſcribes theſe Effects to the Flood, he endeavours anſwering the Objections alledged by many Philoſophers againſt its phyſical poſſibility. This Syſtem does not differ in any thing material from that of *l'Abbé Pluche*, in his excellent Book of *Nature diſplay'd.*

(c) They both affirm, that God, in order to drown the Inhabitants of the World, *inclined the Axis of the Earth towards the North-Stars, or in ſome other manner altered the Motion of our Globe.* (d) "How this could be done without overturning the whole Oeconomy of this Globe, and expoſing along with it to terrible Revolutions, and for ought I know, to a total Subverſion, the whole Machine of the Univerſe, is unanſwerable. Do not Philoſophers agree, that there is a ſtrict

<hr>

(c) Nature diſplay'd. Tom. III. pag. 366.
(d) What is contained between theſe Marks " is taken from *la Bibliotheque raiſonnée.* The reſt is the Journaliſt's.

ſtrict Connexion between it's Parts; and if
ſo, muſt they have all ſuffered for the faults
of the Inhabitants of one Globe?". They
who imagine that our Globe was with re-
ſpect to the Sun in any other Poſition than
that in which it is, do not conſider that it's
preſent Poſition is the only one fit to render
the far greater Part of the World fruitful
and inhabitable. Should the Sun run conſtantly on the Æquinoctial Line, or not
diverge, as it does, from one Tropick to the
other, or in other Words, be always at an
equal diſtance from the Poles, (which theſe
Philoſophers think to have been the primitive Poſition) then our Temperate Zones
would never have Warmth enough to ripen
any thing, and the frigid Zones would be
utterly barren and uninhabitable. Nay it
is even doubtful, whether in that Caſe the
Torrid Zone would not be alſo quite intolerable. In ſhort, the preſent Poſition, as I ſaid
before, is evidently the only one that can beſt
anſwer the apparent deſign of the wiſe Con-
triver. And conſequently, that Alteration
(which our Philoſophers look upon as a very
great Amendment,) would, inſtead of it have
been liable to many Inconveniencies. It appears, that the Phyſical poſſibility of an Univerſal Flood has not been yet accounted for
in a ſatisfactory manner. I will now venture
ſome ſhort Remarks on the proofs our Au-

PART I. H thor

thor draws in favour of his Hypothesis from the Fossils he describes.

I. I ask, whether, supposing the Universality of the Flood, it is possible to conceive that the Waters should have brought together such an immense Quantity of all kinds of Fishes and Plants, and laid them down by Millions of Millions in one single place on a Rock. Suppose the whole Bottom of the Sea should have been overturn'd, and every Fish in it brought up on the Surface of the Waters, is it to be thought they could have left them by immense heaps here and there? Is it not more reasonable to suppose, they should have been dispersed. For tho' those Fossils are found in every Country, yet they are not so universally spread as, I think, they would have been, if distributed by the Waters of the Flood.

II. According to our Author's System, it is not less difficult to determine why these Fossils are found 40 or 50 Feet under Ground, and in as great Numbers as on the Surface. What buried them deeper than it is possible to dig? It cannot be said that the smallest among them were sunk by their own Weight. If you suppose this has been effected by violent Commotions, Overturnings &c. this supposition may serve also to explain the Phænomenon without the help of your System.

III. The

III. The Difficulty is still increased by an Observation of Mr. *Bourguet*. There are petrified Crabs on the Coast of *Coromandel*, and in many Parts of *Europe*, and they are all imperfect; they want either a Leg or a Claw. Some are totally deprived of them. Many Skeletons of Crocodiles, of Fishes, &c. are found in *England*, and in some other Parts of the World, which are all mutilated. Some have their Heads broke, others deprived of them; many without a Tail; the Fins have been transposed in some, others bent as a Bow, many found with one part of the Body separated from the other, Numbers of them have but few remains of what they were, and in some places you will see an odd Collection of Fish-bones and other Fragments. Now all these Instances shew, that these Fishes were in a violent State, more than can reasonably be supposed they would have been in, if they had been brought up, by the Waters of the Flood; or gently left and placed by them, when they begun to return to their former station.

IV. Sea Fishes are found at any Depth, but the like cannot be said of Terrestrial Animals; they are found in the Chinks of Rocks, of Mountains, or not very deep under Ground. From whence proceeds this Difference? Terrestrial Animals are left by Chance on the Ground, or buried in holes by some Accident, or by the Care they

took.

took before they died to hide themselves; and if in such Places there is a petrifying Quality, their impreffions remain. This fhould be the Cafe of Sea Animals, if brought on the Surface of the Earth by the Flood. It cannot be faid they funk by their own Weight, for this reafon would hold with refpect to terreftrial Animals. Then we muft conclude there is a different Caufe.

V. By the foregoing Remarks, efpecially the Second and Fourth, one would imagine that petrified Sea Animals rather came from under Ground than from its Surface. No Body doubts that there are many fubterraneous Canals through which the Waters of the Sea may convey all forts of Animals; any one of them that meets the opening of fuch a Canal muft be hurry'd into it; there may be in fome Places very confiderable Collections of them, fufficient there to ftop the Water; and as this will endeavour to find a vent, where-ever it is ftop'd, the Place muft burft, and in fuch a Cafe it is eafy to conceive, that all the gathered Shells fhould be thrown about on every fide, in the greateft Confufion. We are not without Inftances of this kind, that give fome Weight to this Conjecture. Some Years ago a whole Village in *Piedmont* was buried under Ground. No body has been able to account for fuch a terrible Revolution.

There

There is no Volcano in the Neighbourhood, and it may as well be aſcribed to the Cauſe I have alledged, as to any other. Nay, if the Syſtem of ſome Philoſophers be true, the Difficulty is intirely removed. They ſay that the Sea is higher, or at a greater Diſtance from the Center of the Earth, at ſome hundred Leagues diſtance from the Shore than near it. The manner in which a Ship appears at a Diſtance, certainly proves the Convexity of the Water ; you ſee the Sails and Maſts, and the whole Body of the Ship is not to be perceived. Now if this be granted, the Water of the Sea reaches the Top of the Mountains whenever it meets with Canals to convey it; for we know by Hydraulic Machines, that where-ever Water does not meet with a Reſiſtance it riſes equally, and it may eaſily carry along with it a Quantity of Sea Animals, which may be petrified and produce the Phænomenon ſo much inquired into.

To return to our Author. He advances another Fact in behalf of his Syſtem from the Diſcovery of many Trees on Mountains, or deep in the Ground, in Boggs, Quagmires, and in Places where the Quality of the Air and its Coldneſs oppoſe the Formation of Vegetables, and where no other Agent, excepting Water, could have removed them. But this Fact, if well examined, might probably be accounted for in another

H 3   manner.

manner. Thefe Trees could hardly have been preferved from the Time of the Flood, without being petrified, and there are Examples, as extraordinary as thofe mentioned by the Author, which however cannot be afcribed to the Flood. " *John Huygens* of *Linfchoten* in his Voyage to the *Waeigatz,* fays, that there is in the Rivers of a *Northern* Ifland *a prodigious Quantity of Timber, tho' there is no Land thereabout, where any appearance of either Tree or Plant is to be feen.* Among that Timber he found *the Boards of* a Lodding *of* 38 *Feet, the Holes and the Seams were diftinctly to be feen, for the fide-Planks of the Ruffian* Loddings *are few'd and ty'd together with Cords.* He found far in the Land the Keel of fuch a Lodding 40 Feet long." But the moft furprifing Fact of this kind is related in a Book intitled, *The State of Switzerland,* (e) &c. " In the Year 1460, " *fays the Author*, they found in the Can-
" toon of *Berne,* a Ship a hundred Fathoms
" under Ground in a Mine, at which they
" were Working, and in it forty Men,
" with Sails and broken Anchors. This
" many have feen, and I had my Informa-
" tion from fome that were prefent." Whoever diftinctly accounts for this wonderful Fact, may alfo eafily fhew why Trees are now and then found in Places where
they

(e) *Etat & Delices dela Suiffe.* Tom. I. pag. 59.)

they do not naturally grow. And if fubterraneous Paffages can explain this difficulty,
they may ferve alfo to account for marine
Bodies, and Trees being found at the Tops
of Mountains.

I fhall now conclude this Abftract with
this general Obfervation.— "If there ever
was fuch a total Subverfion, all Men
and Animals being deftroy'd, excepting thofe
in the Ark, according to *Mofes*'s Account,
from whence cometh the Multitude of Animals now exifting?" The Ark far from
being able to receive them all, could hardly
have contained the known Infects. You
cannot fuppofe a new Creation, becaufe
Mofes is filent about it : If there had been
any fuch thing, this Event would have deferved a Place in his Hiftory as well as any
other. His filence in this refpect is certainly a ftrong Prefumption that by the
Flood he mentions, he means only a partial
one. "Befides there is an infinite number of
Animals now on the Earth, that could not
have been tranfported, nor have lived in the
Ark. It is a known Obfervation, that in
America, *China*, *Japan*, *Groenland*, and
new *Zembla*, there are Animals which abfolutely cannot live, but in the Climates in
which they are born ; fince the changing of
Air moft certainly kills them, how could
they have been kept alive in *Noah*'s Ark ?"
How difficult, if not impoffible, muft it

have

have been to find proper food for such a prodigious Variety of Animals, the Natural food of which we hardly know? What a Number of living Animals, must have been kept merely to support the Carnivorous! Without mentioning Lyons, Tygers, &c. the Birds of prey alone (of which there is in all Parts of the World a prodigious multitude of different kinds,) would have required a confiderable Part of the Ark to keep the living Creatures collected for their Food. This, and several other such difficulties, cannot be refolved without fuppofing a Number of Miracles, of which there is not one word in *Mofes*'s Hiftory.

The Tribe of Serpents might occasion many Queftions, which would prove unanfwerable, if you had not a Miracle ready to folve each. — "Another difficulty. — Who went round about the World to gather all thofe different Species of Animals? —Who can account for their return into the Régions they now inhabit?—Who fhew'd every one of them the proper Road to return to the Places fit for them, the White Bears to *Groenland*, the Tygers to the Defarts of *Arabia*, and fo on? How could they crofs over immenfe Seas to go to *Iflands*, where no mortal Man had been before the Difcovery of the New World, and where confequently they were not tranfported"?

Thefe

These Objections, and some others which the Nature of an Abstract will not allow me to mention, appear to me, as yet unanswered. But whatever one may think of the Universality of the Flood with respect to Animals, none of those Difficulties affects it with respect to Mankind. And that is the only Point of Importance.

ARTICLE IX.

La Sainte Bible. Nouvelle Version, *par*

Charles Le Cene, &c.

That is to say,

The Holy Bible. A New Translation by *Charles Le Cene. Amsterdam*, 1741, 2 Tom. fol. Tom. 1. pag. 379, besides the Prefaces and the Project, which contain 223. pag.— Tom. 11. pag. 693.

THE Author of this new Translation of the Bible, publish'd in 1696. a Project of his Work, which Project is known throughout all *Europe*, and has been much admired by some, and as much disliked by others. It was translated into *English* by an unknown Author who gave a second Edition of it in 1727, which was dedicated to the Archbishops and Bishops of *England*. The Work itself did not fully answer the Expectation of those who had

approved

approved the Project ; which might in fome Meafure be owing to this, that the Author died before the Work was printed. His Son, the Editor of it, could not probably fpend upon it as much Time as was neceffary, either to correct fome Defects in the Language, or to produce better Authorities for the many Alterations in it, or enrich it with explanatory Notes which are much wanted. However, the Book as it is, is very valuable, and I believe the only one of the Kind. I intend to give in my next, an Account of feveral of the moft remarkable Additions and Omiffions in the New Teftament according to Mr. *Le Cene's* Opinion, but at prefent I confine myfelf to his Project, efpecially the fecond Part, which now appears for the firft Time, and which along with the Firft is placed at the Head of his Bible, by way of preliminary Differtation.

Before I proceed any further, it will not be improper to abftract the Account of the Author's Life, given by his Son.

Mr. *Charles Le Cene* was born 1647, at *Caen* in *Normandy*, where his Parents, who were in eafy Circumftances, made him go through his firft Studies. He went in 1667 to ftudy Divinity at the Academy of *Sedan,* (a) where he remained till *April* 1669.

After

(a) It was one of the chief Proteftant Academies in *France.* This City lies in *Champaign.*

After a short Stay in his Father's House he repaired to the Academy of *Geneva*, which then had many illustrious Professors. He left that City in *November* 1670, to go to *Saumur*, (*h*) which was not inferior in Fame to *Geneva*. In *March* 1672, he returned to *Caen*, having received from Messieurs *Beaulieu*, *Maurice*, *Mestrezat*, *Turrettin*, *Amyraud*, *Cappel*, *La Place*, *Bochart* and *Morin*, ample Testimonies of his Learning, Morals, and Diligence. I do not know to what Church he was first called. The second was *Honfleur* in *Normandy*, where he marry'd into a Family in easy Circumstances. His Wife's Fortune added to his own, put him in a Condition of giving himself up intirely to the Inclination he always entertain'd for Letters. He had made it his Business to know Books. He bought a choice Library, and then he began to collect Materials for his new Version of the Bible, having formed the Design of it about this Time. This was constantly his favourite Occupation, even at the Time of his greatest Tryals.

He was called to the Church of *Charenton*, but before he could take Possession of his new Office, the Church was shut up by
Order

(*h*) It lies in the Province of *Anjou*, and was the most celebrated Academy the Protestants had in the Kingdom, before the Edict of *Nantz* was repealed.

Order from the *French* King, the Edict of.
Nantz was repealed, all the Proteſtant
Churches in *France* pull'd down, and their
Miniſters forced to leave their Country; &c.
Mr. *Le Cene* fled to *England*, whither he
had the Happineſs of removing his Library,
and carrying off along with him wherewithal to live and be of ſome Service to many other Miniſters, who, as well as he, had
repaired thither to enjoy in full the precious
Liberty of ſerving God according to their
Way of Thinking. There he kept up
with Mr. *Alix*, and others of like Character
and Reputation for Learning, that Intimacy
which they had formed in their own Country. He afterwards went over to *Holland*,
and after having ſtaid ſeveral Years there,
he came back to *London*, where he died in
1703. All his Life was ſpent in carrying
on his grand Deſign. This was his chief Aim,
not only in his conſtant Studies, but alſo in
his Travels, which afforded him an Opportunity of viſiting a great Number of conſiderable Libraries.

The firſt Part of his Project is divided into fifteen Chapters.

The Subject of the I. is expreſſed in theſe
Words. *Too much Care cannot be taken in
giving the right Senſe of the Scripture.* Mr.
Le Cene blames the Tranſlators of all Nations for their being ſo nicely ſcrupulous as

always

always to render the original Verbatim into their own Languages; which unavoidably filled their Tranflation with fuch Hebraifms, and Grecifms, as conveyed no Senfe, or Meaning, to the *Englifh*, *French*, or *German* Reader, who did not underftand *Hebrew* or *Greek*. For Inftance, what Reafon is there for preferving the word *Raca* in *Matth.* v. 22. inftead of the word *Execrable*; which conveys a clear Idea to the Mind. There are Abundance of fuch Words, or Turns, peculiar to the Original, which make our Verfions almoft unintelligible.

The Author enlarges on this fame Subject in the II. Chapter, and fhews that *Mofes*'s, and St. *John*'s forbidding to add to, or take away from, Revelation, does not oblige us to forfake the Senfe in order to give the Words. There are abundance of Occafions where a Tranflator is forced to throw in a Word, elfe no Body could know what his Meaning is.—How many Commentators were puzled at thefe words, 1 *Tim.* ii. 14. Adam *was not deceived, but the Woman,* &c. The Repetition of the Word *firft*, which is in the foregoing Verfe, explains them. Adam *was not deceived firft*, &c.

Chap. III. *The Stile of the holy Scripture is fometimes fo figurative, that a Tranflator is obliged to exprefs the plain Senfe only.* The Writings of the *Eaftern* Nations are ftuffed

with

with Metaphors and Hyperboles. Among many Examples the Author alleges, I shall chuse one only of the last Kind, *viz. Hyperboles.* When it is said that *(c) there is none righteous, none that doeth good,* &c. nothing more is meant than this, that *at the Time this was said, the Corruption was very general;* but those that are not acquainted with this way of speaking are inevitably led into Error, to avoid which, it is proper to translate thus: *There are few righteous,* &c. otherwise you give the Words, but not the Sense of the Text: *(d)* And here is an Example of Figures, which darken the Meaning of the Author to those who are not used to that way of speaking. When St. *Paul* and some others of the sacred Writers speak of the *Jews,* they often make use only of the word *Circumcision;* and when they speak of the *Gentiles,* they mention only the word *Uncircumcision.* Now there are many Readers, who not knowing that by the former is meant the *Jewish* Nation, and by the latter the whole *Pagan* World, cannot possibly understand such Passages. That Inconveniency might be easily prevented, *viz.* by putting the words *Jews* and *Gentiles,* instead of the two others.

Chap.

(c) Psalm xiv.——Rom. iii.
(d) *Remark of the Journalist.*

Chap. IV. *What happened to those that un-dertook to reform the authorized Versions:* Mr. *Le Cene* mentions *Hieronymus, Erasmus, Pagninus, du Jon, Tremellius, Beza,* &c.

Chap. V. *The Necessity of correcting the Versions of the Bible.* Here the Author en-larges on what he said in the four first Chapters.

Chap. VI. *The Abuse of literal Versions is the Source of Superstitions.* Witness what *Origen* and others did in obedience to these Words, *some have made themselves Eunuchs for the Kingdom of Heaven's sake.* (e) Mr. *Le Cene* translates this Text thus : *There are some, who, for the Kingdom of Heaven's sake, live as if they were Eunuchs.*

Chap. VII. *The Faults of Versions have introduced many Errors, and multiplied Con-troversies.* This the Reader may easily apply to many Cases.

Chap. VIII. *The too-literal Versions are of-ten so dark, that the People can make no man-ner of Sense of them.* For Instance, it is said in *Is.* xxi. 12: *The Watchman said, The Morning cometh, and also the Night : if ye will enquire, enquire ye : Return, come ;* which Words our Author renders thus. *The Gentry shall say ; the Morning is come, and so is the Night. Tho' you enquire with so*

much

(e) Matth. xix. 12.

much Impatience, (*f*) *yet you ſhall certainly return.*

Chap IX. *The want of Exactneſs in our Verſions makes the Scripture to contradict it ſelf.* The moſt Part of both *Engliſh* and *French* Verſions ſay, (*g*) that *God was not known unto* Abraham, Iſaac, *and* Jacob *by his Name* JEHOVAH ; and yet *Abrabam* called him by that Name on ſeveral Occaſions. (*h*) Mr. *Le Cene* remarks with *Colomeſius,* and others, that the Hebraic Particle, *lo* is often interrogatory, and this clears up the Difficulty at once : *Was I not known unto them by my Name of* JEHOVAH ? — This Remark may ſpare a great deal of Trouble to many Preachers, if they think proper to apply it to this famous Place in *Ezekiel.* (*i*) *If a Prophet be deceived when he hath ſpoken a Thing, I the Lord have deceived that Prophet, and I will ſtretch out my Hand upon him.* Here again our Author makes the *lo* interrogatory, and the Difficulty vaniſhes : *If a Prophet ſuffers himſelf to be deceived, I the Lord have I deceived that Prophet ? On the contrary, I will ſtretch out my Hand upon him,* &c. Mr. *Le Cene* throws alſo a great Light on the ſecond Commandment by this Criticiſm. He proves that the

Pre-

(*f*) Or *Diffidence,* which certainly renders the Meaning of the Text incomparably better.

(*h*) Gen. xiv. 22. and xv. 7.

(*i*) Ezek. xiv. 9.

Prepofition *lamed* as often means *by* as *upon*, and he tranflates thus. *I punifh the Iniquity of the Fathers, by the Means of their Children,* &c.

Chap. X. *Our Verfions do often confound Things, Places, Perfons, and what concerns them.* They mingle together the four Seasons of the Year, when they fay; *that while the Earth remaineth, Seed-time and Harveft, and Cold and Heat, and Summer and Winter, and Day and Night fhall not ceafe.* (*k*)—The Septuagint have rightly rendered the Original *Kor, Chom, Kayts,* and *Choreph,* by the Words *Winter, Spring, Summer,* and *Autumn.*

Chap. XI. *The Miftakes of our Verfions when they fpeak of Coins and Meafures.*

Chap. XII. *They often confound the Perfons, Countries, and Actions fpoken of in Scripture.* (This is a Continuation of the X*th* Chapter)

Chap. XIII. *They alfo miftake what is faid about Animals, and metamorphofe them into other things.* For inftance, when they transform the *Hyena,* which is a very cruel kind of Wolf in *Arabia, Syria,* and *Africa,* into a *Speckled Bird,* (*l*) which makes a very odd figure among *Lions,* and other *Beafts of the Field.*

PART I.   I   Chap.

(*k*) Gen. viii. 22.
(*l*) Jerem. xii. 9.

Chap. XIV. *The want of exactness in our Versions affords a pretext to bad Men to colour their hardness of Heart, and to Libertines for their Impiety.* Who could avoid being offended at these Words. (m) *The Lord said to* Hosea, *Go, take unto thee a Wife of Whoredoms,* &c. One meets frequently in Scripture with Descriptions made in the present Time, of what Things or Persons were formerly; as for instance; when Jesus Christ says, *the Blind receive their Sight,* (n) tho' he speaks of those that were already cured. Accordingly that Passage of *Hosea* ought to have been expressed thus : *Go, take unto thee that Woman who was formerly a Prostitute,* &c. Again : instead of saying, (o) *the Harlots go into the Kingdom of God before you,* we must read, *those that were formerly Harlots,* &c.—Or that *God justifieth the Ungodly,* (p) we must say, *him who has been ungodly.*

Chap. XV. *The Equivocal expressions of the Original have often lead our Translators and their Readers into great mistakes.* For instance, these Words convey a very dangerous Notion in the Mind : (q) *The Woman shall be saved in Child-bearing,* instead of, *the Woman shall be saved, for her having well educated her Children,* &c.

The

(m) Hos. I. 2.
(n) Matth. xi. 5.
(o) Matth. xxi. 31.
(p) Rom. iv. 5.
(q) 1 Tim. II. 15.

The second Part of Mr. *Le Cene*'s Project is divided into nine Chapters.

This is the Substance of the I. *The Books of the Bible ought to be restored to the order of Time, in which they were wrote*; *for the Time assigned to them by* Jews *and* Christians *serves only to perplex History.* The *Jews* do not agree among themselves in this respect. Some of them have put together the *Pentateuch*, and the *Prophets*, as being worthy of the highest Degree of Respect; and have made a separate Collection of the *Hagiographi*, as requiring a less degree of Veneration. Mr. *Le Cene* finds fault with this Method. I will not pretend to determine whether he is in the right. I think there might be an Use in it. It might, perhaps, be a means to let People know that *the Song of Solomon*, for instance, is not thought so important and instructive, as the *Pentateuch*, or the *Prophets*; and this I humbly conceive would be of more Service to Religion, than the preserving of the Series of History.

The most common division the *Jews* have made of the Bible is into three Parts, the *Pentateuch*, the *Prophets*, and the *Hagiographi*. They give highly the preference to *Moses* over all the other Prophets, for many Reasons, which it would be too tedious to relate. I shall mention one only, because it occasions a Reflection from our Author

which

which it is not proper to pass over. One
of the highest Prerogatives of *Moses*, according to the *Jews*, consisted *in an immediate
Communication with God himself.* This they
ground on what is said, (r) that *God spake
to* Moses, *Mouth to Mouth.* "But, *says Mr.*
" *Le Cene*, these Words do not express an
" immediate Revelation from God to *Mo-*
" *ses*'s Mind, of the things revealed, nor an
" entirely clear and distinct Knowledge in
" *Moses* of God's Nature, Qualities, and
" Actions. For there is no reason why
" these Words should not be ascribed to an
" Angel that represented the Person of God,
" that is to say, it was through an Angel
" that God gave him his Oracles, and ac-
" quainted him with his Will. Nothing is
" more common in Scripture than to refer
" to God, what the Angels do by his Au-
" thority, and when they are honoured with
" the Character of *Angels*, or *Envoys*, the
" Scripture gives them even the Name and
" the Quality of *Gods*, and of *Sovereigns*,
" as may be seen in many Places, which
" *Buxtorf* has collected in his Grammar.
" To be convinced of this, Whatever the
" Rabbins, or some too credulous Christi-
" ans may say, you need only compare
" what is said, *Gen.* xvi. 10. with the 13*th*
" Verse

(r) Num. xii. 6, 7, 8.

" Verse of the same Chapter, and with the
" 12*th* Verse of the Ch. xxii, and what is
" said, *Gen.* xviii. 2. with the 13*th* Verse.
" For the Angel of God who spoke to *Agar*,
" is distinctly named *God*, and *Lord*; and
" we see *Gen.* xxxi. 13. that the Angel who
" spake to *Jacob* is called *the God of Beth-*
" *el*, for it is certainly the Angel that speaks
" in this place, as we may see by the
" 11*th* Verse.

" Perhaps it may be said, that this Angel
" was not called *Jehovah*, but *El*, that is to
" say, the *Mighty*. But this last Name is
" applied to *God* as well as the other; be-
" sides, it cannot be denied that the Person
" spoken of in this Place is called *Jehova*,
" *Gen.* xxviii. 13. So is the Angel with
" whom *Jacob* wrested called *Elohim*, or
" *the Sovereign*, Gen. xxxii. For *Hosea*
" expresly declares it was an Angel, *Hos.*
" xii. 5. and *Jacob* calls him *the Sovereign*,
" adding that *he saw God Face to Face*, and
" calling the Place where this happened,
" *Peniel*, that is to say, *the Face of God* or
" of the *Mighty*. Take Notice that *Hosea*
" does not call him only *Elohim*, or *the So-*
" *vereign*, but *Jehova*, or *God*, ver. 6. ——
" so it is said, *Exod.* xiii. 21. that *Jehova*,
" or God, *went before his People*; and yet,
" for fear of mistakes, it is said that it was
" *an Angel of God*, Exod. xiv. 19. —— xxiii.

I 3   " 20.

" 20.—xxxii. 4.—The Angel fent to *Gi-*
" *deon* is alfo called *Jehova*, Judg. vi. 12,
" 14. 16.

" So thefe ways of fpeaking, *with him*
" *will I fpeak Mouth to Mouth*; and what
" goes before them : *If there be a Prophet*
" *among you, I the Lord will make my felf*
" *known unto him in a Vifion, and will fpeak*
" *to him in a Dream,* but *my Servant* Mo-
" fes *is not fo* ; thefe ways of fpeaking, I
" fay, very well fignify, *I the Angel of*
" *God, who reprefent his Perfon, and who*
" *am his Minifter conftituted to lead and to*
" *govern his People, I fhall for the future*
" *let the Prophets know his will, by Vifions,*
" *or by Apparitions, which I fhall prefent to*
" *their Eyes, or to their Mind and Imagina-*
" *tion and by Dreams ; but I fhall treat more*
" *familiarly with my Servant* Mofes, *with*
" *him will I fpeak Mouth to Mouth ; he is*
" *not to fee God in Ænigmas, Emblems,* or
" *Figures, but he fhall diftinctly hear me*
" *pronouncing what I am to reveal to him*
" *from God.*—This Explanation is not unna-
" tural, and what is related, *Exod.* xxv. 22.
" and *Num.* vii. 8, and 9. confirms it plain-
" ly, and ruins the Interpretation common-
" ly given thefe Words, as if God had re-
" vealed himfelf to *Mofes* without the help
" and participation of his external Senfes,
" of his Imagination, or the Faculties of his
" mind, and that what was revealed to
" him

" him was not reprefented or printed upon
" any one of his Senfes, but by an immedi-
" ate Conjunction with his Mind.   For *Mo-*
" *fes* himfelf declares that God, or the An-
" gel, fpoke to him with an articulate Voice,
" and in the fame manner that Men do con-
" verfe with one another,

" It muft alfo be acknowledged, that God
" had conftituted an Angel over the People,
" not only to guard them on the Road to
" the Land of Promife, but alfo to declare
" his Orders, his Promifes, and his Threat-
" nings ; and to punifh them for their Sins
" and Trefpaffes, or to forgive them when
" they repented ; God having entrufted him
" with his Authority, and even honoured
" him *with his Name* ; Exod. xxiij. 20. 21,
" 22. with an exprefs order to *beware of*
" *him, to obey his Voice, to provoke him not,*
" *for fear he fhould not pardon their Tranf-*
" *greffions* ; and a Promife that if they *obey'd*
" *his Voice, he fhould be an Enemy unto their*
" *Enemies,* &c. which manifeftly fhews that
" all the Revelations, and all the Commands
" *Mofes* was honoured with from God,
" came to him through this Angel, and
" confequently, that the Promifes God made
" him when he told him he fhould fpeak
" to him *Mouth to Mouth,* were to be ex-
" ecuted by means of this Angel.   Add to
" this that God declares he will fpeak to
" him *Mouth to Mouth,* in the fame man-

I 4   " ner

" ner that he appeared to other Prophets;
" and it is certain that when he appeared
" to them in Vifions or Dreams, it was by
" the means of the Angel, as all the Doc-
" tors amongft the *Jews* believe, and conf-
" quently, God fpoke to *Mofes*, *Mouth to*
" *Mouth*, only through the Mediation and
" Interpofition of this fame Angel.

Mr. *Le Cene* thinks this Reflection of
great ufe to folve the Difficulty arifing from
what is fo often faid in Scripture, that God
tempted or tried the *Jews*, to be fully informed of their Difpofitions, as if he had
not thoroughly known them. But fuppofing this difficulty to be as cogent as has
been thought, I do not apprehend our Author's Solution to be of any great fervice.
For it is much the fame thing whether God
himfelf tried *Abraham*, for inftance, or whether he did it through an Angel acting by
his Orders. What is judged unworthy of
God in one Cafe, muft be fo in the other.

Mr. *Le Cene*'s purpofe in the long Obfervation I have related, is to fhew, that the
Jews were in the wrong, in the Diftributi-
on they made of the facred Books into three
Claffes,—that *Mofes* is not greater than any
other Prophet,—and that *Jefus Chrift* alone
enjoyed the glorious Privilege of an immediate Revelation from, and Communication
with, the Almighty.

In

In the II. Chapter, our Author puts the Books of the old Testament in the Chronological Order in which he judges they ought to be, which is the following.

1 Genesis.
2 Job.
3 Exodus,
4 Leviticus.
5 Numbers.
6 Deuteronomy.
7 Joshua.
8 Judges.
9 Ruth.
10 I. Samuel.
11 The Psalms.
12 II. Samuel.
13 The Proverbs.
14 Song of Solomon.
15 Ecclesiastes.
16 Wisdom of Solomon.
17 I. Kings.
18 II. Kings.
19 Jonah.
20 Amos.
21 Hosea.
22 Obadiah.
23 Joel.
24 Isaiah.
25 Micah.
26 Nahum.

27 Habakkuk.
28 Zephaniah.
29 Jeremiah.
30 The Lamentations
31 Letter to the Captives in Babylonia.
32 Tobit.
33 The Prayer of Manasses.
34 Judith.
35 Baruch,
36 Ezekiel.
37 Daniel.
38 Additions to Daniel.
39 I. Chronicles.
40 II. Chronicles.
41 Nehemiah.
42 Esdras.
43 III. and IV. Esdras.
44 Esther.
45 Haggai.
46 Zechariah.
47 Malachi.
48 Additions to Esther.

49 Eccle-

49 Ecclefiafticus.   52 III. Maccabees.
50 I. Maccabees.   53 Supplement of Jo-
51 II. Maccabees.   fephus.

Mr. *Le Cene* is of opinion, that *Job* lived before *Mofes*, and affigns the following Reafons. 1ft, *Job* made Offerings to God (s) as head of his family, according to the Cuftom of the Patriarchs, which he could not have done, had he lived after the Law was given, which confined thofe religious Ceremonies to certain Perfons and Places. (t) 2d, In the Book of *Job* there is no mention made of any Part of *Mofes*'s Hiftory, nor any allufion to it. 3d, *Job* exclaims againft a kind of Idolatry peculiar to the *Chaldeans, Phœnicians, Syrians,* and generally all the *Arabs* among whom he lived.—How far thefe reafons are conclufive, I leave the Reader to determine.

In the III. Chapter, Our Author gives the Books of the New Teftament in the Chronological Order, in which he thinks, after the learned *Lightfoot*, they were written.

1 St. Mat.

(s) Job. i. 5.
(t) Deut. xii. 5, 6.

1 St. Matthew,	14 II. Timothy.
2 St. Mark.	15 Ephesians.
3 St. Luke.	16 Philippians.
4 St. John,	17 Colossians.
5 The Acts.	18 Philemon.
6. I. Thessalonians.	19 Hebrews,
7 II. Thessalonians,	20 St. James.
8 I. Corinthians.	21 I. St. Peter.
9 I. Timothy.	22 II. St. Peter,
10 Titus.	23 St. Jude.
11 II. Corinthians.	24 I. II. and III. St.
12 Romans.	John.
13 Galatians.	25 Revelation.

Mr. *Le Cene* makes many important Reflections on each Book of the Bible, especially those of the New Testament. I could not give a competent Account of them without drawing this Abstract to a too great length. I may attempt it in my next.

Chap. IV. *The common Distinction into Chapters and Verses ought to be reform'd.* This I believe, every Body allows, or if any one had any Doubt remaining, he may have it removed by reading *Locke*'s Preface to St. *Paul*'s Epistles.

Chap. V. *We ought to add to our Editions of the Bible Chronological Tables, representing the Order and Time of the Events related. and a short History of the false Gods mentioned in it.* We have Chronological Tables

bles to fome of our *Englifh* Bibles, and
Author wifhes other Nations would de
fame ; as to the fecond Article, it never
done yet, that I know of.

Chap. VI. *We ought to add by way of
vertifement, at the Head of the Books of
New Teftaments, Explanations of fome
of fpeaking peculiar to it.* This our Au
chiefly applies to many of the Reference
the New Teftament to the Old, expre
in thefe Words, *Thus it is written, &c
this was done that it might be fulfilled w
was fpoken by the Prophet.* (*u*) He looks
on the moft Part of them as bare Allufi
and feems not to like the double Senf
Prophecies fo much made ufe of in all
Books of Divinity. According to his \
of thinking, whatever has been literally
filled at the Time of the *Jews,* tho' m
tioned in the New Teftament as if it w
Prophecy, can be nothing more than an
lufion.] Such as thefe are, as he appreher
very common in all the Antients, and tl
of the New Teftament are but Imitat
of the *Jews,* who ufed to quote their
ered Books in this fame manner. I beli
this Syftem will be relifh'd by few,
thought dangerous by the moft Part of
Readers. But this is a very nice Queftion,

t

(*u*) Matth. i. 22. ii. 15, 17, 23. iv. 14. viii. 17. xii.
xxi. 4. xxiv. 56. John xv. 25. Act. iii. 22. vii. 37.

that would require more time than I can be-
stow at present, were I able to handle it properly. The Subject is far from being exhaust-
ed, and I wish some Lover of true Christianity may take it at Heart, and clear up the
great Difficulties it is, as yet, incumbered
with.

Chap. VII. *An Account of some Jewish
Customs, as far as they are relative to the
New Testament.* I shall only mention one,
out of many given by the Author. It seems
as if there were some Contradiction between
St. *Matthew* and St. *John* in a Circumstance
relating to our Lord's Crucifixion. The
former absolutely denies Jesus Christ's haveing drank what was offered him on the
Cross, *Matth.* xxvii. 34. and the latter as
positively says, that he did drink it, *John*
xix. 29, 30. This cannot be reconciled
without knowing that the *Jews* used to
give two Draughts to the Malefactors when
they were brought to suffer Death. The
first was made of Wine and Gall, or Worm-
wood, to lull them asleep and make them
less sensible. The second, Vinegar, when
they call'd for it, to raise their Spirits. *Jesus*
would not take of that first Liquor; and
this is what St. *Matthew* says; but he took
of the second, as St. *John* relates it, as well
as St. *Mark,* and St. *Matthew* himself,
verf. 48.

I shall

I fhall now end this Abftract with the Titles of the two laft Chapters.

Chap. VIII. *It would be proper to add alfo a Defcription of the Pharifees, and of their Superftitions.*

Chap. IX. *Of the Temper of Mind in which thofe that read our facred Books ought to be.*

ARTICLE X.

Theologie des Infectes, ou Demonftration des Perfections de Dieu dans tout ce qui regarde les Infectes. Traduit de l'Allemand de Mr. *Leffer*. Avec des Remarques de Mr. *P. Lyonnet.* 2 Tom. 8vo. pag. 350. pour le Tom. I. & 317. pour le Tom. II. A La Haye, chez. Jean Swart, 1742.

That is to fay.

The Theology of Infects, or a Demonftration of the Perfections of God, in what concerns Infects. Tranflated from the *German* of Mr. *Leffer.* With Mr. *P. Lyonnet*'s Remarks, &c.

(a) THE Hiftory of *Infects* offers a great Variety of Subjects, naturally exciting

(a) Bibliotheque raif. Tom, xxi. Part I.

citing Admiration and Wonder. The Account Mr. *Lesser* and his Editor Mr. *Lyonnet* give of them is in many respects worthy
the Attention of Naturalists.

The I. Tome consists of an Introduction,
and fourteen Chapters, in which the Author
treats of the following Subjects. I. Of the *Creation* and *Generation* of *Insects*. II. What *Insects* are. III. Of their *Division*. IV. Of their
Number, and the *Proportion* according to
which they multiply. V. Of their *Respiration*.
VI. Of their *Generation*. VII. Of their
Transformation. VIII. Of their *Sex*. IX.
Of their *Abode*. X. Of their *Motion*. XI.
Of their *Food*. XII. Of the *Arms* they are
supplied with to defend themselves against
their Enemies, and the Ways to avoid other
Dangers, they are exposed to. XIII. Of the
paternal Care they take of their *Eggs* and
their *little ones*. XIV. Of their *Sagacity*.

The *Introduction* contains forty four Pages.
Mr. *Lesser* justifies the Study of Insects a-
gainst those that think it more troublesome
than useful.——He draws his Justification
from the Authority of the Fathers,—— the
Pagans,—— and Reason. Out of Mr. *Lesser*'s numerous Quotations, I shall chuse only one from *Pliny*. (b) " How was it pos-
" sible, *(says he)* to find Room in the Body
" of a Gnat, (not to mention smaller Ani-
" mals,)

(b) Lib. xi. *Natur. Hist.* Cap. 2.

" mals,) for Organs capable of fo m
" ferent Senfations?—Where could
" fix that of Sight?—In what
" could fhe find Place to lodge th
" of Tafte and that of Smelling?—
" did fhe find Matter for the Organs
" acute Tone of that little Animal i
" what Art did fhe faften to it Wi
" Legs, and give it a Stomach and
" ftines, with a Thirft after Blood,
" ally human?—With what Indufi
" fhe endow it with Means to fat
" Appetite? She has armed it with a
" and, as if that Inftrument, (almo
" perceptible) was capable of many I
" has made it both fharp and hollow,
" ing at once as an Inftrument to make
" and a Pipe to fuck with.—What
" did fhe give to the (c)Wood-worm
" may judge of it by the Noife it ma
" piercing the Timber defigned fo
" Food?—The Bulk of an Elephan
" prizes us. We fee with Admi
" Towers built upon its Back. We w
" at the Strength in the Neck of a
" and at the Power it has to raife
" Things with its Horns; yet it is not i
" that Nature fhines moft: Her Wifd
" no where more confpicuous than i
" moft minute Things where all her Per
" ons are to be feen united and difplay
" their full Power.

(c) *Teredo.*

To this Quotation from *Pliny*, I may add what Mr. *Reaumur* says in the first *Memoir* of his *History of Insects*. After having shewn that *Natural History is the History of the Works of the Supreme Being*, he demonstrates by a great Number of examples that Inquiries about Insects ought not to be judged useless by those that value only what the undistinguishing part of Men call real Goods, since they may direct us to the way of increasing the Number of such Goods.

If Silk-worms had never been observed; how should we ever have discovered that which so much contributes to our Luxury, as well as our Wants? Could we flatter our selves that the Work of a single Species of Insects should become the Object of one of the principal parts of our Trade; that it could have employed so many Arts, and such a Quantity of different Manufactures? The Wax and Honey of the Bees are certainly of real Use to us. They who observed those industrious Flies in the Woods, and endeavoured to make them Domestic Animals, that transported them into their Gardens, or near their Houses, to make them multiply the more, and conveniently enjoy the Fruit of their Labours, were they not usefully employed.

The Remainder of our Author's Introduction sets forth the difficulty of this Study, the helps to be found in the Closets of the

PART I.   K   Curious,

Curious, the Draughts and Prints; the Defcriptions of the various parts of Infects, and the Hiftory that the Ancients and Moderns have given us of them. There are befides all this, both in the Text and in the Notes, many remarkable things, to which I refer the Reader.

The I. Chapter contains an important Article : How is it that Infects are perpetuated from the Moment in which each fpecies was created ? According to our Author, they multiply by Generation, as all other Animals do. In receiving their Exiftence they receiv'd the Power to produce their Equals, and preferve their various kinds. Mr. *Leffer* fhews afterwards by the Experiments of *Redi* and *Malpighi*, that Infects are not begot, or form'd by all forts of matter, and that the Syftem of *Equivocal Generation*, adopted by the Ancients, is not fuftainable, being grounded on falfe Obfervations.

The general Law, that all Animals multiply by way of Generation, gives Occafion to Mr. *Lyonnet* to make fome Remarks.

How general foever this Rule may be, fays he, *we are not yet certain of it's Univerfality.* The Varieties obferved in this refpect among Infects, give us fome Caufe to remain in doubt. Some are both Male and Female, as Slugs, Snails, and Earth-worms. Others are neither Male, nor Female, and fome

procreate

procreate tho' they are not seen to couple. In some, one single Copulation is enough to produce a Posterity of many Generations. All this may lead us to presume, that it is possible, there may be Insects multiplying without Generation properly so called, and that every Individual of them has by it self the Faculty of producing its kind.

Mr. *Lyonnet* dares not go any further. He alledges the bare possibility of the Fact, without affirming it. *As yet, says he, no Author, that I know of, has demonstrated it by any undoubted Experiment*, notwithstanding those made by *Leuwenhoek, Cestoni, Reaumur*, and *Mery.* The two first pretend, that the *Vinefretter* proves there are Animals that do procreate of themselves. Neither they, nor Mr. *Reaumur*, ever saw any Copulation, nor could they discover a Male in that Species. Yet Mr. *Lyonnet* assures, he saw *Vinefretters* copulating, and insists in opposition to Mr. *Mery*, that the Facts he alledges are not sufficient to prove, that *Pond-Muscles* have not the two Sexes.

The *Solitary*, a Worm that grows in the human Body, and is sometimes sixty Yards long, is perhaps the only Insect, that can be suspected of being self-sufficient to multiply. The most part of Naturalists are in the Dark as to its Origin. 'Tis always alone in the Body it inhabits. There it is formed, no Body knows how. There it remains and

grows

grows old. The like is not obferved in inanimate Bodies. This Worm then feems
to be one of thofe Hermaphrodites now in
difpute. It has the two Sexes, or contains
whatever is neceffary to produce its kind,
fince 'tis always alone. But this fuppofition
does not remove the great difficulties that
may be formed about its Origin. Why is it
never but alone, and through what road do
either its Eggs, or its little ones, go into the
Body of another Man? Mr. *Valifnieri*, one
of the moft exact Naturalifts, fays, that the
Solium is a Chain of Worms named *Cucur-
bitarys*, who hang clofe to one another, and
form the Figure of one fingle Animal.
This Hypothefis is now univerfally received, and was confirmed at *Leyden* by Experiments, made with much care and exact-
nefs by a Phyfician, who chofe this curious
matter for the Subject of a Thefis, at the
taking of his Degree. This piece had the
approbation of Meffieurs *Boerhaave* and *Al-
binus*. Mr. *Lyonnet* is not yet perfwaded,
he wifhes to be convinced by his own Eyes,
and in Cafe he finds any thing againft the
above mentioned Experiments, the Public
fhall be informed of it.

Another extreamly curious Remark of
Mr. *Lyonnet*, concerns that kind of *Polypode*
lately difcovered, and about which Mr.
Tremblay made a great Number of Obfervations and Experiments, all worthy the Attention

tention of the Curious. All Mr. *Tremblay's* Difcoveries about this wonderful Phænomenon were confirmed by Mr. *Lyonnet*, and are in fubftance thus. —

The Form of this Infect fo common in our Ditches, is fomewhat like a grain of feed of Dandelyon. It is generally fixed by its extremity to fome Body, and feldom ftirs from it. Nothing is to be feen that has the Figure of a living Creature. When cut in two, or even in three, Parts, each grows again and becomes what the Whole was, and you have two or three Animals for one. The little ones proceed from its fides by a kind of flow and imperceptible Vegetation; and after growing a while, as Branches, and having often themfelves produced other little ones, they at laft feparate from their Mother, and live alone.

Were you to judge of it by the greateft part of thefe Characters, you might readily place it among the common Vegetables: Yet if you examine it clofer, if you ftir gently the Water it lyes in, you perceive it bends, it fhrinks, it ftretches out, and then you muft allow it a degree above the common Plants, and put it at leaft in the rank of Senfitive ones. But when on cafting now and then your Eyes on it, you find it capable of arbitrary Motions, that is does not remain ftill in the fame place, but knows how to ftir from one to another, by a real,

tho'

tho' a flow, Motion, and that it even endeavours to feek the light; that the Beards placed around its anterior Extremity ferve it by their vifcofity to catch the fmall Aquatic Infects in its way; that thefe fame Beards are as a kind of Arm to convey the prey to the Mouth, and that it fwallows it; then you are forced to acknowledge it a true Animal. Obferve however, that the Vegetable and Animal Kingdoms, are fo near one another in this equivocal Creature, that Mr. *Tremblay*, a very attentive Obferver, was obliged to examine it for many Months before he could decide its being an Animal.

The Increafe of fome Infects affords another wonderful Phænomenon. This Increafe is calculated in the Chapter where Mr. *Leffer* treats of their Number, and of the Proportion according to which they multiply. As his Notion is fomewhat uncertain, Mr. *Lyonnet* made a Remark upon it, wherein he gives a more particular and diftinct Account of this Subject. The Experiment on which his Calculation is grounded, concerns the *Brufhy Caterpillar* mentioned by *Goedard*, by Mr *Merian*, and by Mr. *Reaumur.*—350 Eggs that were laid by a Butterfly of this fort, produced as many little Caterpillars. To avoid confufion, Mr. *Lyonnet* only bred up 80, all came to Perfection, except five that died. Among fo many Butterflies

there

there were no more than 15 Females; probably in another attempt more might be
found. However, on this small Number
of Females Mr. *Lyonnet* makes the following Calculation. If 80 Eggs produce 15
Females able to multiply, then 350 should
have produced at least 65. These 65 Females, supposed as fruitful as their Mother,
would bring forth, for the second Generation 22750 Caterpillars, and among them
at least 4265 Females; which would bring
forth 1492750 Caterpillars, for the third
Generation. It must be remark'd, that this
kind of Caterpillar is not as fruitful as many
others; some of them are at least twice
more so. Yet this is nothing in compari-
son of certain viviparous flies, who bring
forth 20000 little ones at one Litter, consequently one single Fly, supposing the
Number of Females to be equal to the
Males, would produce at the third Generation, a posterity of two Millions of Millions. What are we to think of such a prodigious Increase continued some Years?
The Imagination is soon lost and overwhelm'd, when it attempts to comprehend
such an enormous Progression. This difficulty is not easily answerable by those who
pretend, that God placed in the Body of the
first Insect its whole posterity. If Mr. *Lyonnet's* Calculations be true, this System must
be altogether impossible, for in that Case,

the

the firſt Fly would have contained ſuch a prodigious Number of little ones, that *when come to Maturity, and gathered together, would form a greater Maſs, than what would reſult from the Re-union of all the Globes of the viſible World.* This is not all. As every little one, that a Fly contains, is at leaſt thirty thouſand times ſmaller than it's Mother, and that we muſt ſuppoſe theſe little ones includes Embrios at leaſt thirty thouſand times ſmaller than they themſelves are, and ſo on; there is a new ſort of Progreſſion yet more wonderful than the other, by which each Fly, conſidered by degrees, as nearer its origin, diminiſhes more in ſize, than each Generation made it encreaſe in Number; accordingly ſuch a Worm of a Fly, that is to Day thirty thouſand times ſmaller than it's Mother, was three hundred thouſand Millions ſmaller than her one Generation before, and three Millions of Millions ſmaller, two Generations before. We may judge by this of the infinite ſmallneſs it had, when it's Birth was many thouſand Generations back. Suppoſing that each Fly bears only once a Year, at leaſt twenty thouſand, and many hundred Numbers in a line would be requiſite to expreſs arithmetically, how many times it was ſmaller than a Fly of it's Species, when yet incloſed in the common Mother, out of which this Species derived it Origin. The Phænomenon will

be

be yet incomparably more wonderful, if we suppose, that it is in the *Animalcules* of the Male's feed, that we must look for the Source of this Encrease, since these *Animalcules* are Infinitely smaller with respect to the Male, than the Foetus of the Fly is with respect to it's Female.

This is a terrible Objection against the above-mentioned System. Mr. *Hartsoeker* proposed a parallel one in a Letter he wrote to the Author of *La Bibliotheque Ancienne & Moderne (d)*. This Letter contains a Computation of the infinite smallness of the Seed of a Tree, or a Plant, which is only to appear at the 60th Century of the World. Mr. *Hartsoeker* asserts, that the first Parcel of Seed of the first Plant would be to the last and smallest that should appear the last Year of the 60th Century, as Unity at the Head of thirty thousand Numbers to a single Unit; from which he concludes, that the System is wholly unwarrantable.

(e) Mr. *Bourguet*, a Naturalist, offered a Reply to Mr. *Hartsoeker's* Objection, which may partly serve as such to Mr. *Lyonnet's* Difficulties. He pretends, that Mr. *Hartsoeker* is mistaken in his (f) Way of proceeding; for he reckons the smallness of a Particle

(d) Tom. xviii. Part. I. pag. 144, &c.
(e) See Article VIII. of this Journal.
(f) *Lettres Philosophiques*, &c.

ticle of Seed from the Relation of largenefs, that for Example a Plant acquires in a Year, inftead of reckoning only from the Time neceffary for that Particle of Seed to appear from its Conception to it's Maturity. Mr. *Bourguet* calls *Conception* that State which a Particle of Seed is in, from the Time the preceding Particle came out of it's animal Plant, becaufe we know by Experience, that thefe Plant-feeds are already in the fmall Plant, that they grow there in a certain Proportion, while all the Parts of the Plant that bears them are alfo growing. He pretends, that in the propofed Syftem we muft not fuppofe all the Parts that form the Bulk of a Plant have exifted before in the Seed, and confequently that we muft not judge of the primitive fmallnefs of the Plant-feeds, of the Eggs, or of the fpermatic Worms of Animals, by comparing them with the largenefs the fame organifed Bodies come to, after fome Time, more or lefs.

According to the fame Philofopher's Computation, the Seed that appeared the firft Year of the World was to the one that is to appear the laft Year of the 60th Century, as the Number of Minutes contained in fix thoufand Years is to the Number five. Sixty Centuries have three thoufand one hundred fifty three Millions, fix hundred thoufand Minutes. This, Number is very fmall, if compared to Mr. *Hartfoeker*'s.

Again,

Again, Mr. *Bourguet*, agreeable to the Hypothesis of Mr. *Hartsoeker*, compares a spermatic Worm with an Elephant of fourteen Years, which, when weighed by the Direction of the celebrated *Peiresc* (g) amounted to five thousand *Roman* Pounds, each containing twelve Ounces. The admirable Mr. *Boyle* (h) comparing the extreme Difference between that Animal and the Cheese Mite, (tho' a certain Number of them is requisite to equal the weight of the Grain) calculates on the Supposition that a Mite weighs a Grain, and concludes that the Elephant weigh'd eight and twenty Millions, eight hundred thousand times more than the Mite. Now a spermatic Worm seen with the most excellent Microscope does not appear larger than a Mite seen with the naked Eye, consequently according to Mr. *Hartsoeker*'s Opinion, and his own Calculation, this Elephant must have been fourteen Years before above a hundred thousand Millions of Millions smaller than when it was weigh'd.

The Example will be more convincing yet, if you apply the Computation to the Whale, whose Dimensions have been given. It weigh'd a hundred and thirty thousand
Pounds,

(g) Gassendi *in vita* Peiresci, *pag.* 156.
(h) *Boyle* oper. Tom. II. pag. 598, 599. Tract. *de utilit.* *Philosophiæ. Experim.* Venet. 1697. 4to.

Pounds, and, if compared to the M
and afterwards to a ſpermatic
muſt have been almoſt an innu
Quantity of times ſmaller. Here
Caſes where the Imagination is l
which however are very poſſible.

To be continued.

ARTICLE XI.

ΛΟΥΚΙΑΝΟΥ ΣΑΜΟΣΑΤΕΩΣ ΑΠ
Luciani Samoſatenis Opera cum
verſione *Tiber. Hemſterhuſii* & *Jo*
thiæ Geſneri, Græcis Scholiis, a
omnium proximæ editionis Com
torum. Additis *Jo. Brodæi*, *Jo.*
Lud. Kuſteri, *Lamb. Boſii*, *Hor. Vi*
Jo. de La Faye, *Ed. Leedes*, alliſqu
ditis, ac præcipue *Moſis Solani* &
Geſneri. Tomus I. cujus priorem
ſummo ſtudio curavit & illuſtravit
us Hemſterhuſius. Ceteras inde
ordinavit, notafque ſuas adjecit *J*
dericus Reitzius. Amſtelod. Su
Jacobi Wetſtenii, 1743.

That is to say,

The Works of Lucian, *with the Translation of Messieurs* Hemsterhuis & Gesner, *the Greek Scholiast and all the Notes of the last Edition.* To which are added the Notes of *Brodæus, Jenfius,* &c. with others, that were not published before, especially those of Messieurs *Du Soul* & *Gesner.* 4 Tomes 4°. Tom. 1. has 882. pag. besides 72. for the Prefaces. Tom. ii. pag. 953. Tom. iii. pag. 860.

(a) THIS is a very valuable and long expected Edition of *Lucian.* Messieurs *du Soul,* Hemsterhuis and *Gesner* laboured above thirty Years at this Work. The Bookseller, (Mr. *Wetstein*) dedicated it to the Queen of *Hungary.* The Preface was wrote by Mr. *Reitz* Rector of the *Hieronymian* School at *Utrecht.* The Authors took the trouble to consult the following Editions, the most of which they corrected and collated with old Manuscripts. The Edit. of *Florence* 1496. fol. — of *Aldus* of 1503, — another of *Aldus* of 1522 ; — of *Haguenau* 1526. 8°. — of *Haguenau* 1535. 8°. — of *Venice* 1535. 8°. — two of *Basil* 1545. and 1555. 8°. in Greek ; — and a third Greek and

(a) Biblioth. raif. Tom. 31. P. 1. pag. 1.

and Latin of 1563. — of *Franckford* 1546.
2 Vol. 8°. in Greek ; — of *Venice* 1550.
2 Vol. 8°. — of *Bourdelotius, Paris* 1615.
Greek and Latin, fol. — of *Benedict, Saumur*
1619, Greek and Latin, 2 Vol. 8°. the moſt
correct of all ; — and that moſt faulty one
of *Amſt.* 1687. Greek and Latin, 2 Vol.
8°. — They alſo corrected and digeſted the
old *Scholia*, and added two Greek Indexes :
The Firſt for the *Scholia* and *Variantes*, and
the ſecond for the *Notes*. Mr. *Ch. C. Reitz,*
Rector of *Gorinchem*-College in *Utrecht,*
hath undertaken a third, which, as it contains all the Words and their Conſtruction,
will deſerve the Name of *Lexicon-Lucia-*
nium. It will be publiſhed ſeparately, and
ſo contrived as to ſerve the other Editions
of *Lucian.* Beſides the two Greek Indexes,
there is alſo a Latin one, very large, and a
Collection of critical Remarks on ſome
Treatiſes of *Lucian.* Some of the *Notes*
rather deſerve the Name of *Diſſertations,*
tho' the Author does not in any of them
intend to find fault with the *Notes* of the
former Editions. It would be improper
and tedious to tranſcribe many of theſe
new *Notes*, I ſhall therefore confine my ſelf
to a ſmall Number, as a Specimen of our
Author's way of proceeding.

Tom. I. pag. 36. *Prometheus es in verbis.*
Mr. *Hemſterhuis* treats at large of the word
ϖιτυοκάμπτης Surname of the famous Thief
Sinis,

Sinis, as if the meaning was, *one that bends Pine-trees*. Mr. *Hemsterhuis* approves a Conjecture of Mr. *Wetstein*, *viz.* that *Lucian* calls himself in this place a *Pityocamptes*, for having dared to *bend down* the stiffness of Philosophy, to the good humour of Comedy. Accordingly he reads, εἰ μὴ ἄρα τις ἐμὲ διέλαθε τοιοῦτος πιτυοκάμπτης (intel. οἷος ἐγώ ἐμι) κỳ τραγελάφος κỳ αὐτὸς συντεθεικώς. — On the other hand Mr. *du Soul* reads ἱπποκάμπας which signifies a Marine Monster, represented on some Medals as a Horse, which is a Fish from the Belly; the common Reading being εἰ μὴ ἄρα τις ἐμὲ διέλαθε τοιοῦτος πιτυοκάμπ]ας κỳ τραγελάφος κỳ αὐτὸς συντεθεικώς.

Pag. 239. 61. in the *Dialogue between Mercury and Apollo*, (pag 209. of *Grævius*,) there is in some Manuscripts, ἀπὸ τȣ̃ Ταΰγετον. The Scholiast without any more ado, says, that it is an Atticism, the Nominativus being taken instead of the Genitivus. But Messieurs *Hemsterhuis* and *du Soul*, Correct according to some good Copies— ἀπὸ τȣ̃ Ταϊγέτȣ, without the Atticism.

Pag. 117. 48. (*veræ Hist.* 2 pag. 679. *Græv.*) *Homer* being asked what was his Country, Answers that *he did not know himself*, ὁ δὲ αὐτὸς μὲν ἀγνοεῖν ἔφασκεν. So it is read in every Edition, *ipse se nescire dicebat*. But as a moment after he positively says, that he was a *Babylonian*, called in his Country *Tigranes*,

Tigranes, Messieurs *Gesner, Vorstius, du Soul* and *Reitz* Correct αὐτὲς μὲν ἀγνοεῖν, *illos ignorare,* that is to say, that the Disputants did not know it, of whom *Lucian* says, τᾶτο μάλιϛα παρ᾽ ἡμῖν εἰσέτι νῦν ζητεῖϑαι (b) Might not what *Homer* says of his not knowing what Country-man he was, be look'd upon as an Irony. Some said he was of this; some of the other; he is tired of all those Questions, and through a kind of sullen humuor, he says, *I don't know.* But the Question being afterwards seriously put to him, he answers it at last, *I am a Babylonian,* &c.

Tom. II. Pag. 932, 55. (*de Luctu* pag. 306. *Grævii*), *Lucian* speaking of several Ways of burying the Dead, says, ὁ Ἰνδὸς ὑάλω περιχέει, *Indus vitro circumlinit.* Mr. *Gesner* conjectures, that either the *Indians* had a Composition like the Lacca or Varnish we now make use of, or the Composition of yellow Amber with which *Kerkringius* used to anoint Corps, if we must believe *Morhof,* *Polyh.* 2, 2, 2, 37, 3. He might have added what *Morhof* says in the same Place, that the *Chinese* have a Composition of Rosin, which resembles yellow Amber. To what then may the Word ὑάλω be better applied than to Amber itself?

Tom.

Tom. III. At the Beginning of the Treatise, that has this Title περὶ τȣ̃ μὴ ῥαδίως πιϛεύειν διαβολῇ, Mr. *Gefner* obferves that διαβολή does not fignify *Calumnia*; for in Calumny there muft be fomething falfe; but *Delatio, Accufation,* which may be true in every refpect, and it is this *Lucian* fpeaks of. But Mr. *Reitz,* in the Infcription of the Columns or Pages, kept the ufual Word *Calumnia,* to avoid puzling thofe that are ufed to that Word. He did the fame with refpect to all other Corrections of that Kind.

The moft confiderable Correction is a Tranfpofition of two Sheets in the *Encomium Demofthenis.* The Neceffity of it is look'd upon by our Authors as demonftrated. Mr. *Gefner* propofed it above twenty Years ago to Mr. *Heuman* and it had his Approbation as well as Mr. *Hemfterhuis*'s and Mr. *Du Soul*'s. This laft had already found it out fome Years before. Mr. *Gefner* publifh'd the laft Part of this Treatife, in it's natural Order in his *Chreftomathia Græca* which came out in 1731. The *Acta Eruditorum* mentioned it, and a learned *Englifh* Gentleman feemed to be much of the fame Opinion in the *Mifcel. Obfervat. Eruditorum Britannorum* ; Vol. II. Tom. III. pag. 368. No-body ever found Fault with this Correction ; fo that Mr. *Reitz* was in the Right to receive it in the new Edition, tho' he

PART I.   L   might

might have added the Remark
glish Gentleman above mention
In the Dialogue *Philopatris*
mous Paffage which has occa
Speculations. *Triephon* will
to fwear (b) ὑψιμέδοντα Θεὸν, μ
τον, οὐρανίωνα, υἱὸν πατρὸς, πνε
τρὸς ἐκπορευόμενον, ἓν ἐκ τριῶν, χ
Critias anfwers among other
οἶδα τί λέγεις, ἓν τρία, τρία
Thefe Words were often alledg
that the Expreffions confecrated b
cil of *Nice*, and now made ufe
vines in talking of the *Holy T*
before that Council applied to th
ject. Mr. *Gefner*'s Opinion may
to the following Heads. 1. Th
logue was wrote at *Conftantinople,*
the *Roman* Empire, 2. In the I
Emperor under whom it was p
infult the Chriftians. 3. When
were alfo called *Galilæans.* Thi
the diftinguifhing Character of th

(b) Pag. 770. Græv.— *Critias* fays juft be
ing to your *Way of Thinking, God is a Number,*
Arithmetics, fuch a one as Nicomacus's ;— the
do not underftand your *One-Three,* and your *Three*
was the Reflection of an Infidel who had mad
nefs to ridicule the Chriftian Religion.— With
nefs do they lay hold of our unhappy Difputes
lative Subjects, in order to undermine Religion.
hoped they will have every Day hereafter fewer
ties, or lefs Caufe, to do it.

Julian the Apostate. Mr. *Gesner* shews that this Dialogue was probably wrote by a Sophist, (an Imitator of *Lucian*, whose Expressions he carefully made use of) under the Reign of the Emperor *Julian*, at the Beginning of his War against the *Persians*, upon the first Rumours of the happy Successes of his Arms. He believes it is designed against the dismal Predictions of some Christians, who, fearing lest the Emperor elated by his Prosperity should persecute them at his return, wished his Death, or his Defeat. Mr. *Gesner* having established his Opinion, answers the Reasons alledged against it by Messieurs, *Bull*, *Dodwell* *Moyle*, *La Croze*, *Basnage*, and others, who ascribe this Dialogue either to *Lucian* or to some one living near his Time. Mr. *Du Soul's* Note on the same Subject differs widely from the forementioned. He thinks this Piece of no older Date than the XIIth Century. His Reason is drawn from these Words; *Triephon* says, (c) Οἶδα μυρίας (παρ-θένυς) διαμελεῖς τμηθείσας νήσω ἐν ἀμφιρύ-τη, Κρήτην δὲ τὲ μιν καλέυσι. Mr. *Du Soul* judges that this cannot be referred to any thing but the Fable of the *eleven thousand Virgins*, invented in the XIIth Century (d).

L 2   As

(c) Pag. 769. Græv.
(d) Remark of the Journalist.

As ingenious as this Obfervation may be, I believe it will obtain with very few, for it is univerfally allowed, that *Lucian*'s Stile is well imitated in the *Philopatris*, and who could have been that exact Imitator in that barbarous Age. On the other Hand, it is more than probable that the Dialogue was wrote at the Time of, or foon after, the unhappy Difputes between the *Orthodoxians* and the *Arians*; before that time, there was no Occafion for fuch a Satyr. Mr. *Gefner* fays he has been thirty Years examining his Opinion, and found it every Day more and more probable.

A great many other very curious Notes, Remarks, and Differtations render this Edition vaftly preferable to the former Ones, and tho' the Authors are often of a different Opinion, yet they ufe one another with the greateft Civility. This uncommon Politenefs between, as it were, Rival-Commentators, deferves to be taken notice of. The only thing wanting to this Edition is, an Account of *Lucian*'s Life, and a critical Catalogue of his Works. It is to be hoped one of the learned Authors may be prevailed upon to give the Public that Satisfaction.

ARTICLE XII.

L'Histoire Naturelle, eclaircie dans deux de ses parties principales, la Lithologie & la Conchyliologie, dont l'une traite des *Pierres*, & l'autre des *Coquillages*. Ouvrage dans lequel on trouve une Nouvelle Methode, & une Notice critique des principaux Auteurs, qui ont ecrit fur ces Matieres. Enrichie de figures deffinées d'apres nature par Mr. - - - de la focieté Royale de Montpellier. A Paris ches *Debure*, 4°. pag. 456,

That is to say.

Natural History, illustrated in two of its chief Parts, viz. *Lithology* and *Conchyliology*, the first treats of *Stones*, the last of *Shells*, &c.

(a)THIS Work was publifhed by Mr. *d'Argenville* Mafter of the Court of Accounts in *Paris*. It is rather a Catalogue of *Stones* and *Shells*, with their Names, and an Account of the Authors that give Defcriptions of them, than curious Obfervations which the Title Page feems to promife. Yet as there are Numbers fond of thefe Collecti-

L 3   ons,

(a) See Biblioth. raifon. Tom 31. Part I,

ons, I judged proper to intimate to my Readers, that such a Book exists. As it cannot be abstracted, I will content my self with the bare Mention of some important Articles to be met with in it.

Few Naturalists have treated *ex professo* this part of natural Philosophy. There are not many Books where a sure Knowledge of this Subject is to be found. The Ancients, it is true, as *Aristotle, Pliny, Ælian,* treat of *Animals, Stones,* and *Shells;* but their Writeings want both Order and Veracity. Among the Moderns, *Agricola, Rondelles, Belon,* and *Aldrovandus* addicted themselves much to this study. Yet they have their Faults, especially *Aldrovandus,* who is so full of Digreffions, that his principal Subject makes often the least part of the Work.

Our Author's System is the same as that of *Abbé Pluche's* in his History of Heaven, *viz.* "That the first Principles of Bodies are "always the same, and Chymistry that di-"vides them from those, to which they are "joyned in compound Bodies, is not able to "annihilate them; for Instance, *Crystal* is "still *Crystal;* I mean that the Bodies, "which form the Essence of *Crystal,* re-"main still the same." Chymists divide them into Minerals, Vegetables, and Animals; to which, as every Body knows, they give the Name of Mineral Kingdom, &c.

The

The Author does not examine the Animal Kingdom, and as to Minerals, he treats only of *Stones*, referving others for a Work fubfequent to this.

(*b*) Two famous Botanifts, being perfuaded that every thing in Nature vegetated, were willing to afcribe this Vegetation to Stones; "but, fays Mr. *D'Argenville*, Expe-
" rience has deftroyed their reafoning, for
" thofe that went into a Quarry, with an
" intention to examine Nature, faw Water
" fall from the Vault, drop by drop, and
" congeal, as it were, before them. This
" Water, which is a Collection of drops of
" Rain, differs from common Water; it
" takes up in its way, Salts, Herbs, Straw,
" &c. until it finds a Foundation that ftops
" it, fuch as the beginning of a congealed
" Stone. The horizontal Dilatation in a
" Quarry proves, that Water, falling drop
" by drop, fpreads naturally, and is unable
" to take another Situation, and confequent-
" ly that Stones are formed by an Addition
" of Particles, named *Juxta-pofition*. If the
" terreftrial and faline Particles brought
" along by thefe Waters are coarfe and foul,
" Rocks will be formed of them; if this
" matter fpreads in fmaller Stratas and forms
" thinner Grains, it will make Marble or
" Flint-ftones; If thefe Particles are full

L 4 " of

(*b*) *Tournefort* and *Ferrante Imperato*.

" of Salt and Air, and intermixed in fuch
" a manner that they every way give paffage
" to Light, *Cryftal* will be the refult. If
" they be yet more compact, harder, and
" tranfparent, they will form a Diamond;
" and if this pellucid Matter be filtrated
" through Particles coloured by different
" Salts, or metallic Concoctions, it will then
" form true coloured Stones, Agates, Jaf-
" pers, whofe fundamental Bafis is always
" the Matter of Cryftal."--Such is Mr. *D'Argenville's* Syftem concerning the Formation
of Stones, on which I fhall make no other
Obfervation than this; that it is hard to
conceive, that Water, falling drop by drop,
fhould form thofe Beds of Stones found in
Quarries out of which fome are conftantly
taken, fuch as thofe Quarries that fo abundantly furnifh all the Neceffaries of Architecture, where not even the leaft Sign of
filtrated and congealed Water is to be perceived. How long muft it be before the
Formation of thofe Beds cou'd be effected,
and fhould we not have occafion to com-
plain of Nature, for contriving fuch a tedious way, while fhe feems always to act
fo concifely in things much lefs neceffary.

True Stones, commonly called precious
Ones, are hard and compact Minerals; it is
an acid Juice of Earth coagulated with Matters heterogeneous, terreftrial, faline, ful-

phurous and metallic. Thefe Stones are formed as Knots, among others, in the Chinks of Rocks, and in the Veins of Minerals and Metals.

Such is the Account our Author gives of the Formation of precious Stones. *Cryftal* is ftill their Bafis, but they take a different Colour according to the different Minerals, more or lefs copious in the Place where they are formed. Lead, for Inftance, or Iron, produces the Yellow Colour of Topazes; as Lead and Iron joined together, make the Hyacinth, *&c.* Here our Author adds a Catalogue of Cryftallifed Stones, opaque ones, fome with Figures, and common ones.

True Stones have no other Propriety, befides being fubfervient to Grandeur and Luxury, but as they are natural Phofphorus, and have an electrical Quality; a Quality, whofe ufefulnefs is not yet fufficiently known to us, but ought not however to be neglected, Nature having no other view in the myfterious Favours fhe beftows on Naturalifts, but to put them in the way of deferving more confiderable.

The Formation of Shell-fifh is a great Subject of Enquiry to true Naturalifts. The Opinion of the Ancients about Generation, by Corruption and Putrefaction, has been long exploded; but they have not yet agreed as to the Manner they procreate. Some pretend it is by Eggs, others by Spawn, as

other

other Fifh, and many by **Copu**
fome are of Opinion that **they**
phrodites.

Their internal Structure is lit
they are fuppofed to have **Parts**
to thofe of other Animals, and
form, before their Shell is mad
Humour, that iffues out of their B
they fpread upon one anothe
Stratas, and that in this manner
is formed. Some Shell-fifh h
of Motion, as the one called th
—others as Oyfters and *Pinna M*
not any, and are faftened to 'Ro
the Bottom of the Sea.

The beautiful Colours feen on
ry according to the different Clima
they grow. Our Author afcribes
Minerals, as he does the Colour of tr
to the fame Caufe: The blew Colour
feen in Shells, which an Author (
by many Experiments to be owing
corrofive Salts of the Sea, many
dy'd with Blew, lofing their Colou
analogous to thofe of the Sea.
fame Reafon, River-fhells are not c
ble to Sea ones; frefh Water being d
of thofe Salts that give that Brightnef
others. (*d*)

(*c*) *Bonnani.*
(*d*) I believe the Author is miftaken; the Muf
eep Blue, and fome other Shell-fifhes are within
of a faint Blue. Note of the Journalift.

There are also Foffile-fhells found in the Centre of the Earth, and on the higheft Mountains.—From whence comes this great Quantity of Shells, the moft Part petrified? Mr. *D'Argenville*, after having related the Opinions of many Authors, accounts for this Phænomenon by the Waters of the Sea, the whole terraqueous Globe having been fo overturned in the Time of the Flood, that they could eafily bring thefe Shells along with them to the Tops of the higheft Mountains.

The Method of cleaning and fettling a Clofet of Natural Hiftory, and a Defcription of the fineft ones in *Europe*, make up the reft of this Treatife of *Conchyliology*. This laft Article may be ufeful to Travellers. Nothing can equal the Beauty of the Figures, and in this refpect the Book may be called a Mafter-piece.

ARTICLE

The || Reaſonableneſſe *of the* Ch
on *as delivered in the* Script
an Anſwer to a late Treat
Chriſtianity not founded on
By *Geo. Benſon*, 8vo. 276. pag
Preface.

Remarks on a late Pamphlet, int
ſtianity not founded, &c. In t
to a Friend. By *John Leland*,
I. Letter 84 pag. II. Letter

I Thought proper to join
Works together for brevity
becauſe their Authors write to the
End, and in many Reſpects pr
ſame Way towards attaining it.
ſon's came out firſt, and Dr. *Lel*
his before he had read the former
plainly to be ſeen by comparing th
ther; for tho' many of their Argur
the ſame, yet they are handled i
different Manner.

That theſe Gentlemen are both v
qualified for this Taſk, will, I bel

|| *Reaſonableneſſe.* The Author writes in this ma
Word, and the like. And therefore where-eve
him, I thought fit to write them as he does.

readily granted by thofe who have read any of their former Writings; (a) they before this undertook the Defence of the Chriftian Religion, and they do it now again with Succefs.

The Author of the Pamphlet, thefe Gentlemen have undertaken to confute, has fo well fucceded in involving his real Sentiments, that fome People are yet at a Lofs; whether he meant to prejudice, or to ferve, the Caufe of Religion. I could, fays Mr. *Benfon, alledge fome Inftances of Chriftians, who take him to have wrote ferioufly, in Defence of Chriftianity.* In fact, one would at firft take him for an *Enthufiaft.*— This Queftion Mr. *Benfon* leaves undecided, but Dr. *Leland* feems to have no manner of Doubt about his Intentions (b). He has chofen, " *fays he,* a Manner of writing, which, it " is probable, he fuppofed, might anfwer " his Purpofe; but, which, I think, gives " one no advantageous Opinion of the Sin- " cerity and Candour of his Mind. He " frequently fpeaks with great feeming Re- " gard of our Saviour, of Divine Faith, and

of

(a) Mr. *Benfon* wrote a Treatife concerning the *End and Defign of Prayer*, in Anfwer to the late *Earl of Rochefter,* Mr. *Blount* and other modern Deifts. Alfo a Letter on *Predeftination.*— *The Hiftory of the firft planting the Chriftian Religion,* befides his *Paraphrafes,* &c. Dr. *Leland* is known by his Anfwers to *Tindal* and *Morgan.*

(b) Pag. 2.

" of the Grace of God, and his Holy Spi-
" rit. He makes much ufe of Phrafes that
" have been employed by good Perfons in a
" pious Senfe; but it is plain, that all this is
" managed fo as to expofe Religion, and
" Faith, to the Derifion and Contempt of
" Mankind. He carries the Ridicule fo
" far, as to mix it with his Addreffes
" to the Supreme Being. — I cannot
" well conceive, how any Man that be-
" lieves there is a God, who is a Lover of
" Truth and Goodnefs, and who concerns
" himfelf in the Affairs of Men at all, can
" allow himfelf to be guilty of fuch a fo-
" lemn Grimace and Mockery." This is a
very heavy Charge, and yet I think it hardly poffible to read the Book, that has occafioned it, and not to join with the Doctor in
his Opinion of it. Certainly no Chriftian, of
any Denomination whatfoever would chufe
to fay that *(cc) we ftand in no Need of
any of the Credit of ancient Miracles, or the
Genuinenefs of diftant Records,* which he calls
a very flender and infufficient Ground, &c.
The Difficulty there is in finding out whether that Author wrote ferioufly, or not, is
chiefly owing to the Care he took of ex-
preffing himfelf in the Stile of thofe Divines,
that have depreciated human Reafon, in order to enforce the Neceffity of an irrefiftible
Grace.

(cc) Pag. 59 and 60.

Grace. One would almoft take whole Phrafes interfperfed here and there as Quotations from fome of our old Syftems of Divinity. This, and nothing elfe, has made the Attack dangerous. Otherwife no one, that has his Senfes about him, would be in the leaft tempted to hearken to a Man who intends to banter him out of his Reafon. But People who were often told that the *holy Scriptures reprefent our natural Faculties, as being entirely perverted,* and that *the Spirit of God worketh our Sanctification in us, without any Concurrence of our own,* thofe People, I fay, may fall unawares into the erroneous Notions, which the Author grounds upon thofe Principles. I fuppofe that is the Reafon why our two Authors have taken fo much Trouble. On this Occafion, I cannot help taking Notice of a judicious Reflection of Mr. *Benfon's,* which may ferve to difpel the Apprehenfions of fome People, who fear that fo many Attacks upon Chriftianity might at laft, in fome Refpect or other, prove fatal to it: (c) Thofe Attacks, *fays he,* upon " ra-
" tional *Chriftianity,* muft of Courfe lead
" *rational Believers* to a more careful and
" exact Enquiry into the Nature and Evi-
" dence of their Faith; which cannot fail
" of ending to the Advantage of Truth and
" Virtue. It is poffible, that, upon Exa-
" mination

(c) Preface, pag. v.

" mination, it may be found
" ans have mixed some of t.
" vate Sentiments with the
" of Chrift. And, as fuch
" be defended, they had muc
" with them, than give up *rat*
" nity, or load it with thofe Diff
" afford the moft plaufible (
" gainft it; though in reality
" belong to it. Such Authors a
" ever be their defign) will, pe
" Iffue, help us to get rid of f
" ties and Incumbrances,—whic
" leffe, a very defirable thing.'
join with Mr. *Benfon* in this,
add, that thofe additions he co
are the chief Caufe of fo man
taking a diflike to, or a prejudice a
Religion.' Were it reprefented in
tive Amiablenefs, it would be
ceived by thofe that love Truth
kind, and others would hardly
tack it openly, But as things f
they have fome Pretence for wha
and they fingle out, and fall on th
Parts, in order to undermine tl
Building. This is particularly th
of the Author of the Pamphlet.

The two Anfwers I am abftra
framed very near on the fame
with this difference, that Mr. *Be*
carried on by way of Dialogue,

divided it into three Parts. Part I. contains *the Arguments, for the Truth of the Christian Religion.* Part II. *The Answer to the Difficulties and Objections proposed by this Author.* Part III. *An Interpretation of the Texts which he hath perverted.* Dr. *Leland* in his first Letter, applies himself particularly to confider this Proposition in the Pamphlet; *viz.* " Reafon or the Intellectu-
" al Faculty cannot poffibly, both from its
" own Nature, and that of Religion, be
" the Principle intended by God to lead
" us into a true Faith." In the II. Letter he examines the paffages of Scripture brought in to fupport that Propofition.

The firft thing they fet upon, is to confute the Notion of Faith the Author of the Pamphlet is pleafed to give, and fet down the true one. *With what regard,* fays he, (d) *with what patience rather, can one be fuppofed to attend to Queftions propounded to him,* under the reftraints of Threats and Authority? *to be talked to of Danger in his Decifions, and have the Rod held out with the Leffon, to have Propofitions tendered to his Reafon with Penalties annexed? His Reafon, ever neceffitated to determine juft as fhe does of herfelf, and by her Nature uncapable either of paying Compliments, or giving Offence. He is confcious all the while that he*

PART I.   M   *has*

(d) pag. 8.

has no such free Vote to dispose of, and there-
fore disdains, with all justice, an attempt
equally weak and unjust, of frightning him
into a Compliance out of his Power. — To
answer this Account of *Faith,* our Authors
shew that it is not to be considered as a bare
assent of the Understanding, but also as an
Act of the Will, which implies a Love for
Truth, a desire and endeavours to find it
out, and a steady Resolution to profess it,
even at the hazard of our Lives. *(e)* " Faith,
" *saith* Mr. *Benson,* is a complex thing,
" being partly an Act of the *Understanding,*
" partly of the *Will.* As an Act of the
" *Understanding,* or assent of the Mind up-
" on Evidence, it is necessary, and can have
" no virtue in it. But as it is an Act of
" the *Will,* it derives all its Value from its
" being a virtuous Disposition of the Mind,
" a Candor, or Love to Truth, or a principle
" of Virtue and Piety. *Unbeliefs* on the
" other hand is not a mere doubting, or with-
" holding one's assent, when there is no
" evidence ; but it is a *Vice,* which consists in
" indulging Criminal prejudices, in an aver-
" sion to Truth, or in Men's refusing to
" search and examine, for fear the Disco-
" very of Truth, should condemn their
" Course of Life, — or in refusing to pro-
" fess, and be influenced by, those Truths
" which

(e) pag. 15.

" which they have already difcovered."
According to this Account of *Faith*, it is a
miftake to fay, that *Propofitions are tendered
to our Reafon with penalties annexed*, for
thefe *Penalties are annexed* to *the Want of
regard for Truth*; it is a miftake to fay that
we have no free Vote to difpofe of; on the
contrary the Danger lies, *in not difpofing of
it* according to the Dictates of our Confcience; and if *the Rod is held out*, it is only
againft thofe that refufe to follow what their
reafon hath received. Dr. *Leland's* Notion
of *Faith* is near the fame: He reprefents it
alfo as confifting partly in our affent to
Truth, and partly in thofe Difpofitions that
make us give that Affent, and behave accordingly. The only difference between them
is this, that he is fomewhat more particular on the Neceffity of the firft Act of Faith,
viz. an affent to effential Truths. He dif-
proves this Propofition in the Pamphlet:
*(f) It is impoffible to conceive any the leaft
Connection between the Notion of Duty, and
affenting rationally to any Propofition, however
ftrongly fupported.* " This appears to me,
" fays he, (g) to be a ftrange affertion. It
" is in effect to fay, that no Man can be
" obliged to it as a Duty, to make a right
" ufe of the Reafon God has given him,
M 2   " nor

" nor can God himself require him to do
" fo. He cannot fo much as require his
" reafonable Creatures to believe, and ac-
" knowledge his own Supreme Dominion
" or Perfections, though founded on the
" cleareft Reafon and Evidence, &c."

I fhall beg leave to make fome Obfervations on this Notion of *Faith* confidered as
being partly *an Act of the Underftanding*, or
an *Affent* to fuch, or fuch Propofitions. — I
apprehend the Author of the Pamphlet
might infift, that his difficulty is not yet
folved. — If there are Propofitions that we
are in Duty bound to *believe*, that is, *to give
our affent to*, no matter in what Number
they are, nor what Name you give them,
they are ftill *Propofitions tendered to our Reafon with Penalties annexed.* And why thefe
Penalties? The Propofition either appears
to me true, upon a careful Examination,
or it does not. If true, I muft give my
Affent to it, it is not in my power to refufe
it ; if falfe, no Authority whatfoever will
be able to force this *Affent*, it would be requiring what, in the Nature of things, is
abfolutely impoffible. There is no merit in
doing what I am forced to do ; nor can
there be any guilt in refufing what it is not
in my power to grant. Dr. *Leland*'s Affertion, it is true, is grounded on the Suppofition, that there are fuch Truths which
a Man cannot avoid difcovering, if he makes
a proper

a proper use of his Reason. But I do not
know whether this suppofition is as certain
as it is generally thought to be. I own I
cannot conceive a Man unable to give his
Affent to this Propofition, *There is a God*,
yet I would not abfolutely decide there is
no fuch Incapacity. Much lefs would I
chufe to deny it as to other Truths. There
is fuch a prodigious variety of turns of mind,
and of Circumftances, for which Allowances
muft be made, that it is very difficult to
know whether there may not be fuch a
combination of them re-united in one Man,
as may prevent his perceiving the moft obvious Truth. No Body doubts that there
are People not at all fenfible of the Abfurdity of Tranfubftantiation, and yet what
can be more abfurd ? It is true, we are
apt to think it is in their power to difcover
it, yet I believe any good Man that reflects
on his own Experience, would be very
loth to pafs fuch a Judgment. Perhaps
there is not one of thofe Mr. *Benfon* calls
rational Chriftians, that is, Men whofe *Faith*
is the Refult of earneft Enquiries, and ferious Obfervation, but has been, fome time
or other, in doubt of, nay perhaps ready
to throw off any one of thofe Articles
which he now confiders, as being of the
utmoft Importance to promote his Happinefs.
And it is to be expected that he will be
extreamly cautious, even of fufpecting any

Man.

Man of a want of fincerity, upon account
of his Opinions, let them be ever fo erroneous. — The Queftion about the *Effentials*
of Chriftianity is a puzling Queftion, upon
which it is hardly poffible two Men fhould
agree. Confequently it is hard to decide,
that a Man, who does not give his affent to
any effential Article, does not act fincerely,
or, which is the fame thing, that he is
under the Difpleafure of the Almighty.

Mr. *Benfon*'s Notion of *Faith*, agrees well
enough with what I have laid down here,
with this difference, that he makes it *partly
an Act of the Underftanding*, or *Affent of the
Mind*; and I humbly apprehend that this
Diftinction is not to be found in the Gofpel. As far as I am able to judge of it,
Faith, at leaft the true *Faith*, that *Faith*
which God requires of us, the only one
that deferves that Name, is conftantly taken
for a *Difpofition of the Heart*, *(b)* and not
an Act of the Underftanding. Many truths
are propofed to us, not to be affented to,
but to be examined : It is true the affent
follows of courfe, in cafe the Underftanding
fhould approve what is propofed, but this is
not the thing required. We are to have a
Thirft for Truth, and a Difpofition to draw
practical Confequences, from that which
fhall appear to us to be true, upon a careful
Exami-

(b) See Rom. x. 9, 10.

Examination. It is for the want of this difpofition that *Jefus* upbraids the *Jews*. They would not *believe*, that is to fay, they were refolved not to examine what he told them, and ftill more refolved not to do it. This is the Reafon why he required this *Faith*, from thofe that applied to him for Favours; juft as if he had faid; *Have you that love for Truth, that will make you receive it, if it is properly offered to you, and are you difpofed to ftand by it, for ever after ?* When he found this Difpofition, he gave the evidence, he wrought the Miracle, and them that were deftitute of it, he fends back without granting their requefts; they were deftitute of *Faith*, that is, they had bad Hearts, and confequently it was to no purpofe to give them the Evidence.

If this be what the Gofpel means by the *Faith* it recommends to us, the Objections of the Author of the Pamphlet *fall to the Ground.* There is no fuch thing in Chriftianity, as *Queftions propounded under the reftraints of Threat and Authority*; — *no Propofitions tendered to our Reafon with Penalties annexed*; — *no Danger for us in our Decifions* : — What we are commanded is to be honeft, diligent feekers after Truth, lovers of Virtue, and nothing elfe; and if *the Rod is held out*, it is not *with the Leffon*, but only againft thofe that are determined never to grow wife and virtuous. In fhort,

Exa-

Examination is not to be profcribed, as contrary to Faith, for in that Examination does
the very Eſſence of Faith conſiſt.

To return to our Authors. After having
delivered their Opinion about *Faith*, they
proceed to other Articles. — Upon the Sup-
poſition that the Author of the Pamphlet
ſtrikes at the very Foundation of Chriſtianity, Mr. *Benſon* thought proper to explain
the Grounds on which it ſtands, and to ſhew
that the Doctrine contained in the Goſpel,
its Precepts, and even its poſitive Inſtituti-
ons are reaſonable, as well as its Sanctions.
What he ſays on theſe Subjects is ſo juſt, that
tho' I ſhould treſpaſs the Bounds of an
Abſtract, I cannot help relating Part of two
Articles. The firſt is concerning the rea-
ſonableneſs of the Doctrines contained in
the Goſpel : This is his Opinion of them ;
— (i) " That there is only one God ; that
" he is a pure Spirit, and conſequently In-
" viſible ; that he has almighty Power, in-
" finite Knowledge, and unerring Wiſdom ;
" that he is eternal and immortal, and that
" (in one Word) he is every way perfect ;
" —— that this great Being created the
" World, and continually preſides over it,
" ſupporting and preſerving it in that Order
" and Regularity which we behold ; — that
" he is not only the Governor of all intel-
" ligent

(i) Pag. 21.

" ligent Beings, but takes Care of all the
" fmalleft and inferior Creatures, and that
" none of them are below his Notice, or
" thought unworthy of his conftant Re-
" gard ; — that he created Men in his own
" Image ; and that when Mankind degene-
" rated into Ignorance, Idolatry and Vice,
" he fent among them his only-begotten
" and well beloved Son, a Perfon of great
" Eminence and Dignity ; that by his own
" bright Example, and moft familiar and
" excellent Inftructions, he might recover
" the World to the Knowledge of the true
" God, and the Practice of everlafting Righ-
" teoufnefs ; — that the Son of God, when
" he with this View appeared among Men,
" chofe a ftate of Poverty, Self-denial, and
" Mortification to this World, neither feek-
" ing Riches, temporal Dominion, or fen-
" fual Pleafures, but kept free from all
" Sufpicion of fuch low and ignoble Views;
" — that notwithftanding the great Oppo-
" fition he met with, from the Ignorance
" and Prejudice, the Malice and Wicked-
" nefs of Mankind, he unweariedly *went*
" *about doing good,* and rather fubmitted to
" facrifice his Life, than deny or betray
" fuch important Truths as he had deliver-
" ed ; *(for, furely, no poffible Condefcention*
" *could be too great, to promote the moral*
" *Virtue and Happinefs of intelligent Crea-*
" *tures, and recover a fallen race !*) — that
                                    " this

" this great and eminent Perſon, ʋ
" moſt remarkable Manner, rewar
" his extraordinary Humiliation aɩ
" ferings ; (which was honouring
" warding Virtue itſelf, in the moſ
" ous and excellent Perſon that ever
" ed among Men, and there by in the
" eſt Manner, encouraging us to b
" ous :) — that as by him God mɑ
" Worlds, ſo by him he now gove
" things ; —— that he will, at laſt,
" raiſe the dead, and confer Rewar
" Puniſhments upon Men, according
" have behaved." — Now, *adds Mɩ
ſon,* " are not all theſe things in theɩ
" highly reaſonable ? It is evident thɑ
" makes us the daily Miniſters of good
" another, and chooſes in this Maɩ
" govern the World, not immediatel
" by the Mediation of other intellige
" ings. The *Mediatorical Scheme,*
" fore, has nothing abſurd in it, but ɩ
" wiſe and reaſonable, as the Perſ
" noured with that Commiſſion is thɩ
" lovely Pattern of all moral Perfeɗ
Had the Chriſtian Religion been alwɑ
preſented in this Light, I believe it ʋ
have few Enemies now, if any at all

What Mr. *Benſon* ſays on the *poſitɩ
ſtitutions* of Chriſtianity is as reaſonabl
" ʼ

" These positive Institutions, *says he*, are so
" free from all Appearance of Superstition
" and Vanity, and so wisely fitted to the End
" for which they were designed, that no
" Man can justly, or with any Reason, ob-
" ject against the Things themselves, tho'
" against the Corruption, and Abuses of
" them there has been abundant Reason to
" object. For what considerate and think-
" ing Man can pretend to say, that it is any
" way unreasonable, or superstitious, for
" every Member of any particular Society
" to be solemnly admitted into that Socie-
" ty, by a plain and significant Rite, intitling
" him to all the Privileges, and charging
" him with all the Obligations, which be-
" long to the Members of that Society, as
" such ;— which is the Design of one of
" the *Christian Sacraments?* Or that it is
" unreasonable and superstitious, frequently
" and with thankfulnesse to commemorate
" the Love of their greatest Benefactor,
" who condescended even to lay down his
" Life for them ; and thereupon humbly
" and solemnly to renew their Obligations to
" him ;— which is the Design of the
" other."

Mr. *Benson* insists also on external Attesta-
tions from *Prophecy* and *Miracle*, and afterwards justifies the Authenticnefs of the Books
of the New Testament ; but Time will not

allow me to abftract this Part of his Work. Dr. *Leland* alfo treats of thofe Articles, but in few Words; as he had other Occafions more fully to confider them.

As to the Objections ftarted by the Author of the Pamphlet, in Support of his Syftem, and anfwered at large by our Authors, I fhall only mention thofe that are moft immediately connected with that Syftem, and fet afide fome others difperfed here and there, which are to be met with in all the Books wrote of late againft Chriftianity, fuch as thefe,——falfe Miracles were wrought by defigning Men, which were taken for true ones, ——had the Chriftian-Doctrine been good, there was no Need of Miracles.—— The various Readings in the New Teftament are fo numerous, that it cannot any longer be faid it is the Book wrote by Apoftolical Men.—— That Jefus Chrift's Witneffes were his Friends, *&c.*—— Thefe have been anfwered a thoufand times. Neither need I enlarge upon the other Objections, becaufe they are all, either direct, or indirect Dependencies of the miftaken Notion mentioned before, *viz.* that Faith is an Affent, without Reafon, to all Religious Truths. A Difficulty much infifted upon *is taken from Infant-Baptifm* : He alledges it as a Proof that Reafon has nothing to do with Religion? (*i*) *Can a Man*, fays he, *be baptifed in-*

to

(*i*) Pzg. 9.

to a rational Religion? Or, *where is Reason concerned, when Babes accept the Terms of Salvation by Deputy, and are intitled to all the Privileges of the most extensive Faith by another's Act?* &c. This may be a formidable Difficulty to thofe that afcribe great Benefits to *Baptifm*; but for others there is no Force in it. They look upon it as a meer Ceremony, and *Infant-Baptifm*, as a Declaration from the Parents, that they wifh their Child fhould be a Follower of Truth and Virtue, and that they fhall give him all the Affiftance in their Power for that Purpofe. " The Author of the Objeftion, *fays Mr.* " *Benfon*, knows very well, that fome Chrifti-" ans deny Infant-Baptifm, and he had " much better have done fo, than have given " up his Underftanding, and rational Chri-" ftianity all at once. But others, who are for " Infant-Baptifm, do not fuppofe any Faith " to be required in a Child." This our two Authors treat of at large, and I could almoft fay more than the Argument of their Antagonift feems to deferve.

Another Difficulty he fets a great Value upon, is this: *If the Affent required were to be a rational One,* then Children ought not to be taught Chriftianity, *(m) for it would be highly wicked and unjuft to*

pre-

(m) Pag. 11 and 12.

prepoſſeſs Men's tender Minds in an
before they came to the full Uſe of tl
nal Faculties, &c. Our Author'
may be reduced to this, (*n*) that
Truths agreed upon and receive
whole World, as the Difference
Good and Evil, and ſuch it is hi
per Children ſhould be acquainted
ſoon as poſſible—that Children, by
of their Parents, may be brought t
better and ſooner than they otherwiſ
— that if Bigots and Enthuſiaſts
all Alterations, in religious Affairs, a
rous or heinous, rational Believers
culcate upon their Children, and t
ly and frequently, to learn to ju
themſelves,— and that the educa
Children is abſolutely neceſſary, not
poſſeſs their Minds in favour of a
ticular favourite Tenets, (which is
in Education,) but to teach them l
maſter and govern their Paſſions, an
vent their being led into Immorality.

Another Objection (*o*) *A rationa*
may not come time enough, and if Deatl
overtake us before we have finiſhed o
quiry, what have we to truſt to ?— A
— (*p*) as long as we have not ſu
Evidence we are not guilty, and as ſ

(*n*) *Benſon's* Anſw. pag. 98.— *Leland's* Anſw. pa
(*o*) Pag. 13, &c. (*p*) *Benſon,* pag. 1

we have fufficient Evidence, we ceafe to be juftifiable, or innocent, in rejecting it *(q)* Befides if it be true that by the Word *Faith* the Scripture means nothing elfe, but a moral good Difpofition, fo much the worfe for the Man who lofes that natural Difpofition, our good Father has implanted in his Heart, and who does not take Care to recover it in time.

I pafs over fome other Arguments offered by the Author of the Pamphlet, which are much of the fame Nature as the foregoing, and to which the fame Anfwer may be applied. However, I muft take Notice of one, which is his darling Difficulty, viz. *that Reafon is too weak to guide us in religious Affairs.* The Objections of Sceptics againft the certainty of our Knowledge, and the Affertions of fome Divines, with refpect to the bad Condition of our natural Faculties, ever fince *Adam*'s Fall, are oddly jumbled together by that Author. He chiefly infifts on the Incapacity of the great Number to Reafon at all, and afferts at the fame time, that *the ablest and best of Men are difqualified for fair Reafoning by their natural Prejudices.* The whole is grounded on this Paradox, that *the least Error in Religion is damnable:* This is his grand Topick, as he reprefents Faith as an Affent to every Religious Truth, and concludes that

as

(*q*) Rem. of the-Journ
(*r*) Pag. 23.

as no-body can have fuch a Faith, by the
help of his natural Faculties, ftill liable to
Miftakes, it muft proceed from another
Caufe entirely diftinct from them, and this
Caufe is the infallible Infpiration, and Grace
of God. —Our Authors fhow at large, that
Reafon and Revelation joined together, are
fufficient Rules to lead us to Happinefs;
that thefe Rules far from being oppofite,
afford a mutual Help to one another, and
that God adds to thefe a powerful Affiftance by his Spirit, who acts for us in a
Manner entirely confiftent with our Liberty. To thefe Reafons I fhall take the Liberty to join the following. — Befides Reafon, God has endowed us with a moral
Senfe, or moral Feelings, which never fail.
We are fo very fenfible of the beauty of
Virtue, and the deformity of Vice, that at
the Sight of a moral Object, we cannot
forbear feeling Approbation and Love, or
Difapprobation and Averfion. Thefe Sentiments are found in every individual intelligent Being. They are diftinct from
Reafon, tho' they may be improved by it.
And any one that will follow them, or act
accordingly, fhall moft certainly be accepted
by God, tho' he fhould fall into the greateft Errors or Miftakes. Confequently we
are not left to the Care of an uncertain
Guide, but there is a fure one to any that
has but a willing Heart. If this be allowed

ed (and I believe no Man, who will but mind what paſſes in his own Heart, can ſincerely deny it), the Objeҫtion propoſed is intirely removed.

I ought now to proceed to Dr. *Leland's* ſecond Letter, and the third Part of Mr. *Benſon's* Work, viz. *An interpretation of the Texts which the* Author of the Pamphlet *hath perverted.* But this would draw the Abſtraҫt to too great a Length. I ſhall only take notice that this Author's manner of applying Scripture is palpably unfair. What can be more ſo than taking only part of a Sentence, and joining it to another, that has quite a different Meaning in the Original ; and ſuch like methods which no-body would chuſe to praҫtice, even with reſpeҫt to the Writings of a Pagan Author.

ARTICLE XIV.

LITERARY NEWS.

MUSCOVY.

PETERSBOURG.

Commentarii Academiæ Scientiarum Impe-
riali, Petropolitanæ. 4° 1738. pag. 400.

THE Royal Academy of Sciences of
this City, founded by *Peter* the *Great*
and protected, and much improved under
his Succeſſors, gives every Year *Memoirs of*
Philoſophy and Mathematics. I do not know
for what Reaſon thoſe of the Years 1732
and 1733 were only printed in 1738. I
ſhall ſpeak of each Volume as they come
over, and begin in my next, by the Year
1738.

A very hot Diſpute lately aroſe between
ſome Naturaliſts of this City, eſpecially
Meſſieurs *Gleditſch* and *Siegeſbeck*, on a
Queſtion of Natural Philoſophy, viz. *Whe-*
ther the Plants have the two Sexes. The
former is for the Affirmative, and the latter
is againſt it, and publiſhed a Pamphlet, intitled, *Vaniloquentiæ Botanicæ Specimen,* in
which he gives his Antagoniſts the Name of
Sexualiſts.

Mr.

Mr. *de l'Isle de la Croyere* Brother to the Profeſſor of that Name died at *Kamſchatka,* where he had been ſent to find out a *North* Paſſage to the *Indies.* He ſent from *Arch-angel* and *Kola* in *Lapland* very important Aſtronomical Obſervations.

Mr. *Weitbrecht* gave out lately his *Syn-deſmologïa,* or a Treatiſe *on the Ligaments of the human Body.*

SWEDEN.
STOCKHOLM.

Mr. *Andrew Wilde* has publiſhed a *Latin* Tranſlation, with Additions to *Puffendorff's Introduction to the Hiſtory of Sweden : Preparatio hodegetica ad* Introductionem Puffendorfii in Suecici ſtatus Hiſtoriam *ex Regni Tabulariis accurandam & continuandam,* &c. Acceſſerunt *acta publica de noviſſimo ſucceſſionis jure, et Auctoris Notæ criticæ & politicæ,* cum Appendice *& præjudiciis circa Regalia.* 4°.

Mr. *Bioerner* has juſt publiſhed an Hiſtory of *Gotunheim,* or *Land of the Giants, Specimen Hiſtorico-Geographicum Deſcriptionem* Gotunheimiæ, *ſive* Gigantearum Terrarum *quæ in Suethia Boreali olim ſitæ fuerunt, ſuccincte exhibens.* 4°.

UPSAL.

Mr. *Olaues Rudbeck* died in 1740, after having perfected an *Harmonic-Dictionary of all the Languages both of Europe and Aſia,* in 14 Vol. fol.

Mr.

Mr. *Eric Engmann* publifhed a Differtation wherein he affirms that the Moon cannot be inhabited. *De Luna non habitabili.*

DENMARK.
COPENHAGEN.

The Profeffor *Horrebow* and two of his Sons, have publifhed three Vols. of *Mathematical and Phyfical Obfervations.*

Mr. *Holm* is actually writing an *Ecclefiaftical Hiftory of the Dutchy of Schlefwig*, formed on the Plan of this Book of Mr. *Fabricius : Bibliotheca Cimbrica mediæ & infimæ Ætatis.*

Mr. *Pontoppidanus* lately gave the 3d Vol. fol. of his *Gefta & Veftigia Danorum extra Daniam*, and the 2d Vol. of his *Marmora Danica felectiora.* Thefe Books are much praifed, efpecially the former.

A Society of learned Men is actually employed in compofing a *Metallic Hiftory of the Kings of Dannemark*, in *Danifh* and *French.*

ATTONA.

Mr. *Maternus de Cilano* has printed a Differtation on the Earthquakes in *England* in the Year 1739. He thinks they were caufed, efpecially that which happened at, and about *York*, by the Water contained in fubterraneous Caves, and preffed by an Air in great Agitation. He obferves that Earthquakes are not fo frequent in North Countries as in others, becaufe the North Lands

have

have more openings through which the
prefs'd Air flips out without any great Difficulty.

POLAND.
WARSAU.

Public Spirit for Letters begins to revive
again in this Kingdom, by the Care of the
illuftrious Family *Zaluski*, a Name dear to
the Republic of *Poland*, and more worthy yet
of Efteem in the Republic of Letters. Count
Jofeph Andrew Zaluski has generoufly confecrated to public Ufe his fine and numerous Collection of Books. His Brother,
Chancellor of the Crown, hath affigned the
Funds neceffary to fupport this Eftablifhment, as well as for the Maintenance of a
Librarian, and one of the Houfes of the
fuperb Palace of *Marieville* is defigned for
the Library.

Several Printing-houfes have been erected
in the Kingdom. *Sermons* and *Lives of
Saints* were the firft Books that came out
of them, but they give us Hopes of fomething better hereafter. I do not know in
what Clafs the following Book, wrote by
Palatine *John Jablonowski*, Maternal Grand
Father to King *Staniflaus*, is to be put: *Scru-
pulus fine fcrupulo, vel de Peccatis apud Polo-
nos magis familiaribus, pro peccatis tamen
non habitis.* 8°.

Palatine *Poninski* has given a Collection of
Sarmatides, feu Satyræ 4°.

Jefuit

Jefuit *Nefieck* has publifhed in *Polifh* an *hiftorical Genealogy of all the Families in Poland*, 3 Vol. fol. — It is a pity the Book was not written in *Latin*.

PRUSSIA.
DANTZIG.

Sciagraphia Lithologica curiofa, feu Lapidum figuratorum Nomenclator, Olim a celebri *Joh. Jac. Scheuchzero*, &c. confcriptus, poftmodò auctus à *Joh. Theod. Klein.* 4°. 1740. This Book is much valued. Both the Author and the Editor, have got a great Reputation in the Republic of Letters.

The latter gave alfo a *natural Hiftory of Fifhes*, which is advantageoufly fpoken of by the foreign Journalifts.

Mr. *Martin Adelt* has publifh'd a *Hiftory of the Arianifm*, which was formerly in *Smigla*. If we may judge of this Hiftory by the Title, it is written with a great deal of Moderation and Impartiality: *De Arianifmo olim* Smiglam *infeftante*.

Impoffibilitas Quadraturæ Circuli a priori adferta. This is a Pamphlet 4°. Mr. *Hanon*, the Author of it, defires all the Mathematicians in *Europe*, to pafs their Judgment on his Performance.

Dr. *Kuhn* got the Præmium from the Academy of *Bourdeaux*, for his Latin Differtation on the *Origin of Fountains, the Water of Wells, and other Problems relating to this Subject*. The

ELBING.

The following Work wrote by Mr. *Nathan. Sendel*, the King's Physician, deserves a particular Attention. It is a very curious description of the Amber Closet in *Dresden: Historia succinorum Corpora aliena involventium & naturæ, opere pictorum & Cælatorum ex Regiis Augustorum Cimeliis Dresdæ conditis æri insculptorum conscripta.*

KONIGSBERG.

Mr. *Friese* a Jurisconsult gave out a Dissertation to prove that *Prussia never was subject to the Empire*, and a Continuation of it under this Title. *De actibus Imperii Germanici in Prussiam possessoriis falso venditatis.*

GERMANY.
INSPRUCK.

Anatomiæ Medicinæ Theoreticæ & Practicæ Ministra, 1 Vol. 4°. full of Anatomical Figures, the most part taken from the best Authors, with some entirely new. The Book is wrote by Dr. *Hyeron. Leopold Baccheloni*.

NUREMBERG.

Mr. *Goetz* one of the Masters of this College is extreamly fond of *Apicius*, and endeavours to explain it by a *Lexicon Apicianum.*

ALTORF.

Variæ celeberrimorum Medicorum Observationes, quibus multa loca Novi Testamenti *docte illustrantur.* Mr. *Goetz* is the Author

N 4   of

of this Collection. The firſt Part contains Diſſertations and Obſervations from *Wede-lius, Bartholinus, Baierus, & Conrad Jabre-nius.*

The ſame Author has alſo publiſh'd new Editions of *Cenſorinus* and of *Rutilius*'s Iti-nerary.

Bleeding is generally preſcribed when the Blood is too thick. Here is a Diſſertation of Mr. *Matthias George Pfann,* to recom-mend it in the contrary Caſe : *De uſu venæ ſectionis in rarefactione maſſæ ſanguineæ ni-miâ.*

FRANCKFORT on the Mein.

They print here the following *French* Books. — *Trevoux's Dictionary.* — *Chomel's Dictionary* with Additions, 4. vol. Fol. — *Savary's Dictionary of Trade.* 3. vol. Fol.

Tabularium Eccleſiæ Romanæ Seculi xvi. in quo *Monumenta reſtituti Calicis Eucha-riſtici, totiuſque Tridentini Concilii Hiſtoriam mirifice illuſtrantia continentur.* This Col-lection was made by Meſſieurs *Cyprian* and *Uffel.*

Barchylogus *Juris Civilis, ſive Corpus Legum, paulò poſt Juſtinianum conſcriptum.* Mr. *Senckenberg* Juriſconſult of *Gieſſen* is the Author of this Work.

HERBORN.

Obſervationes Anatomico-Medico-Practicæ variores. A ſmall *Volume publiſhed by* Mr. *Phil. Max Dilthey,* M. D.

GIES-

GIESSEN.

Corpus Juris feudalis Germanici. 8°. by Mr. Senchenberg.

Methodus nova ad Eclipses Terræ & appulsus Lunæ Stellas supputandos. By Mr. *Gersten* Member of the Royal Society at London.

HAMBURG.

Bibliotheca Anonymorum & Pseudonymorum, a *Joh. Ch. Mylio.* This is a Supplement to *Placius's* large Work. Mr. *Mylius* mentions above four thousand Anonymous Authors, or who came out under fictitious Names.

BRUNSWIG.

Mr. *Reimmann* has printed a Literary History of the *Babylonians* and *Chineze.* The later is already known. The former came out for the first Time. *Historia Literaria Babyloniorum & Sinensium :* Illa methodo Chronologica, hæc scientifica Adumbrata, 8°.

HANOVER.

Origines Livoniæ sacræ & Civilis, seu *Chronicon Livonicum vetus, continens res gestas trium priorum Episcoporum, quibus devictæ a Saxonibus, & ad sacra Christianorum traductæ Livoniæ absolvitur Historia : a pio quodam sacerdote, qui ipse tantis rebus interfuit, conscripta, & ad annum* Christi nati, 1226. *Deducta.* One Volume Fol. by Mr.
John

John Dan. Gruber. This Work was entirely unknown, unlefs it be the fame that was in *Petau*'s Library, and now in the Vatican. F. *Montfaucon*, Intitles this laft *De Religione Chriftiana in Livonia.*

GOETINGEN.

The Profeffor *Crufe* has given a fhort fragment of *Eufebius of Cæfarea* on the *Effufion of the Holy Ghoft*, which was never printed before.

De Medulla Spinali, fpeciatim de Nervis ab ea provenientibus ; by Mr. *John James Huber.*

Inftitutiones Pneumatologiæ & Theologiæ naturalis, by Mr. *Hollmann.*

In *December*, 1741. Mademoifelle *Loeber* received the Poetical Crown from the Hands, of the Profeffor *Koeler.* This Solemnity occafioned Mr. *Koeler* to print *Hiftorical Obfervations, on the Diploma* in which the Emperor *Frederic* III. gave to *Æneas Sylvius* the Name of *Coronatus Poeta.*

HELMSTADT.

A Difciple of Mr. *Mofheim* wrote under his Eyes an *Ecclefiaftical Hiftory of the Tartars*, 4°.

De fenatus Confultis Supremorum in Imperio Romano-Germanico Judiciorum, 4°. by Mr. *John Wolfgang Kipping*, J. P. D.

Numophylacium Burcharvianum, Pars I. *Nummos AntiquosGræcos & Romanos continens.* Mr. *Schlaeger* is the Editor of this Catalogue of Medals belonging to the late Mr. *John Henry Burchard*, and which his Heirs are difposed to fell.

JENA.

Theologia naturalis ex Motu corporum de- monftrativa Methodo evicta. 8°. by Mr. *Guft. Eichfeld.* This Book is efteem'd.

Here is a Book much in the Tafte of the excellent *Plain account of the Lord's Supper. De admiffione irregenitorum ad Cænam Domini Commentatio Theologica-biftorico-Critica, & polemica,* 8°. by Mr. *Simon Frid. Rues.* The Author fhews that a Minifter ought not to fcruple receiving to the Lord's Supper, thofe that he judges irregenerate, and that he has no Authority to exclude them.

DRESDEN.

Arcana facra Bibliothecarum Drefdenfium. This is a Catalogue with Remarks, of the Editions of the Scripture contained in the Library of this City, by Mr. *Beyer.*

Mr. *Schoeltgen* goes on with his important work of *Horæ hebraicæ.* He profeffes himfelf an Imitator of *Lightfoot.*

CHEMNITZ.

Hydrocardiologia, five Differtatio Medico- Theologico legalis de liquore Pericardii. Dr. *Gotwald Schufter,* the Author of this Work, Phyfically examines whether *the Water that came out of the fide of Jefus Chrift, came from the Pericardium.* The Author thinks not, and judges there is in this Part of our facred
Hiftory

History fomething that does not agree with the ordinary Courfe of Nature.

LEIPZIG.

Petri Zornii &c. *Hiftoria Bibliorum Ma-nualium*, 4°. Mr. *Zorn*, already known in the Republic of Letters, has made Ecclefiaftical Hiftory his particular ftudy, and this Hiftory *of the Manual Bibles of the firft Chriftians*, was very well received in *Germany*. *Exercitatio hiftorico-Juridica de nundinatione fervorum apud Veteres*, 8°. by Mr. *John Fred. Jugler*.

Here is a confiderable Work wrote by Mr. *John Chrift. Heilbronner*. *Hiftoria Mathefeos univerfæ a Mundo condito ad feculum poft* C. N. xvi.

Mr. *Cofchwitz*, M. D. has wrote a Treatife on *Phyfiology*. *Organifmus & Mechanifmus in homine vivo obvius & ftabilitus*.

The following Treatife of *Statics* by Mr. *J. Leopold*, is reported to be a very ufeful Book. *Theatrum Univerfale ftaticum*, Fol. 332. pages, befides the Preface, the Indexes, &c. which contain 57.

Chriftiani Augufti Haufenii, *Pr. Math. ord. in Acad. Lips.* Novi Profectus in Hiftoria Electricitatis. This Book is in high Efteem in *Germany*.

M. *Abr. Wieling* who has already appeared in the defence of the *Pragmatic Sanction*, wrote lately a Differtation on this fame fubject: Abrahami Wieling *Jurifconfulti & Antecefforis*, De juftitia fanctionis Pragma-ticæ

ticæ Divi Caroli vi. Imp. Aug. Oratio altera, *habita in Auditorio maximo*, A. D. 21. Oct. 1743. *Quùm Jus Publicum Romano-Germanicum profiteri inciperet.* Good Judges think that the Author prove plainly the Justice and Equity of the Pragmatic-Sanction, and consequently that all the Princes, who have guaranteed it, are under a strict obligation to support it. He added to his Speech a bare Copy (without any reflection, or application) of nine Verses of the xv*th* Chapter of I. *Maccabees*, beginning at the 27*th* Verse.

Sacramentorum *in veteris* Romæ *Judiciis follemnium Antiquitates* Illustris Jurisconsultorum Ordinis autoritate in Academia *Lipsiensi* pro gradu Doctoris Juris Confequendo A.D. XII. Maij, A. J. S. MCCXXXX. publice examinandas proponet *Johannes Fredericus Schreiter*, Philosophiæ Magister.— Tho' it is not usual to give Abstracts of small Academical Pieces, yet Mr. *Barbeyrac* has given a full and elaborate Account of this, which has been printed after his Death in a *French Journal.* (*a*)

HALL.

Exercitatio *de optima philosophandi ratione, ex solertiori Dei ejusque admirabilium in Natura operum, & præcipue ipsius Hominis, cognitione petenda.* 4°. The celebrated Mr. *Hoffmann*

(*a*) Nouv. Biblioth. Tom. xix, pag, 187

mann Author of this Book has inferted in it feveral Letters of the late Mr. *Leibnitz.*

Onomafticum veteris Teftamenti, five *Tractatus Philologicus, quo nomina propria ad appellativorum analogiam reducta ex originibus & formis fuis explicantur, cum aliarum gentium nominibus conferuntur, impofitionis ratio, quantum fieri potuit, ubique oftenditur,* &c. 4°. by Mr. *John Simonis* already known by a Work of *Hebraic Philology* which he gave out in 1735. *Arcanum formarum nominum Linguæ Ebreæ.*

A new Hiftory of the Council of Trent lately came out here, it is written by Mr. *Salig,* and moftly taken from feveral important MSS. Pieces, unknown to the Public before and which were taken from the Archives of *Wolfembutel.*

De varia Jurium innovatione per expeditionem Cruce fignatorum, by Mr. *Boehmer,* Privy-Counfellor, *&c.*

Dr. *Baumgarten* propofes to give a new Edition of *Tertullian* in 2 Vols. large 4°. The Firft to contain the Text, according to the Edit. of *Nic. Rigault,* with various Readings. The Second, the Obfervations of the Learned, with thofe of Mr. *Baumgarten,* and Differtations on *Tertullian.*

Mr. *Ludewig,* Chancellor of the Univerfity has juft publifhed the XIIth and laft Volume of his *Reliquiæ Manufcriptorum,* which contain among other hiftorical Monuments

numents, a Chronicle from the Beginning of the World to the Year 1350, by one *John*, whom he judges to be an *English* Man, becaufe he fticks particularly to the Hiftory of *England*. Mr. *Ludewig* has befides confiderable Collections of Diplomas, Chronicles, and other hiftorical Pieces, which he intends to give out under the Title of *Reliquiæ Reliquiarum*.

Ausfurlicher Bericht, von der Trankenbarifchen Miffion, &c. *That is to fay*, A *particularifed* Relation of Miffions in Tanquebár, with 53 Continuations. Hall 1710—1743. in as many Volumes 4°. making about 10000 *Pages*, with Cuts. I fhall begin in my next to give an Account of this Book.

FRANCKFORT on the Oder.

Here is a Differtation that has occafioned many Speculations. *Tentamen Demonftrationis Mathematicæ, qua exiftentiam Corporum Angelorum probat, Carol. Frid. Goede.*

Methodus Cranii offa diffuendi, & machina hunc in finem conftructæ per figuras ligno incifas delineatio. A Pamphlet from Dr. *Bergen* in which he gives the Defcription of a Machine by the Means of which the Bones of the Scull are disjointed precifely at the Places of the Sutures.

BERLIN.

Mr. *Formey* Profeffor in Philofophy has wrote in *French* the Life of Mr. *John Philip Baratier.*

Baratier. This is the young Prodigy of whom Mr. *Whiston,* (b) speaks in the last of the three Tracts he published in 1742. When Mr. *Baratier* was but three Years old, he could read perfectly well. When four, the *Latin* was more familiar to him than any other Language. At five, he was so much Master of the *Septuagint,* as to understand the *Historical Books* in *Greek,* without Translation or Explanation, and near as well as in *French,* or *Latin.* In *October* 1726, (in his sixth Year) he began to learn *Hebrew.* The first of *February,* 1727, he understood perfectly well the first twenty four Chapters of *Genesis.* The twenty fifth of *August* he was at the latter End of the II. Book of *Samuel;* and all this with so much Ease, that according to the Account, his Father (who was his only Tutor) has given of it, he never was employed above three Hours in a Day; and this only in Winter; for in Summer he was so often in Company, that all he could do, was to keep up to what he had learned the Winter before. He was at the same Time of the most chearful Temper, full of Play, and of a very good Constitution. From this to his eighth Year, he gave himself up to a thorough Study of *Hebrew,* and had made a Dictionary of the most difficult Words in the Old Testament,

---

(b) Pag. 43.

Testament, with critical Notes, which were not beneath the Attention of the Learned. At nine Years of Age, he was Master of five Languages. In the Eleventh, he translated the *Itinerary of Benjamin of Tudela* out of *Hebrew* into *French*, and added several Notes and Dissertations in which he modestly takes notice of some Faults committed by *Bochart*, *Buxtorf*, and *Basnage*. After this he applied himself to Ecclesiastical History, and read the chief of the ancient Fathers, and several modern Divines. With this Provision he undertook to confute the Book Mr. *Samuel Crellius*, (c) had wrote under the Name of *Artemonius*, on the genuine Reading of the first Verse of St. *John*. This Answer to *Artemonius* came out in *April, 1735,* and the same month our young Author had got ready for the Press a Dissertation on *Heresies*; but he delayed the Publication of it for some time. He had already made as considerable Progresses in Astronomy, and imagined a Method of finding out *Longitudes* on Sea. He communicated his Discovery to the *Royal Society* of this City in a Letter

PART I.   O   dated

(c) He was Disciple of, and descended from the famous *Crellius*. *Sam. Crellius* disguised himself, on another Occasion, under the Name of *Lucas Mellierus* (the Anagram of his true Name.) Under this borrowed Name he published his *Fides primorum Christianorum, è Barnabæ Clementis, & Hermæ scriptis demonstrata.* D. *Grabe* wrote a Confutation of this Work of *Lucas Mellierus*, and the Book called *Artemonius* is a Reply to Dr. *Grabe*.

dated 21st *January*, 1735. the Da
teenth Year ended. Going thro
he publifhed there (the 8th
fourteen Thefes of Philology, Ec
Hiftory, and Philofophy, which
tained the next Day *(d)* with App
was received Mafter of Arts. I
he repaired to *Berlin.* The Me
the Royal Academy met, he
before them, anfwered extempor
ons to his new Method, prefe
Draught of an Aftronomical I
which he had invented, and was
Member of the Society. He w
as much admired in *Berlin* for I
Deportment, as for his Learning;
he had never ftirred before from his
Houfe at *Swalbach*, a fmall Town
lony of Refugees) in *Franconia*,
Behaviour was as eafy as if he had l
cated at Court. The 29th of
1737, he wrote a very learned
one of the Authors of *La Bibliothe*
manique, on two Works imputed to
fius, viz. his Book *againft the Gen*
his Treatife on *the Incarnation of t*

(d) Under Profeffor *Lange*, who expreffeth hi
in a Letter joined to the *Thefes. Primus es in w*
Academia (puto enim in omnibus aliis) qui vix tri
Spatio triennium Academicum abfolvifti. Primo enin
triculam Academicam relatus, Secundo ftatim Exa
Philofophici fubiifti, & tertio publica difputatione
gifter artium & Philofophia renunciaris.

&c. In this Letter our young Author says, that he had applied himself for two Years to the Study of the Law. In 1739 he inserted the following Article in that same Journal: *The Rules which the Romans observed in conferring* the Proconsular *Dignity.* This same Year he sent to the *Academy of Sciences at Paris* an Account of his Method for finding out *Longitudes on Sea,* and received on that occasion a very obliging Letter from Mr. *Fontenelle.* Mr. *Baratier* had then a considerable Collection of Materials for the Life and Works of *Hippolitus,* and was also preparing *his Succession of the first Bishops of* Rome, which came out soon after (*e*). In 1740 he gave a Dissertation (*f*) on some Writings of *Theodoretus,* in which he shews a vast Erudition. By this time his Constitution was much weakened. He fell into a Decay, and expired the 5th of *October* 1741, aged nineteen Years, eight Months, and seventeen Days. This Account of his Life may be depended upon, as being certified by Mr. *Baratier* the Father a *French* Minister, who communicated it. Rei ....

(*e*) Mr. *Whiston* has made several curious Observations on this Work, in the Book quoted above, and with his usual Candour publickly declares *his having gained by* Mr Barati*er's Book far greater light in several points relating to the Original State of Christianity, than from all the other Writings that have been published these 33 Years, or ever-since he first published his own Works thereto relating.*

(*f*) Inserted in *la Biblioth. Germanique,* Tom XLVIII. pag. 50.

ster at *Hall* in *Brandenburgh*, (
Mr. *Le Maitre*, his former C
Swalbach, two Gentlemen of kn
grity, and by several other Ey
of most Part of the Facts related.

Mr. *Formey* the Author of
Account has translated into *French*
of *Poland*, written in *Latin* by Dr.
of. *Dantzig*, with the *Pacta C*
August III. &c. 8vo.

ULM.

Mr. *Jacob Brucker* has wrote
an *History of Philosophy*, which is
esteemed, and will probably be
lated into *French*.

BAYREUTH.

A new Academy has been ere
with Professors on all Branches of
as well as Masters for bodily Exerc

RATISBONN.

They have re-printed here a
Cardinal *Gotti* against Mr. *John*
De eligenda sententia inter dissid
stianos adversus Joh. Clericum.
is reported to be wrote with M
The Method and Stile of the Au
also praised.

(g) Where he was called from *Swalbach* by t
of *Prussia*, who conferr'd many Favours on him
of his Son, whom he had taken under his Prote

The 3d Tome of, *Scriptores rerum Austriacarum* of *F. Pez*, a Benedictine, is soon to be put in the Press.

TUBINGEN.

Our Dutchess Dowager has honoured one of our public Disputes with her Presence, and has even opposed with a great deal of Wit and Eloquence.

Gnomon Novi Testamenti; a large fol. by Mr. *Bengel*.

Mr. *Osiander* has printed three Dissertations on the *Greek MSS. of the New Testament*.

The Professor *Cotta* is writing a Continuation to *Arnold's Ecclesiastical History*. There is a new Edition of this in 3 Vols. fol.

ALTORF.

Mr. *Goetz* has given a new Edit. of the four Books of *Flavius Cresconius Corippus, de Laudibus Justini Augusti Minoris*; with the Remarks of *Rittershusius* and *Ruizius*.

HEYDELBERG.

Professor *Haurisius* is giving in 3 Vols. fol. a most beautiful Edit. of the ancient *Latin* Authors of the Roman History, with the Remarks of many Learned, and near two thousand Impressions of Medals and Antiquities.

MARPURG.

Specimen Methodi demonstrativæ ad jus Gentium applicatæ de exemptione Legatorum a foro Criminali ejus ad quem missi sunt. The Author, (Mr. *Ab. Dan. Clavel de Branles*, a Native of *Lausanne* in *Switzerland*) exa-

mines

mines only the Cafes that were 1
by *Grotius* and *Binkerſhoek*, and
the whole by modern Examples.

BREMEN.

Several learned Men of this Cit
renewing a literary Society, in
make in common a new Collec
in the Taſte of the *Muſæum B*
of the *Bibliotheca Bremenſis.*

KIEL

De plantis Anthelminticis, A co
demical Diſſertation in which 1
treats of the Plants that ar
cine againſt Worms, and of the
making uſe of them.

SWITZERLAN

LAUSANNE.

Memoires pour ſervir à l'hiſtoire
des Foux, &c. that is to ſay, M
the Hiſtory of the Feaſt of Mad-me
ly kept in many Churches. By Mr.
The Author pretends that this Fea
ed in the Place of the *Saturnalia.*
ſpeaks of other Feaſts, not leſs 1
which were authoriſed by uſe
Churches. The whole is ground
thentic Teſtimonies.

Mr. *de Crouzaz* has given a ne
of his Syſtem of Philoſophy, i
12mo.

The ſame Author has another v
for the Preſs, viz. a Treatiſe on 1
between Body and Soul, &c.

They have printed here *a compleat Collection of Mr. John Bernouli's Works* in 5 Vols. 4°. This Collection contains some pieces never printed before.

Mr. *Bochat* is making another Collection of Inscriptions and other *ancient Monuments to be found in Switzerland*, to serve as a Supplement to *Lauffer, Guilliman Stumpf,* and *Plantinus.*

Here is a new Edition of Sir *Isaac Newton's Opuscula* by Mr. *Castillioneus,* undertaken with the Approbation of the Royal Society in *London,* with the Life of the Author, and a copious Index : *Isaaci Newtonii Opuscula Mathematica, Philosophica, & Philologica : accessit Commentariolus de vita auctoris,* 3 Vols. 4°.

The following Work is soon to be put in the Press : *Commercium Literarium inter* G. Leibnitium & Joh. Bernouillium *in varias Philosophiæ Partes;* 2 Vol. 4° with Cuts.

BASIL.

The Bookseller *Brandmuller* is printing a Supplement in 2 Vol. to his *Moreri,* and a new Edition of Mr. *Otto's Thesaurus Juris Romani.*

BERN.

Young Mr. *John Saltblt,* tho' only fourteen Years old, deserves an honourable Place among the learned. He has published an Analysis of a Section of the Alcoran; *Spe-*

cimen

cimen Arabicum, feu *Analyfis G*
Notæ in Suratam Corani duod
qua Jofephi *Patriarchæ traditur*

Bibliotheca *Selectiffima, five Ca*
brorum, in omni genere fcientiari
morum, quos maximis fumtibus, fu
dio & curâ per plurimos annos co
verò venum exponit Samuel En;
publica Helveto Bernenfi *Bibliot*
marius, qui hunc Catalogum Ori
betico concinnavit, fimul ac notis cr
tuis illuftravit, in Octavo magne
pag. 14. *Libri impreffi,* pag. 1—
nufcripti codices, pag. 167—185.
manici & Belgici, pag. 1—50.
there is not much Dependance on
of Catalogues containing fcarce I
are told that this does certainl
great Number of curious and ra
NEUFCHATE
Effai d'un fyfteme nouveau, &
to fay, *Effay of a new Syftem on*
of Spiritual Beings, partly foun
Locke's *principles.* The Author,
is againft the immateriality of S
ings. — I may perhaps give an
this Book in my next.
ITALY.
MILAN.
Mr. *Muratori* has publifhed
fiderable Collection of Infcriptio
as a Supplement to *Gruterus's,*

Spon's and *Fabretti's Novus* Thesaurus *ve-terum* Inscriptionum, *in præcipuis eorundem Collectionibus hactenus prætermissarum*, &c. 2 Vol. fol. The foreign Journals make a very honourable mention of this Work.

VENICE.

They have printed here a complete Collection of the Works of the celebrated *Malpighi*, a Philosopher and Physician of *Bologna*, and Member of the *Royal Society at London*. Marcelli Malpighii . . . . *opera Medica & Anatomica varia, quibus præfationes & animadversiones instituit* Faustinus Gravinellus . . . . *Editio novissima, prioribus longe accuratior & nitidior, in qua, præter indicem locupletissimum, accessere* Joh. Alphonsi Bonellii, *aliorumque illustrium Philosophorum Epistolæ, nec non* Jo. Bapt. Gyraldi *morborum exitialium, tyrannica sævitia, nobilem mulierem dirimentium Historia Medica. In calce operis adjectæ sunt tabulæ æneæ quàm plurimæ, anatomicarum demonstrationum gratia affabre exculptæ*, fol. 1743.

The vith Vol. of the Collection, intitled *Raccolto di Proze Fiorentine* is come out. It contains the humorous and merry Pieces: *Contenente cose giocose.*

The xxixth Tome of *F. Calogiera's* Collection is also come out, *Raccolto d'Opuscoli Scientifici,* &c. 12°.

POR-

P·O·R·T·U·G·A·L.
L·I·S·B·O·N.

Theatro Hieroino, Abecadario
è Catalogo das mulieres illuſtres,
is to ſay, Theatre of Heroines, hiſ
phabet and Catalogue of illuſtriou
in Arms, in Letters, by their hero
and in the liberal Arts. — By *1*
Froes Perym. 2 Vol. fol.

Vida de S. Jeronymo, Patriarc
Presbytero, &c. *that is to ſay*, *1*
St. Hyeronimus, Patriarch, and
Prieſt, &c. fol. 1743. The T
ſhews what may be expected from
(Brother *John of St. Peter.*) A B
Hieronymus is called a *Cardinal*, iſ
Production of thoſe unhappy
where Inquiſition has ſuch an 1
keep up Ignorance and Falſhood.

F·R·A·N·C·E.
P·A·R·I·S.

Mr. *Lewis Ricoboni* already 1
ſeveral *French* Works, eſpecially 1
of the Italian Theatre, and his *Re*
Moliere and on Comedy in general,
ed in 1743. *A Reformation of*
tre, 12°.

Mr. *D'Auvigny* has given 6 Vc
Lives of illuſtrious Men in Fran
Work is imperfect, the Author ha
kill'd at the Battle of *Dettingen.*

Le vrai Syſteme, &c. or the *true*

Mr. Newton's *Natural Philosophy exposed and analysed, in a Parallel with Cartesius's System,* 4°. 1743. Father *Castel,* (a Jesuit) the Author of this Book modestly expresseth himself thus in his Preface: *I have laid the Ax unto the root of the Tree; and tho' whatever I have heretofore proved against Mr.* Newton *were null, I flatter myself to have catch'd him in his strongest Intrenchment, and to have given a decisive Blow to his System.*

Essai sur les principes, &c. or *an Essay on the Principles of Law, and of Morality,* by Mr. *d'Aube,* 4°. This Book has already received many Contradictions.

They have printed here a new *French* Translation of *Cornelius Nepos,* 12°.

Also a Translation from the *Dutch* of *Aitzema's Civil, Politic, Military and Ecclesiastical History of the United-Provinces.* The Work is to consist of 18 Tom. 4°. There are but few of them out.

Mr. *Winslow* has wrote a *Dissertation* on *the uncertainty of the Symptoms of Death.* I shall speak of this in my next.

Cicero's Works by *l'Abbe d'Olivet* are all complete in 9 Vols. They are printing a new Edition of it in *Geneva.* The Bookseller says it is with the Author's Approbation.

Theory of the Figure of the Earth, drawn from the Principles of Hydrostatics, by Mr. *Clairaut,* Member of the Royal Society in *London,* 1743, 8°.   The

The ancient and modern Government of Egypt, 12°, 1743. *A Description of Corsica, and the History of the last War*, 12°, 1743. *Leſſons de la ſageſſe*, &c. *Leſſons of Wiſdom on the Errors of Men*, 12°. 3 Vols. 1743.

Memoires pour ſervir, &c. or, *Memoirs for the History of the Gauls and of France*, by Mr. *Gibert*, 12°, 1744.

Mr. *Stephen Fourment* has given a *Chineſe Grammar* which is highly valued. This is the Title. *Linguæ Sinarum Mandarinicæ Hieroglyphicæ, Grammatica Duplex, Latinè & cum caracteribus Sinenſium : item Sinicorum Regiæ Bibliothecæ Librorum Catalogus denuo cum notis amplioribus & caractere Sinico editus,* juſſu Ludovici xv, fol. 1742.

Here is a new Edition in 3 Vols. 4°. of all the Latin Poets, with a few choſen Notes and various Readings. *Corpus omnium veterum Poetarum Latinorum ad Manuſcriptos Codices Bibliothecæ Regiæ, alioſque Gallicanos & Italicos, atque ad optimas editiones emendatorum.*

Mr. *d'Hermili* has tranſlated from the *Spaniſh* into *French* a large Work very much eſteemed in that former Language, viz. *Don Juan de Ferrera's general History of Spain*, 9 Vols. 4°.

BEZANCON.

They are printing here a very uſeful Book, viz. *Obſervations on the Epidemic and Pleuretic*

retic Fevers that have been very fatal in Franche-Comté *for some Years past,* 8°. 1743.

Item, A Pamphlet 4°. on the *Contagious Distemper that reigned lately among the Cattle, with Directions to cure the most part of those they are subject to.*

UNITED PROVINCES.

HAGUE,

Memoires de l'Academie, &c. or *Memoirs of the Academy of Surgeons in Paris,* were reprinted here in 2 Vol. 4°.

The following Books lately came out here, viz.

L'Esprit de Monf. de Fontenelle, &c. or, Mr. *Fontenelle's way of thinking,* 12mo. — *Examen d'un livre,* &c. or, *a Confutation of* Mr. *Voltaire's Book on* Sir Isaac Newton's *system of Metaphysics,* 8°. — *Memoires,* &c. or, *Memoirs for the History of the Mind, and of the Heart.* A Periodic work by the *Marquis d'Argens. Lettres, Memoires,* &c. or, *Letters, Memoirs and Negociations of* Count *d'Estrades Ambassador of* Lewis the XIV. to Italy, England, and Holland, *his Ambassador Plenipotentiary at the Peace of* Nimeguen, *with the Answers from the King, and the Secretary of State,* 9 Vol. 12mo. — *Recueil historique,* &c. Or an *historical Collection of Treatises and Negociations,* &c. by Mr Rousset; the 17th Tom, 8°. — *Histoire de* Charles XII, &c. or, the *History of* Charles the XIIth of Sweden, by Mr. *Nordberg.*

berg, the 2d, Vol. 4°. — *Hiſtoir*
de Sicile, &c. or, *a general Hiſtory*
by Mr. Burigny. 2. Vol. 4°.

LEYDEN.

Speedily is to be publiſhed here,
&c. or, *Memoirs for the Hiſtory*
of Polypus, by *M. Tremblay,* Memb
Royal Society in *London,* 4°. wi
This curious Book has had the ap
of Mr. *Reaumur,* who is generall
to be the Reſtaurator of that
natural Philoſophy that concerns
As for Mr. *Tremblay* he is the D
of that kind of Animal, which l
the Deſcription of. *(a)* I ſhall ſpea
Book when it comes over.

The following Books were prin
lately.

Euſtathii Anatomia ex Editione
4°.—*Uteri humani gravidi Anatome*
toria, Authore Willielmo Noortwyk
cum fig. 4°.—*G. Van Swieten, M.*
mentaria in Hermanni Boerhaave *Ap*
de cognoſcendis & curandis Morbis,
adus 4°. — A new Edition of, *Ja*
Inſtitutionum libri quatuor emendat
Editione Jacobi Cujacii, *ac Commentari*
a Coſta, 4°. —Item, of *Velleius Pa*
cnm integris notis & animadverſionibus
rum, curante Petro Burmanno, 8°.

(a) See Article X. of this Journal, pag. 149.

*cum notis variorum ex Editione Dukeri, &
Phædrus cum notis variorum & P. Burman-
ni*, 8°. — A new Edit. of *Hefychius*, in 2
Vol. Fol. with the Notes of many learned
Men, and efpecially of the Editor Mr. *Jo.
Alberti*. — *B. S. Albini* Med. Doctoris, &c.
*Explicatio Tabularum Anatomicarum B.
Euftachii, Anatomici Summi*, Fol. with Cuts,
by the Famous, *J. Wandelaar*. — The 4th
Tome 4°. of *Titus Livius variorum* by *Arn.
Drakenborh*, with *Freinfhemius's* Supple-
ments.

AMSTERDAM.

Lately came out here a new Edition of
Virgil, 8vo. with the Commentaries of *N.
Heinfius*, and of *P. Burmann*. — Another of
the fame in 4 Vol. 4°. — Two new Volumes
of *Ceremonies Religieufes*, or *Religious Ceremonies*, Fol. — Ouvrages divers, &c. or *feveral Works of Mr. Maupertuis*, viz. *Elements
of Geography* ; *Difcourfe on the different Figures of the Celeftial Bodies* ; *Difcourfe on
the Parallel of the Moon* ; *Letter on the Comet*, 12°. — *Cumberland's Law of Nature*,
tranflated into French, with Notes by Mr.
Barbeyrac, 4°. — *Lettres de Calvin*, &c. or
Calvin's Letters to James of Burgundy *Lord
of* Falais *and* Bredam, *and to his Wife* Joland *of* Brederode, large 8vo. Thefe Letters
were lately found among the Papers of
a Gentleman in whofe Family they were
kept very precioufly till now.

ROT-

ROTTERDAM.

— *Recherches Philosophiques*, &c. or, *Philosophical Enquiries* into the certainty of our knowledge, &c. by Mr. *St. Hyacinthe*, Author of *Mathanasius*, or, *Chef d'Oeuvre d'un Inconnu.*

GRONINGEN.

Here is a new History of the Reformation in general. *Introductio in Historiam Evangelii seculo xvi. passim per Europam renovati Doctrinæque reformatæ*, &c. by *Dan. Gerdes* Professor, and Member of the Berlin Royal Society, 4to.

Mr. *Barbeyrac* one of our Professors, and the Ornament of this University, died the 3*d*, of *March* 1744.

GREAT-BRITAIN.
LONDON.

Among the great variety of Books of all kinds constantly printed here, I shall mention only the following.

The Treatise intitled, *Christianity not founded on Argument*, has been answered by several, besides Mr. *Benson* and Dr. *Leland*; among others by Mr. *Tho. Chubb*; by the Revd. Mr. *Tho. Mole*, in his *ground of the Christian Faith rational*, &c. — and by the Revd. Mr. *Randolph*, in his *Christian Faith, a rational Assent*, &c.

Mr. *Muschenbroek's natural Philosophy*, has been translated into *English* by Mr. *John Colson*, Member of the Royal Society, with the Notes of the Translator, 2. Vol. 4°.

A

A Learned Anonymous has publifhed the Plan of a new Edition of the *Book of Job*, with the *Hebrew* Text, and an *Englifh Tranflation*, in 2 Vol. 4°.

Mr. *Warburton* is ftill attack'd about his *Divine Legation of Mofes*. Several Anonymous Writings have appeared againft him. Drs. *Middleton, Pococke, Gray* and *Sykes* are his declared Antagonifts. He wrote lately an Anfwer to the three firft, *Remarks on occafional Reflections, in Anfwer to Drs. Middleton, Pococke, Richard Gray*, and other Authors, 8vo. — Mr. *Tho. Bott* has alfo wrote two Books againft him ; the firft about a *Paffage in Tully's firft Tufculan*, Ch. xvi. on this Queftion, *whether* Therecydes *was the firft Inventor of the Atheiftical Notion of the* To En. The fecond is an Anfwer to the *Divine Legation*, in general.

It feems that our Deifts have thought fome of Mr. *Warburton's* Propofitions favourable to them, fince they have thank'd him, in a Book intitled, *A brief examination of the Revd. Mr.* Warburton's *Divine Legation of Mofes ; by a fociety of Gentlemen.* The following Anonymous Refutation of his Syftem, is wrote with a quite different view, and is much efteem'd on many Accounts : *An Examination of Mr.* Warburton's *fecond Propofition in his projected Demonftration of the Divine Legation of Mofes. In which the faith of the Ancient* Jewifh Church, *touching*

PART I.   P   *the*

the Doctrine of a future state is asserted and cleared from the Author's Objections. *In an Epistolary Dissertation addressed to the Author*, &c.

As the *Moral Philosopher* has thought proper to take the Defence of the late Mr. *Woolston*, in a Pamphlet intitled, *The Resurrection of Jesus confidered in Answer to the Tryal of the Witnesses*, &c. he has drawn upon him several Answers; one especially from the Author of the *Tryal*, &c. Dr. *Sherlock*, Ld. Bishop of *Sarum : The Evidence of the Resurrection cleared from the Exceptions of the Moral Philosopher.* — Mr. *Sam. Chandler*, and the Revd. Mr. *Tipping Sylvester*, have appeared in the Defence of that important Article of our Religion : The first has given us, *the Witnesses of the Resurrection of Christ re-examined, and their Testimony shewn to be entirely confiftent.* The fecond, *the Evidence of the Resurrection of Jesus vindicated against the Cavils of a Moral Philosopher*, &c.

The following Books deferve alfo to be mentioned.

An hiftorical Dictionary of all Religions, by *Tho. Broughton,* 4to. — *Three Treatifes on Art, Mufic, Painting, Poetry, and Happinefs ;* by *S. H.* 8vo. — *A Review of the Advancement of Learning, from* 1300. *to* 1521. *by* Wm. Collins, 4to. — *A Critical and Chronological Hiftory of Sciences,* &c. by *Hen. Winder,* 2 Vol. 4to. — *Of the Rife and Abufe of Parliaments ;* 2 Vol. 8vo. — *The Works*

Works of Saluſt, by *Tho. Gordon* Eſq; — *Salluſt's Hiſtory*, &c. by *Hen. Lee.* — *Guthrie's Hiſtory of* England, — *The Eſſay on Man, and Eſſay on Criticiſm, with the Commentary and Notes of Mr.* Warburton. — *Conſultationes Medicæ, ſive ſylloge Epiſtolarum cum reſponſis Herm. Boerhave.* — Geo. *Edward's natural Hiſtory of Birds,* &c. *with the Figures of ſixty Birds, and Two Quadrupedes engrav'd on fifty two Copper Plates, after curious original drawings from Life, and exactly coloured,* 4to.

This Work dedicated to the Society of Phyſicians in *London,* has been much encouraged by them. Good Judges ſay that by the exactneſs of the Draught, the neatneſs of the Engraving, the Brightneſs and nice Management of the Colouring, in ſhort, by the fine Taſte and exquiſite Art which appears throughout the whole Work, it is beyond any thing of the kind, that has yet been ſeen. . The Attitudes of the Birds repreſented are all natural, gracious, and withal diverſified in the moſt agreeable Manner. — *A brief Account of Calvin burning Servetus.* — *Vanſwiten's Commentaries on Dr. Boerhave's Aphoriſms,* 2 Vols. 4°. — *The Britiſh Empire in America, with a Continuation to the preſent Time,* &c. — *A Letter to* ..... *concerning the Abuſe of Scripture Terms,* &c. The abuſe the Author complains of, is *an Application of Scripture Terms to trifling Subjects.* — *The Golden Calf, the*

Idol

Idol of Worſhip. Being an Enquiry Phyſico-Critico-Patheologico-Moral into the Nature and Efficacy of Gold; ſhewing the wonderful Power it has over, and the prodigious changes it cauſes in the minds of Men, with an Account of the Wonders of the *Pſychoptic Looking-Glaſs, lately invented by the Author,* Joakin Philander, M. A.— This Book is wrote in the Taſte of *Swift's* Works and ſeems to be an Imitation of them. — *The Ladies Aſtronomy and Chronology.* By *Jaſper Charlton.* Second Edit. 8°. — *The Hiſtory of ancient Paganiſm, as delivered by Euſebius,* &c. —The anonymous Author of this Work intends to ſhew by this old Fragment of ancient Hiſtory that all Syſtems whatſoever of Religion are but political Inventions. This Fragment contains the Coſmogony of *Thot,* one of the moſt ancient Monarchs of *Egypt,* the purpoſe of which is to ſhew that the World is a natural Production, owing its Exiſtence and Form, to Chance, &c.—*Five hundred points of Husbandry,* by *Thomas Tuſſer,* 8°.—*Lardner's Credibility of Goſpel,* Five Parts. — *A Letter to the Hon. Col. John in Flanders on the Subject of Religion,* &c. — *Syris,* or the Famous Treatiſe about *Tar-Water* is too well known to require my ſaying any thing about it.

F I N I S.

A

LITERARY

JOURNAL,

For *Jan. Febr. March*, 1745.

A

TERARY

URNAL

A

LITERARY
JOURNAL.

January, February, March, 1745.

VOL. I.

PART II.

DUBLIN:
Printed by S. POWELL, for the AUTHOR,
MDCCXLV.

TABLE
OF
ARTICLES.

a ARTICLE

CONTENTS.

ERRATA.

PAGE 263. line 17. *at the Word*, &c. read *As the* &c. p. 334. l. 7. *to a Monk*, read *to be a Mon.* p. 337. l. 21. *Paderbom*, read *Paderborn.* p. 355 *conformable*, read *comfortable.* p. 362. l. 27. *the l* read *the Nature*, &c. p. 366. l 27. *in some Kids*, &c *some Kids*, &c. p. 367. l. 12. *effected*, read *affected.* p the Note. *Greenland*, read *Groenland.* p. 377. l. 8. 2 *balg*, read *Ziegenbalg.* p. 385. l. ib. dele *in some M* and read *they do more than make amends*, &c. Ibid. read *would not be* such *a shocking*, &c. p. 387. l. ib. *pec* read *peccable.* p. 396. the Note. *quam vos, &c.* read *rei, &c.* p. 442. l. 10. *Translation*, read *Transaction*

A
Literary Journal.

January, February, March, 1745.

ARTICLE I.

Lettres *de* Critique, *de* Litterature, *&c,* ecrites
à divers Savans de l' *Europe* par feu Monfieur *Gifbert Cuper, Bourguemaitre de la
ville de Deventer, Deputè des Etats de la
Province d' Over-Yffel à l' Affemblée des
Etats Generaux des Provinces unies des
Pays-Bas, enfuite Confeiller Deputé de la
meme Province, &c.* Publiées Sur les Ori-
ginaux par Monfieur de B———Amfterdam Chez Smith & Dufauzet 1742.
Grand 4°. Pag. 583, fans les Prefaces
& l' Indice, avec plufieurs figures gravées
en taille douce,

That is to fay,

Letters *of* Criticifm, *of* Literature; *&c.
wrote to feveral learned Men of* Europe, *by
the late Mr,* Gifbert Cuper, *&c.*

THIS

(*a*) THIS is a very valuable Book. Mr. *Cuper* was reputed one of the most learned Men of his Age, and consulted as such from all Parts of *Europe* on the most nice Points of Literature. He was born at *Deventer* in *Over-Yssel* in 1644. His Father was a Magistrate in that Province. His Learning raised him early to a Professorship in History; from which he was promoted to one of the first Magistracies of his Republic. He died in 1716, aged 72. His Character is drawn to the Life in his Letters; he was a sincere Man, a good Friend, benevolent to the Learned, no ways inclined to Ostentation, an utter Enemy to Quarrels, and to all those Ill Usages which so much dishonour the Variety of Opinions, which Variety is so necessary to the Progress of Learning, desirous of Instruction, obliged to those from whom he received any Knowledge, and, above all, of an exemplary Humility.

(*b*) The whole Collection is made up of near two hundred and eighty Letters. The Names of the Learned, to whom they are

directed

(*a*) See Bibliotheque Italique. Tom. 2. pag. 16. & Bibliotheque Françoise Tom. 35. p. 57.

(*b*) The Editor acknowledges his being indebted for this Collection to Messieurs *Royer* and *Chais* Ministers at the *Hague*, Mr. *Dumont* Professor at *Rotterdam*, Mr. *Driebergen* Professor in Divinity among the Remonstrants, Mr. *Peter Marchand*, Mr. *Caillaud* and Monsieur *l' Abé d' Olivet*.

directed, must prepossess the Readers in it's
Behalf. It is not to be supposed, that a
Man like Mr. *Cuper* should write about
Trifles to Messieurs *La Croze, Bignon, Huet,*
&c. The Letters to Mr. *La Croze* have
the first Rank. There are fifty-five of
them which begin in 1708, and end at
the Author's Death. They are of all his
Letters, those in which he opens his Mind
with the most Freedom; 'Tis a particular
Kind of Pleasure to see a Magistrate writing
three or four Times to force out an Answer from a learned Man, who had but his
Merit to draw his Regard and Affection.
They are interspersed with Draughts of
Medals, of Animals, and of some other
Curiosities.——The 52 to Monsieur *l' Abbé
Bignon* begin the same Year, and end also
at the Author's Death. The greatest Part of
'em were wrote in the Time of the hottest War with *France*, and when Mr. *Cuper*
was one of the Deputies of the States-
General in the Army. This Circumstance
occasions now and then some curious Anec-
dotes and Observations.—— Mr. *Le Clerc*
is the Third of the Correspondents, and
the Oldest in Date; his Commerce with
Mr. *Cuper* lasted 21 Years. To keep up
so long a Friendship, a certain Sweetness of
Temper is necessary, in order to support the
Contradictions and Weaknesses of a Friend.
This is certainly very rare in all Classes of
Men,

Men, and more fo among the Learned, as being more expofed to differ in their Opinions, and commonly more eager to defend them. The Reputation of a learned Man is his Land, his Dignity, his Stock; he jealoufly confiders whatever might fully its Brightnefs. The genteel World has other Goods, other Dignities to defend; and is confequently eafier on the Article of Contradiction; for this Reafon the Unpolitenefs of many Learned may be fomewhat excufed.——The Letters wrote to Mr. *Le Clerc* are 23 in Number.——The 11 Letters to Mr. *Bafnage* fhew a little lefs Cordiality; nay a great Part of them is taken up in criticizing that learned Author's *Hiftory of the Jews*; and you find fome Places in the Letters to Mr. *La Croze*, where Mr. *Cuper* decides in his Favour againft the Opinions, and even againft the Manners, of Mr. *Bafnage*,—— There are but 8 of them to Mr. *Nicaife*, and they are of the Oldeft; — 6 to Mr. *Martin* the Minifter; — 4 to Mr. *Jurieu*; — 1 to Father *Banduri*.—— The 13 Letters to Mr. *Van Dalen* are the longeft, and the moft elaborate.——The whole Collection ends with 13 Letters from Mr. *Huet* to Mr. *Cuper*. Tho' the Title of the Work feems to exclude them, yet the Editor hopes no Body will take amifs that they fhould be preferved.——There are now and
then

then some odd Letters to Mr. *Galand,* to F. *Montfaucon,* to *Canon Voffius,* &c.

I am now to give some Particulars of the most important Things contained in this Collection, especially in the Letters wrote to Mr. *La Croze.*

(*c.*) But before I proceed any further, there is an Article in some of these Letters, which I cannot help taking notice of, in Justice to Gentlemen for whose Memory I have a particular Veneration. Mr. *La Croze* had conceived a disadvantageous Opinion of Messieurs *de Beausobre* and *Lenfant,* as if they had been inclined to *Socinianism.* He freely (I could almost say imprudently) opens himself on this Subject to Mr. *Cuper,* and there are now and then Strokes in the Answers of the latter, that have a Reference to this groundless Suspicion. I call it groundless, Mr. *La Croze* acknowledged it afterwards, and those Gentlemens most intimate Acquaintances declare they never heard them say any Thing that might authorize such an Imputation. How Mr. *La Croze,* who really was a good-natured and worthy Man, could forget himself so far, as to form an Accusation generally thought of great Consequence, and that without any Kind of Proof, is not easily accounted for. It is surprising to see

PART II.   B   Men,

(*c.*) Reflection of the Journalist.

Men, who on all other Occasions most
scrupulously avoid doing an Injury, or any
Kind of Disservice, thinking themselves,
in this Respect free from the most common Laws of Charity, nay of Equity itself,
and unmercifully laying at random Accu-
sations of the most dangerous Consequence.
If a Clergyman explains a Truth of Christianity in a somewhat different Manner
from what others have done before him,
or does in the least swerve from the received Opinions, he is immediately accused
of *Heresy*, and branded with the Name of
Socinian. This was the Case of Messieurs
de Beausobre and *Lenfant.* Their Expressions on the Subject of the *Trinity* were
different from those some Divines make
use of. In their New Testament they
give the literal Sense of some Passages,
which are commonly thought to have a
mysterious Meaning, and as Occasion offers,
they freely and honestly tell that such or
such Words are not to be found in the
oldest MSS. or Translations of our sacred
Books. This was enough to draw a *pious
odium* upon them, and yet it was most certainly their Duty to do what they did.

To return to Mr. *Cuper.* His favourite Inclination was Antiquities, Medals,
Inscriptions, ancient Language ; the Government, Clothing, and Manners of the
People of remote Ages. This is what he
delighted

delighted in ; being much less fond of that
Kind of Literature which confists in fift-
ing the Syllables and Words of Authors,
in relating various Readings, and in recti-
fying Orthography. It is eafy to judge
which of thofe two Kinds is the moft ufeful.

At the Head of thefe Letters there is
a *Latin* Epiftle, in which Mr. *Cuper* fharp-
ly takes up the confident Rafhnefs of
Father *Hardouin*. I do not fcruple making
ufe of thefe Expreffions in talking of a Man
who made game of the common Senfe of
Mankind, both during his Life and after
his Death. What an abfurd Syftem, to
pretend to take from us, by one fingle
Dafh of a Pen, all the Poets, the beft Hiftorians, and the Fathers ; to impute fo many
admirable Works to imaginary learned Men
of a barbarous Century ; to accufe of Impofture that Multitude of Infcriptions and
Statues fpread over the Earth ; and all
with a View to erect over the Ruins
of Hiftory an unlimited ridiculous Tradition. It is not without Reafon that Mr.
Cuper makes ferious Reflections on the Order
to which this inconfiderate Author did belong.
Is there not Reafon to think, that this artful Society fuffered thefe Paradoxes to be
penn'd down, in order to prepare the Minds
of Men to hear without Horror fuch
Doctrines, as will to be fure fhock the firft

B 2　　　　　　　Ge-

Generation, but which Councils, Inquifitions, and *Auto-da-fe's* may render Orthodox in another Age.

(d). It may be afked what was the Occafion of the Society's forming fuch a Scheme, and what the Advantage, it might draw from it.—As for the Occafion, I believe it to be this. — The Ignorance of the former Ages has thrown fuch Confufion over fome Hiftories, that it is eafy to conceive how far this Objection might be carried on in fuch good Hands. Nay, they are to be confidered, not as the Inventors, but Improvers of the Scheme for perplexing Mens Underftandings. There have been now and then bold Attempts towards it long before the Society's Foundation; at leaft as to what concerns the Fathers and the Ecclefiaftical Writers. The Number of Interpolations, Forgeries, &c. is fo great, that more than a common Attention is neceffary to be able to gather up a coherent Series of the chief Facts related in that Hiftory.

There are fo many fpurious Works, or fufpected to be fuch; fo many Charges laid by all Sects, or by every Set of Divines againft one another, of Corruptions, Omiffions, Additions in the Writings of the Fathers, that an unprepoffeffed Reader is

(d.) Reflection of the Journalift.

is much at a Lofs where to look for Truth.
And what proves that bare Mifchances, or
Faults of Copyifts, are not the only Caufes
of this Intricacy, is this undeniable Fact,
that the above-mentioned Accufations, or
well-proved Forgeries, do chiefly concern
thofe Articles of Chriftianity about which
there arofe Difputes in the Life-time of
fuch or fuch a Father, or Ecclefiaftical
Writer; and as their Works are much
taken up with thefe Difputes, they have an
Influence almoft on every Thing they wrote.
I do not mean that every one of thofe that
have been guilty of thofe Tricks, called
pious Frauds, did it with a formed Defign
of introducing Ignorance and Slavery. No,
It is probable, at leaft I am willing to think,
that thofe who frankly own the Fact, acted
by no other Motive but a blind Zeal. To
be fure, St. *Jerom* thought he promoted
the Almighty's Glory when he mutilated
Origen's Works in fuch a Manner, that
they could not, with any Shadow of Truth,
be any more called *Origen's Works*; for he
braggs of it as of an Action for which
the Church was much indebted to him :
(e) " Why, *fays he*, fhould I be blamed,
" if in my *Latin* Tranflation of *Origen*,
" I either cut off, or corrected, or paffed
" over

___

(e) *Hieron.* adv. Vigilant. Op. Tom. II. p. 312.
Edit. *Erafm.*

" over what is bad, and gave only what
" is good."—He at the same Time names
the Confessor *Hilarius* and some others, reputed the greatest Men of his Age, who
had done the like.—Whether *Ruffinus*, another Interpolator, may be reckoned among
those that acted *bona fide*, I will not pretend to determine. The learned Dr. *Cave*
seems to think not (*f*) when he expresses
himself thus : *It cannot be denied that Ruffinus, in translating the Writings of others
out of the* Greek *Language, has generally
done it most unfaithfully, by changing, and
curtailing, and adding, till they seem rather
to be new Works of his own, than those of
other Authors. Nor can any One so much
as guess which Parts belong to* Ruffinus,
and which to the Author himself.—The
same Dr. *Cave* says, *That* Ruffinus *translated* Origen's *Comment on the Epistle to the*
Romans *most unfaithfully, that he reduced
it to about one Half, and with great Cun-
ning and Knavery ascribed the Translation
to* Jerom.—However, the Effects of these
Falsifications are equally pernicious, whether they are intended or not, and have
given Occasion since to artful designing
Men to do worse, and embroil every Thing
as much as they could, in order to come
at their wicked Ends. It is chiefly to this
that

(*f*) *Cave* Hist. Litterar. in *Ruffin.* & *Orig.*

that the State the Church has been in for many Ages muft be imputed.—The Example was too edifying not to be followed, the Opportunity too favourable not to be taken hold of by the worthy Society, that modeftly fets out with the bleffed Name of JESUS. Ecclefiaftical Hiftory is in many Parts fo obfcure, in Confequence of the Arts and Frauds aforefaid, that they refolved to make a Handle of this Obfcurity. The Attempt was very bold, and could have been made by no others, confidering how much Times are altered fince thofe unhappy Ages, when any Thing of the Kind might be attempted without Danger. But on the other Hand, as they have yet a very great Number of People refolved blindly to follow them, and others beginning to waver; fo any Thing muft be attempted to fecure the Firft and prevent the utter Defertion of the Laft.—After all, they did not run any great Hazard. If the Scheme fucceeds in any Part, let it be ever fo inconfiderable, that is fo much gained; if not, it will be time then to difavow Father *Hardouin*, to fay he was a mad Man, and to lay the whole Blame at his Door. As to the Advantage they intended to draw from this Chriftian Scheme, probably they aimed at no lefs than overturning the very

Foundation

Foundation of Chriftianity, in rendering the Books of the New Teftament, fufpicious as to the Manner they were conveyed down to us, and by that to make Religion to depend wholly on a Tradition of their own making. What elfe could they aim at ? The Succefs of the Undertaking might have fhock'd fome People and encreafed the Number of Unbelievers, but what do they care for it, provided they have the great Number on their Side. Men will have ftill a Religion ; if not a reafonable, a fuperftitious One, and the good Fathers would have eafily bore fome few Deifts, or even Atheifts, whilft they had the Command over all the reft. — The Trap, it is true, tho' well laid, would have been no ways dangerous to a Man determined to examine Things impartially and with Care. Let Ecclefiaftical Hiftory be ever fo difcouragingly perplexing, this, however, muft be acknowledged by all who know any Thing of the Matter, that no lefs than the higheft Degree of Pyrrhonifm cou'd make one Doubt of the New Teftament's being faithfully tranfmitted to us. The prodigious Number both of Manufcripts found in the three Parts of the World formerly known, and of Tranflations into the Languages of the moft confiderable Nations, are fuch authentic Witneffes, nesses, that an honest reasonableMan can hardly avoid assenting to this Proof. Supposing the Number of Falsificators had been ten Times greater than it really was, how could they have prevailed over the People, who very early had, almost one and all, a Copy of that divine Book, to surrender their Copies and receive new altered Ones in their stead. This could not be effected with respect to an indifferent Book once in the Hands of every Body; much less with respect to a Book, for which Christians had at all Times so much Veneration. The very Proposal would have been more than enough to discredit for ever those that should have made it.—As to the various Readings, they are rather a Proof against, than for, a Collusion; and in short, suppose Christians of all Denominations should agree not to ground any Thing on, or appeal to, any one of those various Readings, the Christian Religion would yet remain sound and safe, both as to its Facts, and as to the Doctrines truly belonging to it. This seems to me a Demonstration that these sacred Books are genuine. This Fact being so well ascertained, it would have been a hard Task for the Reverend Fathers Jesuits to strike at it's Authentickness in a Manner proper to make an Impression on diligent Inquirers. But how few of these are there? And what Mischief may not arise

PART II.　　　C　　　from

from their Projects, if not tim
and vigorously opposed ? I
the best Way to proceed w
that all those that have any
write on Ecclesiastical Histor
tect the Frauds, and lay op
the Mistakes, as they come in
without minding in the least
or such Opinions, this or th
be affected by it, or not. A
but there would remain a suffi
of naked Truths to make up
History. Every Body may
what Advantage might accrue
nity from this Method. — I
on this Article, because it is
oned in the 'Book from whicl
Abstract.

To come now to a Subjec
Kind, Mr. *Cuper* judiciously op
to the pretended Medal of *Phi*
thor of the current Coins in
were too great a Happiness if
such a remote Antiquity, coi
single City, and in a short Compa
had escaped the new Casting, i
of Cities, and all the Accidents tha
turned the Surface of the Earth.—
that Father *Hardouin*'s Explana
Greek Word κοσον, is equally re
Grammar, History, and the Nature

In the eighth Letter he speaks of *Mamouth's* Teeth, the true Teeth of Elephants which are found on the Borders of the great Rivers in *Siberia*. The Illustrious *Sir Hans Sloane* hath proved beyond all Doubt, that they belong to that large Animal. The common Opinion is, that they could not have been carried to those frozen Climates but by an universal Inundation. Others, may be with more Reason, think Elephants may have been brought there, either by the *Chinese* or the *Tartars* in their Wars against the Inhabitants of that Country.

The eighteenth Letter directed to *F. Montfaucon* is a Criticism on some Places of that learned *Benedictine's Palæographia Græca*. There is in it a curious Treatise on the Paper made out of the Palm Tree, and on that made out of Mallows, which is somewhat like that made in *Japan* of a Kind of Mulberry Tree, whose Leaves are like those of Mallows. *Koempfer* hath given a complete and very curious Description of it.

The Learned are divided about the Invention of the alphabetic Letters, some, as Messieurs *Bourguet* and *La Croze*, ascribe it to God himself, and fix the Time of it, when the Law was given to *Moses* on *Mount Sinai*. Mr. *Cuper* does not think so, " It is undeniably true, *says he to Mr*. La " Croze, That the Use of the Tongue

C 2 " was

" was given by God to *Adam*, and it is
" a Joke to talk otherwife along with
" *Lucretius* ; but it does not follow from this,
" that God fhould have given the Al-
" phabet, either to *Adam*, or to other
" Patriarchs, as fome will have it, or to
" *Mofes* as you think. I put this among the
" εὑρήματα by the human Mind's Pene-
" tration, as there are fo many others, which
" according to your Syftem, fhould be
" afcribed alfo to God the παντοκράτωρ.——
To fupport his Opinion he alledges thefe two
Reafons. The firft is grounded on the Explanation all the Learned in the oriental
Tongues give of the Name of the City
Dabir, they unanimoufly render it by *the*
City of Letters. His Authorities are the
Septuagint, the Vulgat, and the Confent of
all Commentators. " Now, *fays he,* if
" this Town before *Jofhua*'s Time had the
" Name of *the City of Letters*, it neceffa-
" rily follows, that *Mofes* could not be the
" Author of the Alphabet, it being impoffi-
" ble that the *Canaanites* fhould have learn'd
" it from the Jews, who were Vagrants in
" the Wildernefs and their fworn Ene-
" mies. Yet they had Letters ; *Cadmus*
" brought them at that Time into *Greece*,
" they have almoft the fame Name as the *He-*
" *brew* ; and the ancient Letters of the
" *Greeks* bear a near Refemblance to the
" *Samaritan*

" *Samaritan* Characters; from whence I dare
" conclude, that they are of greater Antiquity
" than the *Hebrew*; and it follows also that
" *Abraham* and his Posterity have adopted
" these same Names and Characters; except
" you chuse rather to think that the like Names
" were also used among the *Chaldæans*; for it
" appears to me indisputable, that *Cadmus*
" could not take the Names of his Letters from
" the *Hebrews* or *Jews*; but that they were
" known to his People before," &c.— Mr.
Cuper expresses his second Reason in this
Manner, " The Disparity there is between
" those Characters, almost forces me to
" believe, that Men invented them; for
" I am persuaded we should find a much
" greater Resemblance, if they had been
" given by God himself.

The Learned do not agree better as to
the City of *Shalem* or *Shalim*; some place
it on the Territory of *Shechem*, because of
these Words, (g) Jacob *came to* Shalem
a City of Shechem. Mr. *Cuper* finds a
great Difficulty in this Opinion. *Melchisedec*, " *says he*, was King of *Shalem*, but
" if that City had been in the Territory
" of *Shechem*, he would have been the
" King of *Shechem*'s Tributary, for each
" City had it's Sovereign or Petty-King;
                                    " and

(g) Gen. 33. 18.

" and since it appears that *Melchisedec* was
" one of the most Potent, it cannot be said
" with Reason, that the City of *Shalem* was
" situated within the Jurisdiction of *Shechem.*
" If there was a City of *Shalem* in the Terri-
" tory of *Shechem*, *Melchisedec* could not
" be it's King; it must have been sub-
" ject to the *Shechemites*, since it was of
" their Dependency. Besides, the Cities
" of *Shechem* and of *Shalem* were too far
" from one another to be in the same Ter-
" ritory. *Shechem* was situated on the Side
" of *Samaria* towards *Jerusalem*, and *Sha-*
" *lem* was near the *Jordan* towards the *Ga-*
" *lilæan* Sea. *(b)*

We shall mention but one Article more.
Our Author looks upon *Ammian Marcel-*
line as an irrefragable Witness of the Emperor *Julian*'s being diverted by a Miracle
from the Design he had formed of rebuild-
ing the Temple of *Jerusalem (i).* Mr.
Basnage does not make much of that Witness,
but yet believes the Fact, in Consequence
of the Confession of a Jew who acknowledges the Truth of the Miracles that prevented the Re-establishment of the Temple *(k).* Perhaps a Third shall wonder
at the Credulity of these two Great Men.

ARTICLE

(b) A further Illustration of this Subject may be seen in
the *Universal History*, Vol. I. Book. I. Ch. VII. page 446,
447. *Dub.* Edit.

(i) Basnage, histoire des Juifs. Tom. VIII. pag. r63.
(k) Rem. of the *J.*

ARTICLE II.

A Letter to the Journalist.

SIR,

I Read with Pleafure the firft Part of your *Literary Journal*, and heartily wifh you may meet with all proper En-couragement to continue that ufeful Work.

Upon reading your Abftract of Mr. *le Cene*'s important Project, I was induced to fend you the following Interpretations of two notable Paffages of the Holy Scriptures, *viz.* of *Gen.* xlix. 10. and *Jude* v. 6.

The Firft differs in a material Point from all Interpretations hitherto publifhed, or, at leaft, has fome Advantages over them. The Second, tho' offer'd to the Public many Years ago by Mr. *Daillon*, and followed by Mr. *le Cene* in his *French* Tranflation of the Bible, yet will, I believe, be en-tirely new to the Generality of *Englifh* Readers.

For the Firft, I am indebted to a Friend, who gave me a fhort Differtation upon it; fo that neither is an Invention of my own, and as I have no other Hand in them than the Addition of a few Obfervations, I may with lefs Diffidence venture to fee them printed; efpecially if you and your Friends

judge

judge that they deserve a Place in your Journal.

On *Gen.* xlix. 10. *The Sceptre shall not depart from* Judah, *nor a Lawgiver from between his Feet, until* Shiloh *come, and unto him shall the gathering of the People be.* Dr. *Sherlock*, now Bishop of *Sarum*, has given us a Dissertation, (*a*) whereby the great Author makes himself as remarkable for his Modesty, as for his Penetration and Learning. He has considerably illustrated *Junius*, *Tremellius*, *Ainsworth*, and *Joncourt*'s Thoughts, or Comments upon it. But yet, if my Friend be right, the ingenious Prelate has missed a Truth, which casts a clearer Light on the Passage, and extricates it much better, out of all Difficulties.

The Word (*Shevet*) signifies a *Tribe* and a *Sceptre*, as the Bishop observes, but much oftener a *Tribe.* (*b*)

The Word *Mechokek* which has been translated *Lawgiver*, and may be translated *Judge*, as his Lordship chuses to do, signifies also a *Scribe* (*c*) a Scribe invested with

a pro-

(*a*) Dissertation III.

(*b*) שבט לא סור.

(*c*) In several Places it cannot with any Propriety be translated otherwise than by *Tribe.* For Instance, *Gen.* xlix. 16. where the Septuag. translate מטה φυλη. They also do frequently translate the same *Hebrew* Word by *Family*, or *Sons.* Thus ibid. v. 28. שבטי.—Septuag. υἱοι

a proper Authority in the Difcharge of his Office (*d*).

According to that Tranflation the Senfe of the Paffage is plainly this — *Judah* fhall always be preferved in the Form of a *Tribe*, or, in other Words—It fhall never be mixed, or confounded, but on the contrary, fo diftinguifhed, that one may always know the Families and Perfons, belonging to that *Tribe*. There will conftantly be Scribes to keep in good Order the Regifters relating to Families until *Shiloh* come (*e*).

PART II.   D   If

(*d*) If the learned Reader has any Doubt about it, let him confider that חקק (from which the Participle מחקק) fignifies *defcripfit pinxit, exaravit* ; fo that it feems the Word in Queftion does originally mean *Scribens*, or *Scriba*, and more literally fo than *Legiflator*, or *Judex*.

That Tranflation is confirmed by the *Targum of Onkelos*, The Word is there render'd by *Scribe*.

V. Critic. Sacr. in locum.

Accordingly Seb. Munfter. tranflates it *Scriba*.

(*e*) This Interpretation in itfelf, or ftriclly fpeaking, is not new. *Junius* fays, *Prædicit Judæ Tribum diftinctam fore ufque ad Meffiæ adventum, cum reliquæ Tribus difperfæ, & confufæ, effent.* (Vid. Critic. facr. in loc.) But I have found it no where infifted upon as that, which is the precifely true one, nor is that fame Interpretation any where elfe, that I know of, fupported by the right Tranflation of the Word *Mechoebek*. In fhort, I have not met with the Senfe of the Paffage thus placed in a proper Light, fome Hints here and there, fome near Approaches to the Truth, feem'd to me no Reafon to deprive the Reader of an eafy, and fair Tranflation, which, I think, gives him at once the real Meaning of that famous Prophecy.

If with the Bishop we t
Shevet a Government in the Ti
tho' we confine that Governr
Tribe, and thereby entirely
many Difficulties, which the
received Notion of *Judah's*
the other Tribes labours und
Objections will remain, which
to think, cannot be thoroughl

The Difficulty arising from
Years of the *Babylonish* Captivit
in a great Measure, solved by
Observation, and Reasonings (
I doubt, whether they are alto
factory, and here is another mo
rable, which has not been ta
of.—The *Hasmonean* Princes we
Tribe of *Judah*. What the
(p. 265.) is not to be denied.
what Propriety of Speech can
that the Government subsisted in
of *Judah*, when Persons not of
were the Governors of their
Nation ? The same Difficulty oc
under the Reign of *Herod*.

(f) See his III Differt. p. 292.

Now upon my Friend's Scheme there is no period of Time, no Event, that can create any such Difficulty. It has been all along the Tribe of *Judah*'s special Privilege to have their Archives, and Records, in good Order. The ten dispersed Tribes cou'd not keep them so; and we have a particular Account of the Tribe of *Levi*'s not carefully preserving theirs. It is related in *Ezra* 11. 61, 62. that the Children of *Habaja*, *Rotz*, and *Barzillaï*, look'd for their Registers in Order to know their Genealogy, but they were not found; wherefore they were put from the Priesthood. This is confirm'd by *Nehem.* vii. 63, 64.

As to the Word *Shiloh* I refer the Reader to the Bishop's Dissertation, and the Authors quoted by him.

All I shall say, and endeavour to prove in a few Lines, is, that the Interpretation, (g) or Notion, *Finis* (an End) appears to me not only very jejune and far-fetched, and incongruous, but utterly inconsistent with the Words, that follow,

D 2   viz.

(g) That is the late learned Mr. *le Clerc*'s Opinion; and I am sorry to find Mr. *le Cene* seems to prefer it to all others. See *Bible de la Cene Projet. Ch.* 1. p. 2.

viz.—Unto him shall the gathering of the People be. And as those Words make one of the most essential Parts of the Prophecy, I beg leave to make a few Observations upon them.

1. *Shiloh* is either the *Thing* or *Person,* (I do not at present examine which of the two) in which the Blessing conferr'd on *Judah* chiefly consists ; and therefore, tho' *Judah* is particularly concerned in this Place, or tho' it is he, and his Family, to whom the pleasing Promise is made, yet, according to the Rules of Criticism, I humbly conceive 'tis to *Shiloh,* and not to *Judah,* one ought to refer the Words — *To him shall the gathering of,* &c. The Grammatical Construction strongly favours that Opinion, *Shiloh* being the last Word before the Phrase aforesaid, *To him shall,* &c. and at a considerable Distance from the Word *Judah.*

2. If you refer said Words to *Judah,* you make of the Prophecy a very odd Sentence, and give it a very poor Meaning, especially in the Sense of those, who by *Shevet* understand the Power of a Lawgiver, or a Judge ; for then it will run thus—Judah *shall preserve the Power of a Governor until* Shiloh *come,* that is, *until that Power be entirely at an End ;* and

to the same Judah *still governing, or while his Power lasts, shall belong the bringing together* (or, as others translate it, *the Obedience*) *of his own People* (*b*), a Sort of Tautology of little Significancy; for, pray, what comfortable Promise does that add to the foregoing —*The Scepter shall not depart*, &c.

3. I think it absurd to make *Shiloh* a *Thing* and not a *Person*. 'Tis evidently so if you interpret the Promise, as I do, thus,—Judah *shall always remain a distinct Tribe until* Shiloh *come*; for then the Promise implies, that that *Shiloh* was to be of the Tribe of *Judah*, the chief Reason why the Preservation of that Tribe is here mentioned being, because it wou'd, when the *Shiloh* appear'd, be a Proof that that same *Shiloh* (whose coming from, or belonging to, *Judah* was the greatest Honour, that cou'd be conferr'd on said Tribe) was really a Descendant of *Judah*.

But

(*b*) By the Word *People* here, as has been intimated before, some understand the whole Jewish Nation, and think that the Scepter, or Power, of *Judah* shou'd extend over the twelve Tribes.—Others, and among them the Bishop of *Sarum*, for very cogent Reasons confine it to the Tribe of *Judah*, and for Reasons still more convincing that Authority cannot be but what the same great Author makes it, an Authority vastly inferior to Royal Power. So that there is here a small Degree of Power, and only over a handful of People.

But fhou'd you maintain that the *Shevat* means not a Tribe, but a certain Degree of Power, and that the Words —*The Scepter fhall not depart*, &c. fignify, Judah *fhall preferve a certain Authority until*, &c. then I own the above Argument wou'd not have the fame Strength. But in that Cafe if you make *Shiloh, Finis, the End of* Judah's *Power* (lay afide the Kind of Tautology of the Words following, and even fuppofe them to import much more than they certainly do) you reduce the Prophecy to fomething, that was not very comfortable.— Why truly the Tribe of *Judah* wou'd have a Power for fome Ages, and then that Power wou'd be utterly deftroyed. Well, but, you'll fay, that Power wou'd end only at the coming of the Meffiah. I might anfwer, that according to the Interpretation, I am here confuting, that glorious Manner of the Ending of *Judah's* Power is, at the beft, but very obfcurely hinted. But were it never fo clearly foretold, pray, what particular Prerogative, or Advantage, is that to *Judah* after the Lofs of his Power, if the Meffiah is not to come from him, and thereby not only continue a Power, but greatly encreafe it, or alter it for the better, in the fame Family? And in Mr. *le Clerc's* Senfe there is not, cannot be, here any Thing to fhew

that

that the Meffiah fhou'd be of *Judah*'s Family, or Tribe.

4. The Word *Hammim* (*i*) Signifies the Nations in general.

Had *Jacob* intended to exprefs that the *gathering*, or *keeping under Obedience*, a few *Ifraelites*, fhou'd belong to *Judah*, wou'd he have made Ufe of the very Word, that implies the greateft Univerfality? (*k*)

5. It is very likely, that this Prophecy intimates the very Bleffing promifed to *Abraham, Gen.* xii. 3. and repeated to *Ifadc, Gen.* xxvi. 4.—*That all the Nations of the Earth fhou'd be bleffed in his Seed*: Nay, *Jacob*'s Expreffions do in fome Degree explain what that Bleffing fhou'd confift in, *viz.*—That *Shiloh* (*a* (*l*) *grand Pacificator, an extraordinary Perfon, that was to be fent, One, who fhou'd be eminently titled* the Son of GOD, *One, by whom the great Things in referve in the Hands of Providence were to be perform'd*) fhou'd gather, or *bring to Obedience*, or *re-unite*, all the Nations of the Earth, and thus make them but one happy People. *Jacob* adds, that

<hr>

(*i*) עמים

(*k*) Vide Buxt. & Critic. facr. on that Word in the plural Numb.

(*l*) In this Parenthefis I include the Chief, and moft probable Meanings given by Dictionaries and Commentators, to the Word *Shiloh*, excluding only Mr. *le Clerc*'s ill conjectur'd *Finis*.

that this *Shiloh*, to the particular Honour of *Judah*'s Family, was to defcend from, or belong to, it ; and in Order to prevent all Doubt about it he foretells at the fame Time, that that Family fhou'd have the peculiar Privilege of remaining all along a diftinct Tribe, or Family, known as fuch by authentic Regifters, until the coming of that glorious Perfonage.

Thus, methinks, the Whole hangs well together, and makes up a Prophecy fo much the more important, as there are few, if any, in the Old Teftament, that can better afford us for the Caufe of Chriftianity that Kind of Support, which may be expected from the Prophecies of that Book.

I cou'd enlarge on my Arguments for that Interpretation, but hope there is no Neceffity for it ; and I am loath to detain you any longer on that Subject.

Let us now fee how we are to underftand the other Paffage, *viz.* in the Ep. of St. *Jude*, v. 6.

In our *Englifh* Bibles, it is tranflated thus — *And the Angels, which kept not their firft Eftate, but left their own Habitation, he hath referved in everlafting Chains under Darknefs unto the Judgment of the great Day* (m).

There

(m) It is to the fame Purpofe in all the *Latin, French*, &c. Bibles, except Mr. *le Cene*'s new Tranflation.

There are in the *Greek* three Words, which may have occasion'd a total Misapprehending of the Sense of this Passage. If the Generality of Interpreters have miss'd their real Signification, no wonder they shou'd here give us a Sentence quite foreign to the Apostle's (*n*) Meaning; and if Mr. *Daillon* did luckily hit upon it, then surely 'tis his Interpretation we ought to follow.

Those Words are, 1. The *Greek* Word, (*o*) which is render'd in *English* by *Angels*, 2. The *Greek* Word (*p*) which is render'd by *Estate*. 3. The *Greek* Word, (*q*) which is render'd by *Habitation*.

All those, who have any Knowledge of the *Greek* Tongue, know that the Word we translate *Angel*, signifies literally, and properly, a *Messenger*. Probably those intelligent Beings, which we call *Angels*, have got that Denomination from their chief Office with Respect to Mankind, *viz.* their being sent by the Almighty to execute his Commands.

In the Revelation of St. *John* the Pastors of the seven Churches are called *Angels*,

PART II.   E   for

(*n*) I say *Apostle*; for 'tis not my Business here to examine whether that Epistle was really wrote by St. *Jude*, or to dispute about it's authentickness.

(*o*) Ἀγγελος.

(*p*) Ἀρχη.

(*q*) Οἰκητήριον.

for this Reaſon, no **Doubt**;
were the Meſſengers, or **Mi**
Word of **GOD**, that is, **Pe**
declare it.

In ſhort, the Word *Angel*
rally nothing elſe than **a Meſ**
it is to be obſerved, that **for t.**
it is applied only to Meſſenge
nary, or of an eminent **Rank.**

The Word (*r*), we have tr
Eſtate, and in the *Latin*
Tranſlations is render'd by *Ori*
ſignifies properly, literally, (*s*)
Priority. In a more remote,
phorical Senſe, but which, howev
frequently has, it means *P.*
(*t*) *Authority*, and in the remoteſ
Senſe, it may, or does intimate *fi*
or *Origin.*

As to the Word, which is re
Habitation, it ſignifies juſt that, a
fore of itſelf cou'd not occaſion
ficulty. 'Tis by mere Accident,
the equivocal Meaning of the ʃ

(*r*) Ἀρχη.
s) Thus St. *John* 1 v. 1. Ἐν ἀρχῆ ἦν ὁ λόγος, Ε
Beginning was, &c.
(*t*) *Luke* xx. 20.——ἵις τὸ παραδοῦναι αὐτὸν τῇ d
That ſo they might deliver him to the Power and Auth
See alſo 1 *Cor.* xv. 24. *Eph.* i. 21. *Coloſſ.* ii. 10, &

Words, that it has thrown a little Darkness on this Paſſage.

As the Word Ἄγγελος in the Holy Scripture, often denotes that Sort of intelligent Beings, which St. *Paul* calls *miniſtring Spirits*, our Tranſlators without Heſitation receded from the proper Meaning of it, and tranſlated it *Angels* inſtead of *Meſſengers*.

As the next Word might, tho' improperly, ſignify *firſt Eſtate* or *Origin*, they thought fit to chuſe that Interpretation, becauſe it ſeem'd more agreeable to the Notion of celeſtial Beings; and to the following Words, than the Word *Priority*, or *Authority*, wou'd have been.

At the Word render'd by *Habitation*, ſignifies really that, or in general any Place of Abode, ſo of Courſe it is here taken for that Place, which the *Angels* inhabited before their Fall.

Having once taken the Word *Angels* in that Senſe, which it now conſtantly has in all our modern Languages, there was no room to underſtand by the Word *Habitation*, any thing elſe than Heaven, or whatever is the *Angel's* Place of Abode.

And thus the Senſe generally given to this Paſſage, and concerning which, the Learned (being perhaps miſled by a fortui-

tous

tous Relation between two or three Words, or by the Multitude of Interpreters, that went before them) feem to entertain no Manner of Doubt, is, that the Angels or celeftial Beings, who rebel'd againſt GOD, and thereby forfeited the high Rank, in which the Almighty had placed them, were baniſh'd that bleſſed Abode, and are kept in Chains (*i. e.* Priſoners) for the great Day of Judgment.

There are ſtrong Reaſons to ſuſpect, that this is one of the Effects of the prejudiced Opinions, which were of Old introduced into Chriſtianity by Rabbinical Dreams, and Heatheniſh Notions about Dæmons. Not that I would deny the Fall of Angels. Nothing more poſſible, or even more probable, than ſuch an Event. I conceive indeed, that the very Idea of a *moral finite Being*, excludes Impeccability. But the Queſtion is only whether that Event be here mentioned, or not ; nay, whether this Paſſage refers at all to thoſe intelligent celeftial Creatures.

Here is an Interpretation of it, which agrees better with the plain, or moſt common, Meaning of the Words in the Original.

In the XIIIth and XIVth Chapters of *Numbers*, we read, that *Moſes* by GOD's Command, ſent twelve Men, one of each

Tribe

Tribe of *Ifrael*, and every one of them the *Head*, *Chief*, or *Ruler* (*u*), of his Tribe, to go, and fpie out the Land of *Canaan*: That all thofe Meffengers, except *Jofhua* and *Caleb*, by their cowardly and falfe Report, difpirited the People, and thereby raifed againft God, and againft *Mofes*, a Mutiny more general, and more formidable than any, that *Ifrael* had been before guilty of.

It is to thefe Meffengers my Author applies this Paffage. The Senfe runs fmoothly thus:

GOD *referves for the Day of Judgment thofe Meffengers, who did not act according to their Dignity and Truft; but inftead of fhewing good Example, and leading the People of* Ifrael *as they ought, did vilely renounce their Habitation,* that is, *that comfortable Place of Abode, which* GOD *had appointed for them and promifed.*

It may be of fome Weight to obferve, that if thefe Words,—*but left their own Habitation,* be applied to the Angels, then the Apoftle's Expreffion is not only very weak, but really quite improper; for according

---

cording to the commonly re
on the Fall of Angels, and i
as we can judge, according
of Things, the bad Angels
bellion muſt have been ban
and driven out of the glorious
Bleſſed ; and can it with any
Speech, be ſaid of ſuch as ar
their Habitation, that they
ſaken, or renounced it ? The
ing, forſaking, or renounci
tary ; and therefore had the
the Baniſhment of the falle
wou'd have expreſs'd it oth
by *they quitted*, or *left* their
tion (*x*).

Whereas when the ſame
applied to the unworthy N
foreſaid, it is viſibly both en
juſt.

Another Obſervation, whic
to perſuade the Reader, is, th
Verſe, that precedes the Paſſ
pute, the Apoſtle ſays, *that t*
ing ſaved the People out of
Egypt, *afterwards deſtroyed t*
lieved not. Now an Inſtance
what really happen'd in the

(*x*) ἀταιτόντα: ἀπολείπω ſignifies to for
to give over and certainly implies volunt

after the Deliverance from the Bondage of
Egypt feems to be abundantly better connected with the foregoing general Saying,
and fitter to make an Impreffion, than a
wonderful Affertion about what happen'd
to the Angels no body knows when;
confidering efpecially, that that Event is
not mention'd any where, that we know
of, in the Holy Scriptures, and that when
the Apoftle mention'd it, it muft have been
quite new to his Readers, or, if known,
was taken either from Tradition, or fome
Book which is not among the facred Writeings of Jews or Chriftians.

To which let me add, that the Crime
here mentioned, is that of *not believing*,
or *not trufting in GOD*. The Apoftle puts
his Readers in mind of the difmal Effects
of it. It was for that (*y*) Crime, he fays,
GOD deftroyed thofe, he had fo gracioufly
delivered from the Bondage of *Egypt*.
Now, as the following Verfe is fo link'd (*z*)
with the former, that the two feem to
make but one Sentence, it is very likely
he does here purfue the fame Thought,
and only gives a more particular, and more
terrible Inftance, to enforce the fame
Truth. Upon that Suppofition the Apoftle,
befides calling to the Chriftian Reader's

Re-

(*y*) Τοὺς μὴ πιςεύσαντας ἀπώλεσεν.
(*z*) Grammatically by the Particle (τὶ) and by the Con-
text, according to the foregoing Obfervation.

Remembrance, that the unworthy Meſſengers periſhed alſo in the Wilderneſs, *(a)* informs us, that becauſe they had been in a ſpecial Manner guilty of Diffidence, and Diſobedience, and had thereby occaſioned the People's Rebellion, GOD intends to make a ſpecial Example of them in the Day of Judgment. And if ſo, here is a ſhort, and clear Paraphraſe of the two Verſes.

GOD deſtroyed thoſe among the Iſraelites, *who wou'd not truſt in him, and as to the Meſſengers, who behaved ſo unworthily, he not only cauſed them to periſh in the Wilderneſs, but keeps them in Cuſtody againſt the Day of Judgment to inflict upon them a ſeverer Puniſhment.*

I muſt not omit taking Notice, that this Place of St. *Jude's* Epiſtle ſeems altogether to be copied from the 2d Ep. of St. *Peter,* ch. II. v. 4.

St. *Jude's* Words being fuller than St. *Peter's* may ſerve to explain them ; and both Places, no Doubt, ought to be taken in the ſame Senſe.

I am,
Reverend S I R,
&c.

ARTICLE

___

(a) That is implied in the Deſtruction of the Unbelievers in general, and particularly mention'd in *Numb.* xiv. 37.

ARTICLE III.

The Theology of Insects by Mr. Lesser, with Mr. Lyonnet's Remarks, &c. II Abstract. (a)

WE have seen in the former Abstract that Mr. *Lyonnet*'s Remarks make a considerable Part of this Work, and perhaps the most Curious. On the Chap. VI. he treats at large of the Formation of the *Foetus*, according to the System of *Lewenhoec* and his Followers. This curious Observer found in the Seed of Man, and many other Animals, a prodigious Number of Animalcula which serve to encrease the Individuals of the Species in which they are contained. Mr. *Lyonnet* strongly attacks this Hypothesis, and the Author of *La Bibliotheque raisonnée* defends it as warmly. As this Opposition may serve to the Illustration of this Subject, I shall relate some of the Objections and Answers, as concisely as possible.

I. Mr. *Lewenhoec* pretends, that no Spermatic Worms or Animalcula are to be found in the impotent, the decrepid, nor in those who

PART II.　　　F　　　　labour

labour under some particular Disorders, but always where the Qualities requisite to Prolification subsist. *No less,* says Mr. *Lyonnet, than a great Multitude of Experiments is requisite to establish a Fact of this Nature.*

Answer. Mr. *Lyonnet* ought to have shewn, that his Adversary's Experiments are actually contradicted by others. It may happen, that the Seed of a very fruitful Animal does not contain at every Instant the necessary Conditions to impregnate, or, to speak according to *Leuwenhoec*'s System, it may sometimes want the Animalcula necessary to produce the *Foetus.* Every Copulation, even with the most fruitful Animal, does not succeed. Consequently, some few contrary Experiments shou'd not destroy the proposed System. If it could be proved, that Seed became prolific in one particular Case, tho' it then contained no Animalcula, this Experiment alone would demonstrate *Leuwenhoec*'s System to be grounded on a false Hypothesis. The Impossibility of the Proof is manifest.

II. Supposing, *says* Mr. *Lyonnet,* it should be proved, that no other Seed than what is fruitful contains these spermatic Worms, why are we to conclude that these Animalculas are the Cause of Fruitfulness, rather than infer that it produces them ? For Instance, standing
ing

ing Water nourishes an infinite Number of Animals extreamly small, which are not to be found in that which runs; must we conclude, that these Animals made the Water stand, or that the Water standing produced them.

Answer. There are Facts, the Probability or Certainty of which depends on the Concurrence of many Circumstances. This is of that Number. By the same Way of Reasoning, I might shew, that it is uncertain whether the Seed contained in the spermatic Vessels is really the Cause of Fertility. If I should only say, *There is in those Vessels a certain Humour, therefore, that Humour is the Cause of Fertility :* Would this Argument be thought convincing ? Yet it is certain, that without this Humour, without this Seed, there is no Fertility. But this certainly depends on other Circumstances, which are to be verified. This Kind of Argument is a Sophism, called by Logicians, *enumeratio imperfecta.*

III. *Great and small Animals,* says Mr. *Lyonnet, are to be found in all the other Parts of the Body, under the Skin in the Mass of Blood, on foul Teeth, &c. Now these Animals are not the Cause of Fertility, why should those of the spermatic Humour be so ?*

An-

Anſwer. Here is ſuch anot
ment which Mr. *Lyonnet* is def
ſwer, and his Anſwer ſhall ſolv
culty. *There is in all the other*
Body different Sorts of Humours
a great Analogy with the Seed.
Humours are not the Cauſe of Fe
then ſhould the ſpermatic Humour

IV. The Defenders of *Leuw*
pinion add Strength to their Syſte
Reſemblance there is between
tic Worm and the *Foetus,* in a
the Head of each is large in Propo
reſt of the Body. Mr. *Lyonnet* r
Conſequence they draw, and reduc
Argument to this Syllogiſm ; *The*
have a large Head, the Foetus *has a*
therefore the Animalcules *makes*

Anſwer. If the Syllogiſm b
in the following Manner, it wi
great Matter of Triumph. Ever
fecundated by the Male's See
neither ſmall Worm, Embry
other Corpuſcle that can becom
After Copulation you find in t
a particular Place, a ſmall W
what like thoſe ſeen in the S
is it not probable, that is is o
that were ſwimming in that
which has ſerved it as a Vehic
ſport it to the Egg, where i

metamorphofed, and open'd, as Seed thrown in the Ground, where it is contained as in a Womb, and from which it receives it's Nourifhment and Accretion? Thefe and fome other Circumftances put together, will be more than fufficient to take off the Ridicule to which the above Syllogifm has been expofed.

V. Mr. *Swammerdam* judges it a Fact undeniable, that the *Foetus* of Infects (from the Formation of the Egg, and confequently long before Copulation) fills the whole Capacity of the Egg, in which it is found. If fo, the *Foetus* owes not its Origin to a fmall Worm in the Male's Seed, which could not enter the Egg until a long Time after its Formation. Here then are *Foetufes* formed without the Help of fpermatic Worms, and that even in Animals that have them.

Anfwer. Granted, if the Fact be true. Mr. *Lyonnet* is defired to point out the Place where he found this Affertion of *Swammerdam.* The Obfervations of the celebrated (*b*) *Malpighi* on the Origin and Formation of a Chicken are quite favourable to *Leuwenhoec*'s Syftem. In his Opinion, every Egg fecundated by the Seed of the Cock, contains a *Foetus*, or fmall *Embryo,*

(*b*) Malpighius *de Formatione pulli.*

Embryo, and every Egg not impregnated contains no fuch Body. This *Embryo* is included in a *Bag*, or *Follicule*, of an Oblong Figure, and this *Follicule* is itfelf contained in the *Cicatricula* of the Egg, which is a Spot, or a fmall white Point, of an orbicular Figure. *Malpighi* repeated often his Obfervations, and always difcovered the fame Thing *(c)*.——Add to this great Difcovery the Relation and Refemblance confpicuous between fpermatic Worms, and the Embryos of Chickens, Frogs, and Men, Compare thefe Worms, fuch as they are defcribed by *Leuwenhoec (d)*, with the human *Foetus*, and that of Rabbits, and you'll be convinced at leaft of the probability of his Syftem. As to the human *Foetus*, examine if you pleafe, the Defcriptions given of it by *(e) Riolan (f)*, *Harvey (g)*, *Ruyfch*, and *(h) Dodart*.——All thefe Facts united form a very ftrong Prefumption in favour of a Syftem adopted by many great Men, and particularly the celebrated *Boerhaave*,

(c) Epift. ad *Oldenb.* 1672.
(d) *Epift. Phyfiol.* pag. 390, fig. 5.
(e) *Mif. Anat.* Cap. 13.
(f) Liber *de generat. Animal.* Exercit. 56.
(g) *Thefaur. Anat.* VI. Tab. II. fig. I.
(h) Hift. de l' Acad. Roy. des Sciences, an. 1701. pag. 23.

Boerhaave, who after giving the Description of small Worms, or little Eels, found in the Seed of Men, Quadruped, Birds, Fishes, amphibious Animals, and Insects, adds the following Words.

Si hæc conferuntur cum mole, figura, loco, permutatione, Carinæ Pulli apud Malpighium descriptæ, & cum observatâ naturæ lege in generatione Ranarum, probabile fiet, Animalcula hæc Masculini seminis continere rudimenta corporis futuri humani; in primis, cum testibus, aut hoc humore, deficientibus Sterilitas semper a parte maris adsit. Animalcula hæc erescunt demum, et explicantur, ubi calor, motus, nutrimentum Subtilissimum, locus denique aptus, conspirant simul ita, ut latentes hic adumbratæ partes evolvi queant; veluti avium, Insectorum, Testudinum, Plantarum, ova, dies, menses, annos, inertia, fæcunda tamen, quiescunt, donec longa dies, conditiones enumeratas addat, vitamque Suffocatam excitet (i).

VI. Mr. *Lyonnet* suppofes, that these *Animalcules do multiply in the Bodies where they are found*, and asks whether *they are formed in them by an immediate Production*, or whether *they multiply by the Way of Propagation?*

Answer.

(i) *Boerhaave*, Instit. Med. pag. 327, 328. par. 651. Edit. 1734.

Answer. Another **Suppof**
bable than his may **be in**
which will fufficiently **anfwer**
All the Parts of organifed.
Day brought to light **have**
created from the Beginning o
there is therefore in **the whol**
Propagation, or **Generation**
called, but only a **Manifeftati**
ifting Bodies, whofe **prodigi**
efcaped our Senfes. Thofe **Pa**
fpread over the vaft **Expanfe**
mofphere; or perhaps **containe**
Individual of each **Species, whe**
out of the Hands of the **Creator.**
be above the Reach of all **th**
great Bodies are expofed to, i
laft find out a Subject proper to i
perceptible to the Senfes. The N
Abftract does not allow me to
longer upon this Subject.

VII. *Is it not very ftrange,*
Lyonnet, That the fpermatic An
fo quickly enlarge in the Womb,
do not grow in the Semen, *tho*
furrounded by a Subftance in whic
born, and from which they receive
and it's Prefervation?

Answer. Mr. *Lyonnet* fuppofes
bryo is already quite formed in
before the Copulation, before

Sexes are mixed. Now I afk what Purpofe Copulation anfwers according to this Suppofition. The *Embryo*, in the Egg, lies in the Womb adapted to it, it receives the Humour proper to nourifh it, to bring it forth, to make it grow. What does it want more? What Effect hath the Seed of the Male on this *Embryo*'s little Body! Is it to put it in motion? It has Motion, fince the Humours circulate in the Veffels of this little Body, as well as in the Parts that furround it, in the Ovarium, in the Tubes, in the Womb, &c. I own I cannot conceive of what Ufe the Seed of the Male is, if the *Embryo* be not contain'd in it. The Syftem of Animalcules is not liable to the fame Difficulty, fince the fpermatic Veffels are the Womb of their laft Manifeftation; this is the Egg of the Female, where they find a lodging fit for a new Metamorphofis.

VIII. *Leuwenhoec*'s Syftem, fays Mr. *Lyonnet*, fuppofes that GOD, in Order to produce one fingle perfect Animal, was obliged to form fo many hundred Millions of defective ones, that the Imagination is frightened at the Number. Does this Conduct correfpond with that uniform Way in which Nature acts, where all Things proceed to their End, the moft direct, fhort, and plaineft Way?

PART II.   G   *Anfwer.*

Anſwer. This Objection has been made a thouſand Times, on account of the prodigious Quantity of Seed ſcattered every where with a Profuſion, reſembling an entire Loſs. Here is another Miracle in Nature no leſs wonderful than the prodigious Number of ſmall Worms, which Mr. *Lyonnet* is ſo much alarm'd at, and which nevertheleſs Reaſon is forced to admit. I mean the *Elms* ſurpriſing Fruitfulneſs, according to the the Experiments and diſcoveries of the famous *Dodart* (*k*).

This ſkillful Naturaliſt judges, that in an *Elm* of ſix Inches Diameter, and twenty Feet high from the Ground to the upper Part of the Trunk, there are as many Times thirty-three Millions of Seeds, as there are ſix Lines in the Height of twenty Feet, *viz.* 15840000000 Seeds, and that this Tree actually has in it ſelf wherewithal to be multiplied and produced again to that wonderful Number of Times. Add to this, that each Seed of a Tree contains in itſelf a ſecond Tree, which includes the ſame Number of Seeds,—That you never can come at one Seed that does not contain more Trees, nor at a Tree that does not contain more Seeds, or that contains leſs than the preceding, conſequently here is a

Geo-

(*k*) Hiſt. de l' Academ. *An.* 1700. pag. 88.

Geometrical encreasing Progreffion; the firft Term is 1, the Second 15840000000; the Third the Square of 15840000000; the Fourth its Cube, and fo on without End. *Reafon, and Imagination,* fays Mr. *Fontenelle, are equally loft and confounded, in this immenfe, and, as it were, more than immenfe Calculation.*

Now let Mr. *Lyonnet* explain, why GOD placed in a fingle Tree fuch a prodigious Number of Seeds, or, if you will, of imperfect little Trees. Would it not be enough, that this Tree fhould contain a fufficient Number of them to propagate and multiply according to the ordinary Courfe of Nature? Certainly of a thoufand Seeds, here are nine Hundred and ninety-nine loft, (if it be a Lofs never to arrive at Perfection) and that by a Kind of Miracle in Nature.

But, according to Mr. *Lyonnet's* Opinion, fince GOD always accomplifhes his Defigns the fhorteft Way, what need was there, that amongft Animals and Plants there fhould be Males and Females? Could not Multiplication be without the Union of two Sexes? and is not that *the moft direct, plain and fhort Way?*

After all, does Mr. *Lyonnet* really believe that the Lofs of fo many Millions of fmall Worms, or Men in Miniature, affects in the

leaft

leaft the OEconomy of the Univerfe? Their Creation coft not the Almighty more than that of a Grain of Sand. They are fo many little hydraulic Machines produced to return foon to that State from whence they were brought.

IX. *Of what Nature*, fays Mr. *Lyonnet*, *is the Soul of thefe little Men? Is it a brute Soul? Is it a reafonable One? If reafonable, what is to be its Fate after this Life?* In the Opinion of the Church of *Rome*, all thefe little Men are Reprobates, condemned to Hell-fire, or at leaft confined in the *Limbus* as they are not baptized.

Anfwer. Here is a Man of Parts uneafy about the Nature of the Soul of a fmall Worm, of a little human Seed, who at the fame Time knows not what his own is. For my Parr, I am fatisfied about it. I have thought fo much, examined fo freely, and confidered fo frequently the Nature of my Soul, without comprehending any Thing about it, that I am no way tempted to make ufelefs Inquiries about the Souls of fpermatic Worms. I perceive that I think I feel that my Thoughts proceed from my Brains, this is all I know. Did Mr. *Locke* know more, becaufe he anatomized and diffected the Soul. Mr. *Boulier*, who wrote fo much, and fo well, on the

Souls

Souls of *Beasts*, who spoke of them with so much Sagacity, what Discoveries has he made ? None.

But what is to be the Fate of these Souls ? Why should I perplex my self about what I cannot know, much less remedy. If the Gentlemen of the Church of *Rome* are inhuman enough to damn them, or to confine them to a Place of Sadness and Despair, I cannot but wonder at the unaccountable Error and Weakness of the human Mind, when it attempts to go beyond it's Sphere. It is more prudent to recall our Imagination, than inconsiderately lose ourselves in dark and impenetrable Futurity.

(*l*) Having related, as exactly as I possibly could, the Reasons alledged on both Sides, I shall now close this Abstract with one Reflection.—The two Systems proposed are yet liable to very great Difficulties. I could willingly give the Preference to *Leuwenhoec*'s, if it was not carried, as I apprehend, somewhat too far. Mr. *Malpighy*'s Observations, Dr. *Boerhaave*'s Remark on them, and Mr. *Dodart*'s Experiments, are certainly of great Weight, and the Consequence drawn from the Last seems to me to be just. I can reflect very
quietly

(l) The Author of this Abstract.

quietly on the Lofs of an inr
Quantity of inanimate Seeds of
for a fingle One that comes to
on. But the Cafe alters when
is applied to Men. The Belie
Immortality of the Soul, I own,
if not wholly, grounded on the E
of it's Faculties; and thefe Fac
-nothing yet in a fpermatic Wor
it feems that we may, without R.
admit the Deftruction of fuch
nificant Being; for certainly that's
that can happen. But is not t
on even of that fomewhat dif
And where is the Neceffity of
Suppofition? Is not the Almigh
Interpofition requifite neverthele
Philofophers have been endeavou
Century paft, to reconcile all
rations of Nature to general L
blifhed from the Beginning by
preme Author of all Things.
Syftem, they aimed at giving
Notion of his Power and Wifdo
have fucceeded, at leaft as to w
cerns the mechanical World.
Laws of Nature, that anfwer all
pofes of a conftant Intervention,
ly fomething more admirable,
Intervention itfelf. Or to ma

again of the Comparifon fet forth at the Beginning of this Abftract, a Watch with a perpetual Motion would require more Art, and give us a higher Opinion of the Workman's Skill than our common Watches do. All this muft be granted.— What then? Can this be applied to the moral World? Does not the Non-interpofition deftroy the very Notion of Government? A Providence by general Laws, once fetled and no more minded, is no Providence at all. We are carried away in the Middle of a Series. Our Actions are as neceffary as the Effects of Gravitation.—Or if you allow Free-agency, you muft allow alfo a Government fitted to this Faculty of the Beings fo governed, a Care properly fo called, a continual Interpofition adapted to the Alterations our Liberty occafions.

Now this particular Providence is as requifite in the Formation of Men as in any Cafe whatfoever, becaufe this is as free an Act of ours, as any other. Why then fhould we not fuppofe, that at the inftant GOD is pleafed that a Man fhould exift he creates a Soul? This is as eafy to him, as to permit that a Soul already made fhould animate fuch a Body. This Syftem anfwers the fame good Purpofes,

poſes, and is not liable to
Inconveniencies that attend the I
of an infinite Number of
ing deſtroyed, without having
Thing to deſerve ſo frightful a
As to the Pretence of raiſing o
ration of the divine Power
dom, by the Syſtem of gene
I have allowed it to be right
mechanical World, but is very
being juſt when applied to th
For one ſingle Act of Goodn
particular Care, &c. by much
all the poſſible Beauty of a
The oftner we conceive our
ther coming to our Help, direc
a Manner ſuitable to our Natur
Faculties, the higher is the Notic
have of his moral Attributes, o
nevolence, &c. Nothing can be
hilarating in our preſent Circt
than the Thought of his continual
ing over us, and providing for us, in
ſtrict Senſe theſe Expreſſions
And if we allow this in one Caſe,
allow it in all. Time will not p
inlarging on this uſeful Subject.

A R T

A R T I C L E IV.

L' Orthopedie, *ou l'art de prevenir & corriger dans les Enfans, les difformités du Corps,* &c. 2 Tom. 8°. *Bruxelles,* 1743.

That is to say,

Orthopædia : Or the Art of amending and preventing Deformities in Children by Means, which Parents themfelves, and all Perfons, who are employed in the Education of Children, may eafily put in Practice. By Mr. *Andry,* Profeffor of Phyfic in the *Royal College,* and Senior Dean of the Faculty of Phyfic at *Paris,* with Cuts. 2. *Tom.* 8°.—*Tom.* I. *pag.* 304. *Tom.* II. *pag.* 310. befides 84 in a Preface, &c.

THIS Book, perhaps, one the moft ufeful that has been written thefe many Years, was tranflated into *Englifh* foon after it came out abroad. It contains many Facts that are not to be found but in Books of Phyfic, which are underftood or look'd into by the Gentlemen of that

PART II.　　　　　H　　　　　Pro-

Profeſſion only, and if this is read with Attention by all thoſe that want ſome of the Inſtructions contained in it, we may expect to ſee the next Generation reap the Benefit of it.

" (a) It is not only allowable, *ſays Mr.*
" *Andry*, to take Care of the Gracefulneſs
" of the Body, but this Care, while it is
" confined within certain Bounds which
" Reaſon preſcribes, and which every Body
" is well acquainted with, ought to be en-
" joined. We are born for one another,
" and ought to ſhun having any Thing
" about us that is ſhocking ; and even
" tho' a Perſon ſhould be left alone in
" the World, he ought not to neglect
" his Body ſo as to let it become ugly ;
" for this would be contradicting the In-
" tention of the Creator. It is on this
Principle, that the *Orthopædia* (b) is founded. The Author hopes that few Parents are like that whimſical Mother,
who

(a) I took this, and the other Quotations, out of the *Engliſh* Tranſlation.
(b) This Title is formed of two *Greek* Words ; viz. Ὀρθὸς which ſignifies *Straight, free from Deformity*, and Παιδίον, *A Child.* The Author made uſe of the Expreſſion *Orthopædia* in imitation of two celebrated Authors. One of them gave the Title of *Pædotrophia* to a Treatiſe upon the Manner of ſucking Infants ; and the other that of *Callipædia*, to a Poem upon the Method of getting beautiful Children.

who feeing her Daughter have a Set of
very beautiful Teeth, made her pull out
the fineft of them, left they fhould make
her vain, and fo prove an Obftacle to her
Salvation.—Or like another Mother *(c)*,
who having a very beautiful Daughter,
was always bidding her to hang down
her Head, bend her Neck forwards,
and walk with her Feet inwards, for this
Reafon, that one ought to avoid pleafing
the World.

The Author writes for Parents of better Senfe than thefe. His Purpofe is
to give feveral plain and eafy Methods,
for preventing and correcting the Deformities of the Bodies of Children. He
confiders only the external Defects; the
others he leaves to the Management of
Phyficians and Chirurgeons. For Inftance,
when he fpeaks of the Defects which
concern the Eye, he does not tell in what
Manner a *Gutta ferena* is cured, or how
a *Cataract* is to be couched; thefe Defects require the Light of Phyfic, and all
the Dexterity of Chirurgery to manage
them. But what he writes is to fhew
Parents what they may practife themfelves, with regard to their Children, fo as
to give them a ftreight and agreeable Look,

H 2 and

(c) Dionis, Cour d' Operations de Chyrurgie.

and prevent, or cure, their Squinting, winking, &c. This excellent Work is divided into four Books. The Firſt contains a general Notion of the external Parts of the Body. The Second has for it's Objeƈt, the Art of preventing and correƈting in particular the Deformities of the Shape, with Reſpeƈt to the Trunk of the Body. The third Book concerns the Deformities of the Arms, the Hands, the Legs, and Feet. The Deformities of the Head make up the fourth Book, *viz.* Firſt, the Deformities of the Head properly ſo called; Secondly, thoſe of the Hair; and Thirdly, thoſe of the Face. Mr. *Andry* conſiders the Face firſt in general, with Reſpeƈt to its Air; then in particular, with Reſpeƈt to the different Parts which compoſe it, ſome of which are obvious to the Sight at firſt, as the Fore-head, the Eye-brows, the Eye-lid, the Eyes, the Noſe, the Cheeks, the Ears, the Lips, the Chin, the Skin; others of them again are not ſo conſpicuous, as the Gums, the Teeth, and the Tongue. He talks of this laſt Organ, with regard to Dumbneſs, Liſping, and Stammering, and other ſenſible Defeƈts of the Tongue, as far as concerns the Speech.

The whole Work is very methodical, interſperſed with curious Remarks and Examples,

-amples, always adapted to the Subject in Hand, and which make the Reader go thorough it with Pleasure. Tho' the first Book is but a Kind of Introduction to the other, yet it is a very useful One, as it contains a complete Enumeration of the external Parts of the Body, the Proportion of those Parts, the Variety which may be remarked in the Make of some of them, —and the Tastes of different Nations upon this Subject; but I am obliged to confine my self to more important Articles, extracted out of the other Books.

What Care ought to be taken of the Clavicles *and the* Chest *in Children.*

A Well proportioned Chest is one of the greatest Ornaments of the Body, and it has the requisite Proportions, when it is sufficiently raised in the Fore-part and at the Top, especially in Women, when the *Clavicles* (d) are not too crooked, when it does not jut out backward,
nor

(d) The *Clavicles* are two little Bones, which form the upper Part of the Vault of the Chest.

nor incline more to one Side
other; in ſhort, when it is likе
raiſed in the Fore-part, and at
and plain behind.

To preſerve this Form our At
this Caution to Mothers, w
ſwadle their Infants, not to
Shoulders too tight; for this
Clavicles more crooked than they
and hence the upper Part of th
contraçted;—and when Childrе
Gowns, he would have them
made, that the openings of the Sl
allow them ſufficient Liberty to
Arms outwards. And, as ſoon
are a little grown up, he adviſе
to give them a ſtick of a proper
to hold by the two Extremities
Arms ſtretched out; for this ſma
if it is frequently repeated, will
to make the *Clavicles* long and
rents ought beſides to make their
thruſt forward the *Cheſt*, and accuſtе
to uſe this Exerciſe frequently.
tion which they make to accomр
will puſh their Arms backwards,
a neceſſary Conſequence will lengt
Clavicles.

The Means to prevent the Bellies *of
Children projecting too much forward, and how to keep their* Back
ftreight, &c.

FOR this Purpofe two Things muft be
obferved ; the Firft, to hinder Children from fitting crooked upon their Seats;
the Second, to take Care, that the Bottom of the Seat, upon which they fit, be
not hollow in the Middle, but quite plain.
The beft Way, *fays Mr. Andry,* is to make
the Seat of a Piece of Cork-Tree that is
very even ; for, befides that the Chair is
thereby render'd lighter, it has this
Advantage, that it preferves Children
from the falling of the *Anus,* to which
they are fo fubject, which is well worth
minding.

Here follows a great Number of ufeful
Directions, on the following Heads.———
*How Children are to be taken Care of,
with refpect to their* Shoes *and* Stockings.
——*In what Pofture* young Girls *ought to
few, read, work in Tapeftry,* &c. — *What
fort of* Tables *Children ought to write upon.*—*How they ought to lie in* Bed *with
refpect to* Bolfters.—*The Importance of frequently*

quently beftowing new ftitch'd
them.—The Method to prevent t
out the Backfide too much. 9
to prevent their carrying th
wrong.

Of the Neck *crooked or* ft
particular Method for r
the Necks *of Children,*
Shoulders, *&c.*

WHAT Mr. *Andry* fays on t
is too ufeful to be paffed ov
hinder the *Shoulders* from growi
you muft take Care to keep th
well back, placed over the *Hips,*
Cheft forward. The Perfon fhou
flat in Bed as poffible, and if on
is too thick, he fhould always
the oppofite Side: for the *Shoul*
which one lies always projects be
Plane of the *Back.* —Nurfes, We
Children, and Governeffes, who c
fufpend Children by the Leadin
lifting them up in the Air, mal
liable to have the *Neck* funk bet
Shoulders.—Thofe Mafters and M
who teach Children to read or w
on too high a Table, which rife

their *Elbows* (for it ought to be two Inches lower) expose them to the same Deformity. —The same must be understood of eating Tables, &c. When you observe, that a Child inclines to sink his *Neck* between his *Shoulders*, you should never allow him to sit upon an Elbow-Chair: For these Chairs, while he makes Use of them, make him raise up his *Shoulders*, and hence it happens, that his Neck sinks betwixt them.——A Method of managing a Child when he either raises or depresses one *Shoulder* too much, is to put some sort of Burthen upon the *Shoulder* that is lowest, and let the highest quite alone, for, the Weight upon the low *Shoulder* will oblige him to raise it up, and at the same Time will make him depress the other.

Here follow Prescriptions on the Deformities of the Body, which proceed First, from Children's being wrong swadled. Second, from their being wrong laid down in the Cradle. Third, from their being wrong carried in the Arms.

The Body too thick:

SOME young People to procure themselves an easy Shape, put Vinegar into every Thing that they eat, and even drink it sometimes. This Remedy is extremely

dangerous. Among many Inft
thor alledges, I fhall only relate

A young Lady of great
joyed a perfect State of Healtl
ago ; fhe was pretty fat,
Appetite, and a blooming
She began to be fufpicious of
fat, for her Mother was ve
and fhe was afraid of gro\
fame Size. A Woman, whom
upon this Subject, advifed
every Day a fmall Glafs of V
did fo accordingly, and the F
nifhed. Charmed with the Su
Remedy, fhe continued it m
Month. At length fhe began
Cough, and as it was dry at firft, i
upon as only a flight Cold wl
go off again. In the mean Ti
very dry Cough it came to a
flow Fever fucceeded, with a I
Breathing, and her whole Hab
grew lean and confumptive. N
came on, with Swellings of the
Feet, and the Difeafe ended with
nefs. When her Body was o|
Lobes of the Lungs were foun
of Tubercles. The Lungs re|
Grape, and the Tubercles repref
Stones ; during the Courfe of h
the *Peruvian* Bark was made uf
alfo febrifuge alkaline Opiates, th

of Affes Milk, and Broth of Cray-fifh; to. which were added the pectoral Herbs, to prevent an Ulceration of the Lungs. But the Confumption ftill continued its Courfe 'till fhe died.—Mr. *Andry* advifes young People to reflect upon this Cafe.

To prevent the Body's growing too thick, or to cure this Deformity, he prefcribes the following Ways, Firft, Not to fleep too much. Second, To drink plenty of Tea and Coffee. Third, To abftain from Chocolate, Beer, and every Thing that is capable of producing too nourifhing Juices. Fourth, To eat and drink vey moderately, and if you muft drink Wine, let it be white Wine. Fifth, To take a great Deal of Exercife on Foot. Sixth, To take every Day, for feveral Weeks, a little of the Afhes of Cray-fifh, mixed with a frefh Egg, or diluted with Broth. Thefe Afhes are very effectual to hinder the Body from growing too fat; the Dofe is half a Drachm, if the Perfon is above twelve Years of Age. But in Cafe the Perfon has fo great a Difpofition to grow fat, that he muft have fomething ftronger, you may add to the above Afhes, thofe of Sea-fpunge, and of the Pith of Sweet-Brier, fo as to make a Powder; the Dofe of which ought to be half a Drachm. This Medicine is fo extenuating, that it fometimes occafions too

great

great a Meagerneſs; and her
it, you ought to have a
gard to the Diſpoſition of
takes it, for unleſs he is afr
to an enormous Size, he had
have Recourſe to the laſt Po
tent himſelf with the Firſt,

The Body too ſler

MR. *Andry* treats of the
ſo far as it proceeds fr
in a Child, ariſing from the l
ing too great a Fondneſs t
their Children.——The Remedy
every Body.

The Nature of an Abſtract
low me to enlarge on the foll
cles. 1. *The Arms and Legs*
too long. 2. One *Leg* or *A*
than the other. 3. One Arm
thick. 4. How to manage wh
does not touch the Ground eaſily.
Shape the Arms, Hands, Fingers
ought to have, to appear han
Roughneſs of the Hands, Hairineſs
Hands. 7. The *Hand crooked*.
on the *Hands*. 9. *Hardneſs* of t
10. *Shaking* of the *Hands*. 11.
of the *Hands*. 12. *Chilblains*
Hands.

To prevent them our Author prescribes the following Method,—to rub the Hands during the Month of *October*, with white Wine, in which Rocket has been infused for the Space of two Days.) 13. The *Itch* upon the *Hands* and *Arms*. 14. Deformities of the *Nails*. 15. The *Right-Hand* weaker than the *Left*. 16. The *Legs* crooked. 17. The *Feet* wrong turned.

The 2d Volume begins by the Deformities of the *Head*. To this the Fourth Book is designed. I shall relate those Articles only which appear to me the most useful or entertaining. The Author, speaking of the *Face in general, with respect to the Air and Mien*, expresses himself thus: " The Air of the Face depends upon the " Sentiments of the Soul. Are you de- " sirous that your Children should have " a noble Look, an agreeable and pleasing " Air ? Inspire them with Sentiments " noble and humane, and these Senti- " ments will represent themselves upon " their Faces.—The Face, so to speak, " takes the Features of the Soul, and " moulds it self by them.—When a Child " is bred up in the Maxims of Honour, " the Features of his Face are found in- " sensibly thereupon, and become at last " indelible, provided this Education is pro- " tracted so long as till the Features are " quite confirmed. The transient Senti-
" ments

" ments of the Soul make or
" Impreffion upon the Counte
" its habitual Sentiments, fu
" contracted in a good or bad
" by good or bad Habitudes, t
" by redoubled Impreffions, im
" the Face fuch deep Char
" they are never afterwards to
" It is this that makes the g
" Countenance. When a you
" is naturally of a choleric T
" there is no Pains taken to
" Paffion in him, his Face is f
" ceive the Impreffion of th
" and Frowns which Anger
" the Marks of which will n
" pear ; but even, when he is
" will difcover his paffionate
" and give him a rough Air."—
may be faid of all the other
and from this we may infer,
rents are, as it were, the Maft
Children's Countenances, becauf
depends upon the Sentiments of
the Sentiments upon the Educ
the Education upon the Pare
" the Child's Features are no
" the Parents cannot give the
" Regularity ; but it lies in th
" to form the Mind and the
" the Child, and it is by the formi

" that they are able to mould the Air of
" his Face."

Of the Eye-Brows.

THERE are fourteen Conditions neceffary to *handfome Eye-brows*.

1. *They ought to be fufficiently furnifhed
with Hair*. If they have too little Hair,
" You muft begin with fhaving them, *fays*
" *Mr. Andry*, fo as not to leave the leaft
" Down upon them, and afterwards fo-
" ment the Part that is fhaved feveral
" Times a Day, with a Decoction of
" Worm-wood, Betony, and Sage, boiled
" in white Wine. Continue this a Month,
" or at leaft for three Weeks ; after which,
" fhave the Part a-new, and then anoint
" it with an Unguent of Honey, Wax,
" and Eggs, mixed together ; and repeat this
" Unction for a Month every Night before
" you to go to Bed, putting a Linen-Cloath
" upon the Eye-brow, to keep the Ointment
" applied to it."

2. *The Eye-Brows ought to be only moderately thick*. If they are too thick, burn
a Cabbage, make a *Lixivium* of the Afhes,
and with this *Lixivium*, rub the Child's
Eye-brows frequently.

3. *Each*

3. *Each Eye-brow*, fhould form upon the Forehead, a Concave Line in the Shape of an Arch, the Hollow of which ought to make a fmall Vault above the Eye, fuch as Mr. *de Voiture* defcribes in the following Stanza, where he paints the Eyebrows of a young Lady, whom he met with at a Ball.

> Sur un front, blanc comme l'yvoire,
> Deux petits arcs de couleur noire,
> Etoient mignardement voûtés,
> D'où ce Dieu qui nous fait la guerre,
> Foulant aux pieds nos libertés,
> Triomphoit de toute la Terre.

> *Beneath her Ivory Front, juft o'er her*
>   *Eyes,*
> *Two fable Arches elegantly rife,*
> *Where perch'd on high the God of plea-*
>   *fing Pains,*
> *His haughty Empire o'er the World*
>   *maintains.*

4. *The upper Part of the Eye-brow ought to be thicker planted with Hair, than the lower.* When this is not the Cafe, it may eafily be helped. The Method of doing this to fhave the Part as fmooth as poffible ; as the Hair will grow again, after it fprouts fhave it a-new ; it will not need fhaving

a

a dozen of Times, provided you take care to rub the Part that is fhaved with the Unguent of Eggs and of Wax.

5. *The Interval, or the Space between the Eye-brows, fhould be quite free of Hair.* When they are thus joined, the beft Method for removing that Deformity is that prefcribed above for the Eye-brows when they are too thick.

6. *The Hairs muft not ftart up, but lie flat in fuch a Manner, as they may point from the Nofe towards the Temples, and not from the Temples towards the Nofe.* When the contrary happens, we cannot too quickly fet about the removing of fuch a Deformity. " As foon, *fays Mr. Andry,* as " ever you obferve a Child have the Hair " of the Eye-brows turned the contrary " Way, they ought conftantly to be " ftroaked with the Finger, from the " Nofe towards the Temples, and this " muft be continued every Day for a long " Time. You muft likewife make ufe of " a little Brufh, fuch as People rub the " Teeth with, the fame Way. This is " all the Method that needs to be ufed, " and it is no lefs effectual than it is " fimple.

7. *The Hairs ought to be fhort, and leave no bald Spots.* To make them fhort when they are too long, the only Method is to

PART II.　　　K　　　cut

cut off what is too much with a Pair of
Sciffars; As to what concerns thofe Parts
where the Hair is interrupted, the only Thing
to be done, is to fhave them from time to
time.

8. *The Hairs of the Eye-brows ought not to
ftand on End, or ftart out from one another.* When this is the Cafe, you muft
fhave the Eye-brow two or three Times,
and take Care after it is fhaved, to pafs
the Fingers frequently over it, from that
Part which is called the Head, to the other
named the Tail, and this will foon make the
Hairs lie fmooth, without over-topping one
another.

9. *The Eye-brows fhould be of a black
or Chefnut Colour, and not reddifh, nor
red.*

10. *Each Eye-brow ought to make an entire Arch.*

11. *This Arch ought to be only moderately
raifed.* When it is too high, it gives
the Face an Air of Affurance, which does
not become every Body, efpecially the Fair
Sex.

12. *There ought to be one Eye-brow on
each Side of the Forehead.* To have only
one Eye-brow, is a great Deformity, which
may be cured when it proceeds from the
Defect of the Humour, which ferves to
nourifh the Shoots employed by Nature
for

for the Production of the Hair of the Eye-brows. For that Purpose you muſt have Recourſe to the following Compoſition, which ſhould be renewed every Day for three Months. This Compoſition is made of the Oil of Honey ; the Oil of Worm-wood, and that of bitter Almonds, of each two Drops ; of the Perſon's own Urine three Drops ; mix them together, and make them Milk-warm, and with this Liquor rub the Part ſeveral Times a Day, till the Points of the Hair begin to appear upon the Eye-brow, and after that continue the ſame Method till the Eye-brow is quite grown.

13. *Neither of the Eye-brows ſhould be quite bare.* When they are both naked, you may try to remove that Deformity by the ſame Method propoſed in the foregoing Article.

14. *The Eye-brows ought not to be double one above another.* This Deformity is very difficult to correct.

The Deformity of the Noſe.

1. THE want of a Noſe. 2. The Noſe flat or broad. 3. The Noſe like the Foot of a Pot. 4. The Noſe awry. 5. The Noſe full of red Pimples. 6. The Polypus

of

of the Nose. 7. The Nose full of little Holes. 8. The Nose too large. 9. The Nose slit. 10. The Nose resembling that of a Horse. 11. Convulsive Motions of the Nose.

Among these Articles I shall select only the Seventh. —— " There are, *says our* " *Author*, Noses all prick'd full of small " Holes, like the Shells of Almonds. It " is generally believed, that these little " Holes are Apartments for Worms, and " upon this Notion it is usual to pinch " these Places between the Nails, to " squeeze out the pretended Worms, " which are nothing else, than a greasy " Sort of Stuff hardened within these " Holes. The pinching with the Nails " squeezes out this Stuff effectually; but " then, on the other Hand, it produces " three very bad Effects, the First is, that " of making the Nose red; the Second, that " of making it too large; and the Third, " is that of raising Tumours upon it some-. " times.

Mr. *Andry* pretends, that the best Method of obliterating these little Holes is, to rub a little of the Oil of Nutmegs with the Finger, or a small Brush, all along the Nose. This Oil applied several Times a Day for some Weeks, softens that stuff which is pent up in these Holes, and makes

it

it ooze out, only by rubbing the Nofe with a bit of Linen Rag. After this a few Drops of the Vinegar of Rofes, rubbed gently upon the Nofe, fhuts up thefe little Holes, that they do not appear any more.

Of the Eyes.

I Shall fay nothing of the Deformities the *Eye-lids* are fubject to, and proceed directly to thofe of the *Eyes:* Our Author mentions feven Deformities attending them. 1. The Squint-Eye. 2. The enflamed Eye. 3. The wandering Eye. 4. The fcaly Eye. 5. The winking Eye. 6. One Eye lefs than the other. 7. The fierce Eye.

As for the Squint-Eye (or *Strabifmus,* for fo this Diforder is called) it is very feldom incurable ; when it is contracted after the Birth, it is always owing to the Fault of Nurfes, who lay down their Children in falfe Lights, that is, where the Light does not fall fo directly upon them as it ought, inftead of laying them down in fuch a Manner, as they may have the Light, whether Day-light or Candle-light, directly oppofite to them. — Another Fault of Nurfes is, that when they want to

ftill

ftill a crying Child ; they hold
their Eyes fome Toys, which they
one Side to another, and which
dren cannot look upon fo ne:
fquinting.

The firft Thing to be take
in order either to prevent or cu
order, is, never to let Children
Thing that is either too near, o
at a Side, or fituated directly
Eyes.

The fecond Method to be m
is, to make the Child look a
Eyes, in a Looking-glafs, abou
of an Hour, Evening and Morr
veral Days ; but with this
that each Eye fhall look at that
correfponds to it in the Mirr
no great Piece of Slavery, and
be expreffed how efficacious it
recting this Deformity of the Ey

What Mr. *Andry* prefcribes
inflamed Eye, and the *fcaly Eye*,
me to require the Advice of
to be properly put in Practice
I fhall fay nothing about it.

There is nothing contributes m
Children wandering Eyes, than
to their View a great Huddle of
Motion. This Deformity is fo
more a Misfortune, as a P

has an unfettled Look is generally fuppofed, though often unjuftly, to be of
as unfettled a Mind. For this Reafon,
Mr. *Andry* advifes Parents, never to allow the Nurfes, or Servants, to carry their
Children to Places where there are great
Crowds of People.

When a Child is new waked, he ought
not to be expofed immediately to a ftrong
Light, for this makes him wink very
clofe; and when People will not trouble
themfelves to correct it, this Winking by being repeated every Day, turns into a Habit, and the Child winks all his Life afterwards, juft as if a Grain of Duft had
got into his Eye. This violent and habitual Winking, when it is of a long Standing, is not eafily cured; but however difficult the Cure may be, it is not abfolutely impoffible, and where the Cure is
practicable, the following fimple Remedy
is very good for effecting it. It confifts
in applying upon the Eye-lids, and alfo
round them, a fmall Linen Cloth dipt in the
Juice of Purflane, and this muft be
repeated feveral Times a Day, for fome
Months.

Mr. *Andry* afcribes the *Menopia*, or the
Deformity of having one Eye lefs than
the other, to every Exercife or Play, that
requires the fhutting of one Eye; therefore,

fore, he advises young People n
Use of perspective Glasses, till th
at a proper Age.

The *Haggard,* or *fierce Ey*
monly the Effect of a bad Educ
allowing Children to look ang
who contradict them. We m
this, what was already said
Face in general, with respect to
Mien.

Of the Ears.

I Shall pass over what the *A*
about the *Cheeks,* and proceec
the *Ears.*

They are a great Ornament t
when they are well shaped, do
a certain Size, are neatly placed
dered, and have all those little
Turnings and Windings, which c
external Parts of this Organ.

When the Ears are too lar
Fault not to be corrected, an
Method in this Case, is to con
or, at least, not to keep them
posed, which is easily done.
Pains cannot be taken to make
Children lie neatly. A skillful An

(*e*) *Winslow's* Anatomy.

obferves, that *thofe Ears which have not been tied down in the Time of Childhood are naturally bent forwards.* Where the Ear is right placed, it lies fo clofe to the Head, that you cannot put a Piece of the thinneft Paper between it and the Head without moving it.

Amongft the Women of the Kingdom of *Aftracan*, the longeft Ears are reckoned the moft beautiful; and to make them long, they prefs them with Rolls of Parchment, which they make larger from time to time, and are fafhioned in fuch a Manner, as to make the End of the Ear reach down to the Shoulder. This fhows how eafily the Ears may be ftretched. On this Occafion Mr. *Andry* juftly exclaims againft the barbarous Cuftom of pulling Children by the Ears, by way of Punifhment, which not only ftretches them, but fometimes occafions Dullnefs of Hearing, and even Deafnefs.

Deformities of the Face.

THOSE that are independant of the Small-Pox are the following.

1. *The Face full of red Pimples.* In order to remove this Deformity, the Mafs of Blood muft be fweetened and diluted,

PART II.   L   which

which may be done by the Ufe of Chervil and Crabs in Broth, made with a little Veal and Mutton, but not Beef. It muft be ufed fcarce Milk-warm, and never hot.

2. *Freckles.* They are commonly occafioned by the Heat of the Sun, and hence we ought to take Care of expofing Children to it.

3. *Marks upon the Face.*

4. *The Complexion brown, pale, yellow, tawny,* &c. When it is naturally fo, there is no poffibility of changing it thoroughly, all that young Girls can do in this Cafe is, to have Recourfe to Palliatives; not to red and white Paint, which they commonly make Ufe of in *France,* and which hurts the Complexion, but to Things that are more harmlefs, fuch as, amongft others, a little Afs's Milk, or Talc-water applied to the Face.

Mr. *Andry* fpeaks much againft white and red Paint, and quotes Mr. *La Bruyere,* who fays, that if Women want only to pleafe their own Eyes, they may embellifh themfelves according to their Tafte; but if it is the Men that they would charm, he protefts that he has counted the Votes, and declares to them, on the Part of all Mankind, or at leaft of the greateft Number, that the white and red

Paint

Paint makes them frightful and difgufting; and the red alone makes them look old, and difguifes them.——— So that we may fay *Paint* draws it's own Picture to the Life, in the following Verfes of a *French* Poet.

Par tout où l'on m'employe, on me
    cache avec foin,
Le grand jour m'eft un peu contraire,
Si je fers d'abord fans befoin,
Je me rends bientot neceffaire.
Tant que je fuis caché bien fouvent
    mon Emploi
M'attire des Cajoleries :
Mais je furprend des flateries,
Qui ne s'adreffent point à moi.
Je fers en aparence, & je fais mille
    maux,
Je fuis d'un facheux voifinage,
Et je ronge enfin jufqua'ux os,
Ceux que je flatte davantage.

Whene'er you employ me, you carefully
    hide me ;
I'm fo ugly that none by Day-light can
    abide me.
If at firft I am ufed for Fancy alone,
Yet a while, and without me there's
    nought to be done.

But

But tho' thus concealed, y
    caress'd,
Tho' it is not to me the fo
    address'd ;
Only so far the Praise fron
    I claim,
That without me she ne'er
    got such a Name.

They mistake me, who fan
    I appear,
Tho' I make those who u
    I'm sincere,
I'tell them like Angels I'l
    to shine,
While slily their Beauty I
    mine.

5. *The Complexion wan.*
6. *The Complexion coarse.* It
the being much exposed to th
and the Wind, especially in *S*
too long and frequent Sweatin
7. *The Complexion shining.*
" would have a beautiful *(*
" *says* Mr. *Andry*, it ought n
" but should resemble that B
" you observe upon certain F
" they have been handled.
" *the Bloom of Complexion,* b

" *Luftre*, becaufe this does not belong to
" it. The Lilly is white, but it has no
" Glofs, tho' you fay the Brightnefs of
" Lilly. Snow is likewife white, but it
" does not glitter ; tho' you fay the
" Brightnefs of Snow. Rofes, with all
" their Brightnefs are not in the leaft glofly.
" You fay of a fine Complexion, that it is
" *compounded of the Rofe and Lilly*, without
" meaning that it fhines ; and in the fame
" Manner, you fay a fnowy Complexi-
" on, without fuppofing that it glit-
" ters."

Mille fleurs fraichement eclofes,
Les lis, les œillets & les Rofes,
Couvroient la neige de fon'teint.

Her Beauty to the Eye difclofes,
A thoufand frefh-blown Flowers and
  Rofes,
Lillies and Pinks, which fweetly grace
The fnowy Whitenefs of her Face,

Says Mr. *de Voiture.* Alabafter does not
fhine, though it is white, and when the
Poets fpeak of a *Breaft of Alabafter*, they
do not thereby mean that it is fhine-
ing.

As this Abftraét is perhaps already too
loag, I fhall end it with the Titles of
                                        the

the remaining Articles in the
Deformities of the Gums.——
of the Teeth, with the Means
them to push out —and of
and beautifying them. —— *De*
Tongue, with Respect to the
The want of Speech occasioned
&c.

After this is to be found i
a *Thesis* defended under Mr.
Whether moderate Exercise is
Preserver of Health.

ARTICLE

Histoire civile du *Royaume* de
duite de l' Italien de *Pierr*
Juris consulte & Avocat
avec de nouvelles notes, ref
medailles fournies par l'
qui ne se trouvent point dan
Italienne. 4°. 4 Vol. La H
Pierre Gosse & *Isaac Beaureg*

That is to say,

The *Civil History* of the K
Naples, translated from the
Peter *Giannone,* a *Neapolita*
an and Advocate, &c. Th

is divided in 8 Books, and contains 656 pages, befides the Bookfeller's Advertifement, the Dedicatory Epiftle, and the Introduction, which make up 28 pages.

(a) THIS is the *Tranflation* of a Work that appeared in *Italian*, in the Year 1723, Dedicated to the late Emperor *Charles* VI. The Author is Mr. *Peter Giannone*, a Man well known in the Republick of Letters, for his exact and judicious Knowledge, and for a certain candor, modefty, and fimplicity of Manners, in the old Tafte.

This Book is the more curious, as it is not a bare Hiftorical Narration, but a political Defcription, wherein the Origin of Revolutions is reprefented, and the Laws and Alterations in the Government are traced up to their Beginning; with an Account of Ecclefiaftical Affairs intermingled with them (b).

When

(a) See Bibliotheq. raifon. *Tom.* XXX. I *Part. pag.* 26. —Biblioth. Francoife *Tom.* XXXVI. II *Part. pag.* 328, &c.—And Biblioth. Italique, *Tom.* IX, *pag.* 231.

(b) This Part of Mr. *Giannone's* Work drew upon him the Refentment of the Clergy. They incited the Mob against him, and he was obliged to flie to *Vienna*, to avoid being tore to Pieces. The Emperor granted him his Protection. But having left *Vienna* fometime after, as he was travelling

When this Book firſt appeared in *Ita-lian*, it was the more agreeable to the Public, as beſides the Exactneſs and Fidelity with which it is wrote; they were charmed to ſee a complete Hiſtory of the Kingdom of *Naples*; no Body before having ever undertaken to do for that Kingdom, what ſo many others did in other Parts for the Honour of their Country; a very ſurpriſing Negligence to be ſure in a Country ſo large and ſo full of Virtuoſos, whoſe Works even ſhew, that no Science was better improved among them, than that of the Law.—The Author begins the Hiſtory of that Kingdom from the *Romans*, to whom the Provinces, of which the Kingdom of *Naples* is now compoſed, were formerly ſubject. He propoſes to give, by way of Preliminary, a Sketch of the Form and Conſtitution of the *Roman* Empire,

travelling from *Venice* to *Geneva*, he was unhappily arreſted by a *Piedmonteſe* Officer; and ever ſince, tho' he is actually living, and is treated with great Clemency, through the Generoſity of his *Sardinian* Majeſty, he has been loſt to the Public. In the very Beginning of the Book, there is one of thoſe Strokes, which, without doubt, the Holy Mother was highly incenſed at; " *The Church,* ſays he, in incroaching on the Temporalities of Princes, did by its Statutes and Settlements ſo well intrude, and- as it were incorporate itſelf in the State of Empires, that there is no Poſſibility of reminding the Alterations that happened in one without the Knowledge of the other. See *Biblioth. Francoiſe,* Tom 36. II Part. p. 329, and 324.

pire, and of its Laws, to point out the various Methods taken by different Emperors to bring them to Perfection, and give a concise Account of two celebrated Academies then existing for the Study of the Law, the one at *Rome* for the *Weſt*, and the other at *Beryte* for the *Eaſt*. His intent is to furniſh wherewithal to judge of that Kingdom's decline, and of the Revolutions that happened in it, ſince *Conſtantine* thought proper to tranſer the Imperial Seat to *Conſtantinople*, and by that Means to form two Empires out of one.

All this may be look'd upon as a Digreſſion, which could be placed in any other Work full as well as in this. But it muſt be owned at the ſame Time, that this Part of the *Roman* Hiſtory is ſet in a very agreeable Light.

Mr. *Giannone*, after giving a Deſcription of *Naples*, beſtows this Encomium on the Government and Laws of the *Romans*, that all Nations have look'd upon them as general Laws, and adopted them into their particular Syſtems.

In the Beginning of the firſt Book the Author treats of the different Condition of the *Italian* Towns, as theſe Towns were not equally treated by the *Romans*: from hence aroſe the Diſtinctions and the different Degrees they granted them; ſome having the Privileges of Citizens of *Rome*, others being called municipal Towns, Co-

PART II.   M   lonies,

lonies, Rights of *the Latins*, Prefectures, and allied Towns. They all enjoyed different Prerogatives. — The Author treats afterwards of the Condition of the Provinces, of the Empire's Difpofition under *Auguftus*, of the Difpofition and Form of the Provinces which now compofe the Kingdom of *Naples*, of the State of that City under his Reign, and of *Naples* as it is at prefent the Capital of the Kingdom ; and he fhews that in that Time it was neither a Republic intirely free, nor Independant of the *Romans*, who had granted its Inhabitants extraordinary Prerogatives, which they enjoyed as Favours and Rewards for their Faithfulnefs to them, and as the natural Effect of the agreeable Time they fpent in that City, according to this Paffage of *Paterculus* fpeaking of *Naples* and *Cumæ*, in the firft Book of his Hiftory. *Utriafque urbis eximia femper in Romanos fides facit eas nobilitate atque amœnitate fuâ digniffimas.*

Talking afterwards of illuftrious Writers, " It were difficult, *fays the Author*, to " give an Account of the great Number " of high Geniufes, of fublime Wits, " that owed their Birth to the above named " *Italian* Towns, or who, by their Refidence " in them, and cultivating of the Sciences, did improve their Talents ; Philofophers,

" lofophers, Mathematicians, Orators, and
" efpecially Poets, whofe Works contain-
" ed whatever Antiquity produced in thofe
" feveral Kinds worthy of Admiration,."

The Elogy he pays to the Profeffors of the
civil Law and their Books, fhews how much
that Science was improved among them.
He proves that the Study of the civil Law
was no where fo much honoured and
efteemed, as among the *Romans* ; and it
is to the great Efteem Men of the firft
Rank had for the Study of the Laws,
that the Authority they got, and the great
Regard paid to them is chiefly owing,
and with Juftice ; for who is to be compared to the Civilians of *Rome* ; *Claudius*,
Sempronius, the *Scipios Mucius*, *Cato*,
Brutus, *Craffus*, and fo many other Names
equally illuftrious.

The laft Part of this Book contains the
Inftitutions of the Princes, the *Papyrian*,
Gregorian, and *Hermogenian* Codes ; and the
famous Academies of *Rome* in the *Weft*, and
of *Beryte* in the *Eaft*.—What he fays of
thefe two Academies deferves a Moment's
Attention.

Before *Adrian*'s Reign, *Rome* had no
Academy ; Mafters taught Youth in private Houfes, and the Place they received
their Scholars in, was named *Pergole*.

Even

Even the Civilians did not decline thefe Functions, independently on their chief Occupations, which were to explain the Laws, to write, to anfwer, to give Advices, but they taught young People the Laws in their Houfes. *Cicero* fays he had been Difciple of *Quintius Scevola*, Son of *Publius*, tho' that famous Civilian *nemini ad docendum fe dabat*. *Adrian* was the Firft that founded a College at *Rome* to teach in public the Sciences and *Belles Lettres. Alexander Severus* inlarged and adorned that Eftablifhment; he affigned a Maintenance to the Rhetoricians, Phyficians, Grammarians, and to all the other Profeffors; he founded public Auditories, and Penfions for Scholars, whofe Relations were poor, but free born.

The Reputation of this famous Academy brought to *Rome*, from all Parts of the Empire, an infinite Number of young People there to ftudy Sciences, and in particular the civil Law; and tho' the *Greeks* feemed to have a good Opinion only of themfelves, and of what belonged to them; yet they acknowledged that to be well rooted in the Practice of Virtue, the firft Principles of it were to be got from the *Roman* Laws.

The Emperors beftow'd a particular Attention on whatever concerned the Profperity

perity of the Academy at *Rome*. When that City fell from its ancient Splendor, the Academy fell along with it, but *Valentine* the Elder reſtored it to its firſt Luſtre, and by that *Rome* did really deſerve, even in the moſt barbarous Times, the Praiſes of many Authors of thoſe low and degenerate Centuries, which *Savaron* has collected in his Notes on *Sidonius Apollinaris*.

As to the Academy at *Beryte*, which is a City of *Phœnicia* in the *Eaſt*, it is not certainly known by whom it was founded, but it is not to be doubted, that it had been famous many Years before the Reign of *Dioclefian*. The Proof of it is to be found in an Inſtitution of that Prince, which the *Juſtinian* Code mentions, as directed to *Severine*, and to other Students of *Arabia*, which lived at *Beryte* to be inſtructed in the Law.

About the Year of Chriſt 350, under the Reigns of *Conſtantius* and of *Conſtans*, the Academy at *Beryte* was yet flouriſhing. *Juſtinian* gave it the Name of the *City of Laws*, and ordered, that as the civil Law was only to be taught at *Rome* in the *Weſt*, the Academy at *Beryte* ſhould alſo alone enjoy the ſame Priviledge in the *Eaſt*, along with the Academy at *Conſtantinople*, which
had

had already been eftablifhed
the Younger, in the Year 42 5
. In the fecond Book, the
in the Beginning of the I
(the Chriftian Æra) and in
the following Years, the
Roman Empire.

The Reafon he alledges
Romans, formerly brave and
became cowardly and effemir
and Faction fucceeded in the Pl
tues that had been fo much
them. That Nation who
the whole World, was cor
Turn, and expofed to the mof
volutions.

The Declenfion of the E
lefs remarkable in the *Eaft*
the Provinces were fubdued.
may ferve alfo for the
Belle-Lettres, which were rui
the Empire.

In the Sequel of this Boc
mentions the new Laws, an
ftem of Laws under the l
fantine and his Succeffor
blifhment of an Academy a
the Inftitutions of the Prin
the *Theodofian* Code was fo
and Authority of that Cod
and in the Provinces of th

Naples.—Here is a fhort Account of what he fays on that Subject.

Theodofius after having quite reftored, in the Academies, that Knowledge of the civil Law, which had been decaying and entirely neglected, thought it was neceffary to difpel the Darknefs diffufed over that Science by the great Number of Law-Books, and the Multiplicity of Imperial Inftitutions contrary to each other. To fucceed in this, he took the Refolution to make a new Code, to the compiling of which, he gave all his Attention. To that End, he cut off whatever was fuperfluous, and admitted nothing but what was neceffary for the Decifion of Law-Suits; it was publifhed in 438. Eight Civilians, of known Probity and confummate Learning, were employed in this Work; their Commiffion was to gather together the Inftitutions of fundry Princes hardly known, to make a Body of them, to correct their Faults and Alterations, and to form an Abridgment of them as concife as they poffibly could. Their Work neverthelefs required no lefs than 16 Books, for it contained all the Inftitutions during the Courfe of a hundred and twenty-fix Years, *viz.* from 312 to 438, under the Reign of fixteen different Emperors. No Part of either public or private Law was neglected in the compiling

compiling of this Code, nor even the
Ecclefiaftical Law, which takes up a whole
Book. It was no fooner publifhed, than
it was received in the two Empires. Tho'
Theodofius did not reign in the *Weft*, yet
this Work was approved and received there.
Before he undertook it, he had communi-
cated the Project to *Valentinian* his Collegue,
who gave him all the Affiftance in his
Power.

After a long Defcription of the famous
Theodofian, Code of it's Ufe, and of it's
Authority in the *Weft*, and in the Provinces, which now compofe the Kingdom of *Naples*, our Author mentions at
large the Alteration brought into the Ecclefiaftical Polity by *Theodofius*'s Converfion.'
—It fecured the Peace and Tranquillity of
the Church. By this Event, the Bifhops,
who, during the three firft Centuries, had
continually been expofed to the fatal Effects of Perfecution, were enabled hence-
forward to make a public Profeffion of
their Faith ; they founded Churches, they
erected Altars, and in Proportion to the
Importance of the Cities, where thefe
Churches were fituated, the Bifhops who
conducted them, took different Ranks, and
rofe to greater, and never heard of before,
Dignities. Then only began to be known
thofe Titles of *Metropolitan*, of *Primate*,

of

of *Patriarch*, who, in spiritual Affairs had under their Jurisdiction the same Provinces, as the Governors or Prefects in civil Affairs. So it was under the Reign of *Constantine*, that the Ecclesiastics began to leave off the Simplicity of the first Ages; and that Ambition, the Desire of Power, and amassing Wealth, took Place of Charity, Poverty, and of Moderation which were formerly the only Arms they had to oppose to Persecution. So that is may be said that *Constantine*'s Reign was the Epocha of the Church's Grandeur, and that this Prince himself laid the Foundations of that ambitious Power, which for many Ages challenged to himself the Right of deposing Kings from their Throne, of putting their Kingdom under Interdiction, of absolving the People from the Oath of Allegiance to their Sovereign, and which has even attempted to obtain over the Temporalities of Princes, an Authority no less absolute than over their Spiritualities.

Every Body knows, that the *Goths* invaded *Italy*, about the latter End of the fifth Century. *Theodoric* their King received the Sovereignty of *Italy* from the Emperor *Zeno*. Mr. *Giannone* speaks very advantageously of the *Goths* in general,

PART II.　　　　　N　　　　　and

and of *Theodoric* in particular. He re-
establish'd the *Roman* Laws, and order
ed, they should be observed both by
the *Romans*, and the *Goths*. He put at
the Head of the Courts of Judicature,
Men famous for their Integrity and Reputation. These Judges were approved of
by the People (a singular Privilege which
he generously granted them.) He had
all Qualities requisite to form an excellent Prince. Tho' *he was an* Arian, he
never persecuted nor disturbed the *Atha-
nasians*; so far from it, that he even protected them in their Opinion. We see
by *Cassiodorus's* Letters, that this Prince
was just, humane, honest, very sober, according to the Use of his Nation at that
Time, and very plain in his Dress.
Equally fit for Peace and for War, he
was always successful in the one, and never
failed in the other, of heaping Favours
upon all his Subjects. It is remarkable,
that the warlike Nation of the *Goths,*
never neglected the Exercise of Justice,
even in their hottest Wars. They have
been unjustly accused of Inhumanity.
They gave a full Liberty to the People
they conquered, to live quietly under their
own Laws. *Grotius* says that the *Germans* called this Nation *Goten,* or *Guten,*

that

that is to fay, *Good*, becaufe they practifed Hofpitality towards Strangers.

In the third Book, the Author fpeaks of *Juftinian*, who fucceeded *Juftin* Emperor of the *Eaft*, and who deferved, by his noble Actions, the Name of *Great* that was given to him. This Prince was equally illuftrious in Peace and in War. He reftored the Empire to its priftine Majefty by the Actions of *Belifarius* and *Narfes*, his Generals, and by the Care and Labours of the Civilians he employed. He formed a Defign of giving a more perfect Syftem of the civil Law, and in the fecond Year of his Reign he publifhed an Edict, ordaining the compiling of a new Code, and committed this Work to thofe that had got the greateft Reputation amongft the Magiftrates, the Profeffors, and the Counfellors. The famous *Tribonianus* was Prefident of this Commiffion. They were to collect the Conftitutions contained in the *Gregorian, Hermogenian,* and *Theodofian* Codes, to add to them the Laws publifhed fince, and to compofe out of that whole Work one fingle Volume, which was ended and publifhed at the Beginning of the third Year of *Juftinian's* Reign, in the Month of *April* 529. From thence the *Theodofian* Code fell into Difufe in the *Eaft*, but it had a better Fate in the *Weft*, efpecially in *Italy*, where

N 2

the

the *Juftinian* Code was not received as long as the *Goths* were Mafters of it.

After giving this Account of *Juftinian* as Legiflator, he takes a View of his military Affairs, in which he was every where fuccefsful. In the great and difficult Undertaking of the Laws, he had the Happinefs to be affifted by excellent Civilians, fuch as *Tribonianus, Theophilus, Dorothæus,* &c.—In the military Way, he had Generals of confummate Skill and Bravery ; *Belifarius, Narfes,* and fome others, to whofe Victories over fo many Nations, he owed his Titles of *Alemanic, Gothic, Francic, Germanic, Alanic, Vandalic,* and *African,* which were given to him. He conftantly had good Succefs, till having fufpected *Belifarius*'s Fidelity, he recalled him, and fent in his Place into *Italy, John* and *Vitalis.* The Valour and Skill of thefe Generals were fo much inferior to *Belifarius*'s, that the *Goths,* refuming their Courage, elected *Totila* for their King. This Prince by his Merit and Valour, repaired in a fhort Time the Lofles the *Goths* had fuftained. He routed the Imperial Army, and retook the moft Part of the Provinces *Belifarius* had made himfelf Mafter of.

Till then the Bifhops of *Rome* had not intermedled in State Affairs. Far from domineering over Princes, they did not even

take

take Notice of their Quarrels. The Popes *Vigilius*, and *Sylvester* gave the first Example, and they have been but too well imitated by their Successors. *Vigilius* left no Stone unturned to prevail over *Justinian*, to send *Belisarius* back to *Italy*, to oppose the Progress of *Tolita*. *Belisarius* was sent, but with Forces so much inferior to the Enemy's, that this second Expedion, far from adding to his Glory, rather impaired the great Reputation he had acquired in the first. *Totila* made himself Master of *Rome*, in sight of his Army, but, not being able to keep it, laid it in Ruins, drove out the Inhabitants, and carried away the Senators with him. He died after having reigned about ten Years. After the Death of *Totila*, *Justinian* recovered what he had lost during his Life; but he had no sooner delivered *Italy* from the *Goths*, but he was obliged to give all his Attention to his second War against the *Persians*, and to repulse the *Huns*, and soon after (in 565) he died, aged 82. He reigned 38 Years and 8 Months.

Justinian's Death was the Epocha of the Fall of his Projects, ever after the Fortune of the eastern Emperors was on the decline. The Pandects, the Codes, and all their Laws shared the same Fate. *Italy* and the Kingdom of *Naples*, fell again under the Yoke of the *Lombards*, who

were

were defended from the G
the young Son of *Vigilant*
Justinian, succeeded to the
out inheriting the great Qua
Predeceffor. He was a Prince
Parts, and entirely under the G
his Wife *Sophia*, he recalled
Italy, and sent in his Place *Longi*
568.) who, under the Title
committed there all Sorts c
which greatly haftened the I

When the *Lombards* con
they proclaimed *Alboine* their
(in 579). The whole Ceremic
in lifting up the new King
in the Midft of the Army,
claiming him their Sovereign
Shouts of Joy, and putting in hi
Pike, which was the Symbol of

Rotari was the firft of t
that gave them written Law
left the *Romans* at Liberty to
own. The Government of the *L*
very mild. They hated Perfe
Rotari's Time, there were i
the Cities of his Kingdom, tw
the one *Athanafian*, and the othe
and they both enjoyed a free Exerc
Religion.

Mr. *Giannone* fixes to this
Origin of the Fiefs in *Italy*.

this intricate Subject in a very clear
Light.

The Remainder of the Book treats of
the Succession of the Kings of *Lombardy*,
and of the Expedition of *Conſtans*, the
Emperor of the *Eaſt*, into *Italy*. This
Prince was Son of *Conſtantine*, who had
kept the Throne only four, or ſix Months,
Martina, his Step-Mother, having put him
to Death, to place on it *Heraclian* her
own Son, who was depoſed ſix Months
after, and baniſhed with his Mother.

Conſtans ſucceeded him in 642. This
Emperor ſo paſſionately wiſhed for the
Re-union of *Italy* to the eaſtern Empire,
that he thought he could not with Honour wear the Imperial Crown, until he
had retaken from the *Lombards*, all their
Conqueſts. Unwilling to truſt this important Enterprize to his Generals, he
left *Conſtantinople*, and put himſelf at the
Head of his Army, but from his bad
Succeſs, loſing all Hopes of getting the
better of the *Lombards*, overwhelm'd with
Grief, he went to *Rome*, and tho' well
received by the Pope, he ſtrip'd the
City of its moſt precious Ornaments, carried away the moſt valuable Things found in
it, Gold, Silver, Braſs, Marble, and put
them in Ships to be carried to *Conſtantinople*;

After

After this he went back again to *Naples*, and from thence to *Reggio*, where his Troops were again defeated; at laſt he repaired to *Sicily*, and was murdered in a Bath, by his own Servants in 660. The immenſe Riches he was carrying away from *Rome*, and from other Places, fell into the Hands of the *Saracens*, and were carried to *Alexandria*.

Bardanes was the firſt, that publiſhed an Edict againſt the worſhipping of Images, but *Leo*, the *Iſaurian*, who then poſſeſſed the eaſtern Empire, was ſo warm againſt it, that he got the Surname of *Iconoclaſt*. He ſent word to the Pope, *Gregory* the 2d, that if he did not leave off the worſhip of Images, he would depoſe him, and name another Pope in his Place. For ſome time *Gregory* was in hopes, that the King of the *Lombards* would protect him againſt the Emperor, but he ſoon perceived, that this King had not ſo much the Pope's Preſervation at Heart, as a Mind to make Uſe of the favourable Opportunity thrown in his Way by thoſe Diſſentions, in Order to extend his own Dominions. *Gregory* in that Extremity, thought of bringing the *Romans* over to his Party; he ſucceeded by the Dread he gave them of the Ambition of the Emperor

and

and the *Lombards*, and engaged them to acknowledge him for Sovereign, which they did. This was the Origin of that temporal Sovereignty; which the Popes at prefent enjoy in *Italy*. The Emperor prepared with a numerous Army to take a fevere Vengeance both of the Pope and of the *Romans*.

The Pope, in this Extremity, refolved to apply to the *French*; who had embraced the Chriftian Religion about fifteen Years before. *Charles Martel* governed the Kingdom. The King, unable to govern, had committed his Authority to this great Man, who was Mayor of the Palace. It was to this true Mafter of the Kingdom that *Gregory* fent a fumptuous Embaffy. No Pope had ever done the like before. *Gregory* intended by this Mark of Diftinction to engage *Charles Martel*, to give him the Succour he ftood fo much in need of, and he fucceeded ; *Charles Martel* promifed to march to *Italy*, to defend the Church and the *Romans*, in Cafe they were attack'd. Our Author enlarges much on this Article, on purpofe to fhew what was the Origin of the temporal Power of the Popes, their artful Compliance when they wanted the neighbouring Princes to keep up their Authority, and the Means they afterwards made ufe of to ftretch it, even to the Prejudice of thofe that had prevented their Ruin.

PART II. O *Leo*'s

Leo's Death happened about this Time, as well as *Gregory*'s ; and the King of the *Lombards*, did not furvive them long. *Conftantine Copronymus* fucceeded *Leo*, *Gregory* III. *Gregory* II ; and *Rachis* was chofen King of the *Lombards*, but he foon abdicated the Crown to a Monk of *Mount-Caffine*. It was about this Time that the Crown of *France* was transferred from the *Merovingian* Line, to the *Carlovingian* ; I fhall have foon occafion to fpeak of this Event.

Rachis having abdicated the Crown, the *Lombards* gave it to *Aiftulphus*. This Prince was formed by Nature with a Genius equally capable of defigning and executeing grand Enterprifes. He made himfelf Mafter of *Ravenna* and the whole *Exarchate*, which had been in the Hands of the *Greeks* for about a hundred and eighty-three Years. The *Exarch*, after haveing for a while ftood the Siege of *Ravenna*, unable to hold out any longer, fled to *Greece*. *Aiftulphus* puff'd up with his Succeffes, look'd upon the Dutchy and City of *Rome* as a Dependance on the *Exarchate*. He fent Deputies to *Rome* to the Pope, haughtily menacing, that if they did not fubmit, and pay the annual Tribute of a Crown a Head, he would forthwith ranfack and lay wafte the City, and put the Inhabitants to the Sword. The
Pope

Pope fecretly difpatched a Man of Truft,
to *Pepin* King of *France*, to reprefent to
him the Straits to which he was reduced,
and his Defire to take Sanctuary in
France, in Cafe Ambaffadors fhould be
fent to him, with whom he might go on
his Journey with fafety. *Pepin* agreed to
it, and fent two of the chief Lords of
his Court to bring him to *France*. When
thefe Ambaffadors came to *Rome*, they
found the *Lombards* ready to inveft the
Town. They then conducted the Pope to
France, where he was received with the fame
Honours, that could be paid to the greateft Prince upon Earth. *Pepin*, in order
to be more refpected by his Subjects, and
to fecure the Crown to him, and to his
Family, had himfelf crowned by the Pope.
After this Ceremony was over, he fet out at
the Head of his Army for *Italy*, forced his
March over the *Alps*, routed the *Lombards*,
purfued their King to the Gates of *Pavia*,
where he befieged and forced him to reftore
the Dutchy of *Rome*, with *Ravenna*, and
twenty other Cities which were joined
that Year (154) to St. *Peter*'s Patri-
mony. This is the fecond Time the
Pope applied to *France* in his Dif-
trefs.

In the fixth Book is to be feen what
paffed at *Charles the Great*'s Election to the
Roman Empire. Here is a fhort Abftract

of

of what our Author fays about this great
Event, — Whilft *Pepin* and *Grimoaldus*,
waged a bloody War together, *Charles the
Great*, who had fubdued the *Saxons*, and
over-run feveral Places included in or
belonging to his vaft Dominions, ftop'd at
laft, in the Year 795, at *Aix La Chapelle*,
being greatly delighted with the Situation of
that City, and the adjacent Parts. There
he received the News of *Adrian* the Pope
being dead at *Rome*, the Year 796, and
of *Leo*, Prieft and Cardinal, being elected to
fucceed him, who took the Name of *Leo* III.
This new Pontiff fent Ambaffadors to
Charles the Great, to affure him, that, con-
formably to the Example of his Predecef-
fors, he would acknowledge none but him
for his, and the Church's, Protector ; at
the fame Time, he fent him as *Patrician
of Rome*, the Standard of the City, with
many other Prefents, and defired him to
fend one of the Lords of his Court, to
receive in his Name the Oath of Fidelity,
which the *Roman* People were willing to
tender to him.

Charles the Great accepted both of the
Prefents, and the Homage offered to him
by the firft City in the World. He chofe
his Son-in-law *Anghilbert*, to go and receive the Oath of Allegiance from the
Romans, and from that Time he was Sovereign

reign inftead of Patrician of *Rome* ; Juftice being adminiftered both by his Commiffaries and by himfelf.

The Pope's good Offices highly deferved fome Reward ; accordingly, *Charles the Great* fent him a confiderable Part of the immenfe Treafures he had got in the War againft the *Huns* ; which were happily ended by the Conqueft of *Pannonia. Leo* had great Enemies, who entered many Heads of Accufation againft him ; but not being able to prove them, rufh'd upon him one Day as he was performing a public Funftion, wounded him in feveral Places, dragg'd him afterwards in the Streets, endeavouring to pluck out his Eyes, and cut out his Tongue, but he happily got out of their Hands, and the Duke of *Spoletta* having haftened to his Help, he conducted him to *Charles the Great*, who received him at *Paderbom*, with all the Magnificence poffible. This Prince thought proper afterwards to fend him back to *Rome*, and to name ten Commiffaries to go with him to have a legal Hearing of this Affair ; a fhort Time after, he went to hear himfelf the Accufations laid againft the Pope. Without entering into any more Particulars, it is enough to fay, that it turned to the Pope's Advantage.—It was at this Time, that

that the moſt artful Contrivance, that can
be imagined, was put in Practice, to engage *Charles the Great* more and more to
ſupport the Intereſts of the Holy See, a
Contrivance, which *Leo*'s Succeſſors made
ſuch a Handle of, that a Function,
which, in its Beginning, was nothing elſe
but a bare Ceremony, they made Uſe
of afterwards, as one of the ſtrongeſt
Proofs of the Sovereignty, which they pretend belongs to them, and which they claim
over all the Catholic Countries. The
Pope declared *Charles the Great Roman
Emperor*, and crowned him as ſuch. After he had put the Crown on his Head,
he gave him the ſacred Unction, and
cloathed him with a long Royal Mantle in
the *Roman* Faſhion, and this Prince was acknowledged as Sovereign, after having received the ſame Honours, that were paid
to the ancient *Roman* Emperors. He took
the Titles of *Auguſtus* and of Emperor, which he tranſmitted to his Poſ-
terity.

The declining State of the *Lombard* Princes,
the Re-eſtabliſhment of the Authority of the
Greek Emperors in the Provinces of the
Kingdom of *Naples*, the Irruptions and Ha-
vocks the *Saracens* made in it, are the
Subjects of the ſeventh Boook.

Here

Here is to be feen a Succeffion of fatal Events, which reduced thofe Provinces to the moft deplorable Condition. The *Lombard* Princes, divided among themfelves, foon ruined their own States, already weakened by their Difcord ; they were obliged to yield to the Authority of the Emperors of the *Weft*. On the other Hand, the *Saracens* compleated the Defolation of the Country.

Among the moft remarkable Events mentioned in the eighth and laft Book of this Work, are the Tranflation of the Empire from the *Italians* to the *Germans* and the Origin of the Electors of the Empire. The Sovereigns, who abufe their Authority and give themfelves up to Tyranny, in fpite of all Precautions they may take, have always Reafon to dread the juft Refentment of a People, fenfible of their Unhappinefs, and made defperate by Oppreffion. The Kingdom of *Italy* being tranflated from the *French* to the *Italians*, *Berenger*, called the *Young*, and *Adalbert* his Son, made the People groan under their Oppreffion. This Situation forced them to implore the Affiftance of *Otho* King of *Germany*. This Prince had already fubdued the *Saxons* and *Sclavonians*, and, by a Number of great Actions, had acquired through all *Europe*, a Reputation not at all inferior to *Charles the Great*. *Otho* went

to

to their Affiſtance, defeated their
and was declared Emperor. Th[
is ſtiled the Tranſlation of t[
from the *Italians* to the *Ger*[
us ſee now what concerns th
the Electors of the Empire.—
commonly referred to this T[
pretend, that *Otho* the Third, [
Male Iſſue, foreſeeing the Tro[
his Death might occaſion in [
of a Succeſſor, thought of prev[
and choſe accordingly by the [
under the Approbation, of *G*[
mong the Multitude of *Ger*[
who all concurred formerly t[
peror's Election, ſeven of the
derable, who, for the Future,
that Right before the others
the ſeven Princes now called
the Empire.—*Bellarmine* after
Eſtabliſhment was made by
Authority of the Popes. [
trary is proved by this Reaſ[
ther the Emperor, nor the [
Power to deprive the *Germ*[
the Right of giving their [
Election, without their Con[
proved further from the be[
who are unanimous in this, tha[
formed the electoral Colle[
Conſent of the Princes of *G*[

Court of *Rome* claims its Authority in this
Refpect from the Emperors ufually going
to *Rome* to be crown'd by the Pope.
But is there any more in all that, than
what is practifed to this Day by the Kings
of *Italy*, of *France*, or of *Spain*, who are
crowned by Bifhops of their Kingdom,
and their Subjects. No Body will fay,
that thefe Princes think they hold their
Crown from the Bifhop, who confecrates
and crowns them. The Emperor *Maximilian* made a Speech to the Electors, in
which he told them ; " I am going to
" *Italy*, there to receive folemnly the
" Imperial Crown, according to Cuftom,
" which is a mere Ceremony, and without
" any Power, as it is well known ; I acknow-
" ledge, that it is wholly from your Elec-
" tion, that the Imperial Dignity and Au-
" thority proceeds."

Tho' it be true, that the Electoral College was inftituted in the Time of *Otho* III.
the Election of *Henry*, Duke of *Bavaria*,
was neverthelefs made by all the Princes
and Prelates of *Germany*, according to the
old Cuftom. The *Italians*, at the Death
of *Otho*, who left no Succeffor, took Advantage of the Circumftances to feize on the
Empire and Kingdom of *Italy* ; but *Henry*
fent there *Otho*, Duke of *Saxony*, at the
Head of an Army to expel *Arduine*, who

PART II.   P   had

had got himſelf proclaimed Em
ſoon after he repaired thither
with a powerful Army, and t
via, where *Arduine* had re
Place was ſoon taken and ranſa
Emperor triumphant and dr
crown'd King of *Italy* by t
ſhop of *Milan*, and ſoon after
to *Rome*, and was there crown
by the Pope and proclaimed *A*
is in this Manner that the 1
the Kingdom of *Italy* went
Houſe of the *Othos*, to the
the Dukes of *Bavaria.* ——— 1
this Book contains the Eccle
lity during the tenth Centu
Arrival of the *Norman* P
made ſuch Alterations in i
thought proper ; when gro
Maſters, they reunited ſuch a
ber of various States, to
potent Monarchy. This we
in the following Volume of
ſtory.

A f

ARTICLE VI.

Mr. *Keifler's* Travels continued *(a)*.

I Shall fay nothing about the Defcription our Author gives of *Rome*. It is a Labyrinth of fuperb Buildings, of magnificent Ruins, of excellent Works of Art ; fuch a Defcription cannot be abftracted.

A Manufacture of the Ancients has been renew'd at *Tarento* and *Regio*, in the Kingdom of *Naples*. It is a Kind of brown Silk, which is found tied to a Shell. They make of it Caps, Gloves, Stockings, Waft-coats, warmer than the Woollen-Stuffs, and brighter than Silk itfelf.

Our Author went to the Mount *Vefuvius*. Unhappily the Smoak prevented his going up to the great Opening of the Bafon, out of which the inflamed Matter iffues. He adds nevertheless, many remarks to thofe of Travellers, who had the fame Curiofity before him. —The Stones which the *Volcano* throws up contain Iron-particles ; the Load-ftone attracts them. O-

P 2 thers

(a) See the Part I. of this Journal, pag. 57.

thers are covered with a glaffy vitriolous
Cruft; I call it vitriolous, becaufe the
green Varnifh, that Stone is covered with,
preferved its Moifture whole Years, and
it eats Paper, as foon as the Moifture of the Air reaches it. It has precifely the fame Effect as that fine Vitriol,
of the livelieft green Colour, which hangs in
the Form of a Pyramid down the natural
Roofs of *Rammelfberg*'s near *Goflar* (b).
Mr. *Lemery* has explained the Nature of
Volcanoes, by an Experiment made with
Iron and Brimftone; that Experiment is
confirmed now; for Iron is found in *Vefuvius*; as for Brimftone, no Body had
any Doubt about it.

Men have done more than Nature itfelf to
deform thofe fine Climates. A *Volcano* does
Mifchief but once or twice in a Century,
Affaffins, Poifon, and the Inquifition, work
continually to the Deftruction of Mankind.
The Author affures, that the abominable *To-
phania* was yet alive, when he was at
Naples. She poifon'd a thoufand People
with a Water that deftroyed a Man at a
fixed Hour; fhe gave it *gratis, and for
Charity fake* to Women tired of their
Husbands. When fhe was difcovered, fhe

run

---

run into an Afylum, and they were fatisfied with locking up this deteftable Creature, that deferved all the Torments that
could have been invented, whilft a poor
Heretic, or a Jew, is burned in folemn
Pomp, tho' he be accufed of nothing but
an Error of the Underftanding.

Public Women are much more dangerous yet than the *Tophanias*. Every Body
knows, it is from *Naples* comes that fhameful
Sicknefs, capable of deftroying all Mankind,
had it preferved its firft Fury. The *Nea-
politans* have no Spleen againft thofe univerfal Poifoners, they keep ten Thoufand
of them, and the Clergy feems to contribute to their Safety. What an Abomina-
tion! "The *Nuncio*'s Auditor, *fays Mr.*
" *Keiſler*, was furprifed by the *Shirres* on
" *Venus*'s Dominions. He was known and
" immediately releafed. Not fatisfied with
" this Lenity in the Judges, he had the
" Infolence to demand Satisfaction, and the
" *Nuncio* the Weaknefs to back his De-
" mand. The *Vice-Roy* feverely punifh'd
" them in granting their Requeft; the
" *Shirres* were led about the Town,
" with a Paper on the Cheft, fignify-
" ing, that they were fo ufed for have-
" ing difturbed the *Nuncio*'s Auditor in his
" Pleafures."

Every

Every Body has heard of the
of St. *Januarius*. The Author
it very naturally. It is a thick O
is liquefied by. a Degree of Hea
the Concourse of People, War
and the Hands of the Prieft
give it. St. *Januarius* was too
the *Bourbons* in 1734, to deferv
neration of a true *German*.
Neuman of *Berlin*, has invented
with which he can at any Tin
the fame Miracle *(c)*. The pro
Duke of *Tufcany* was prefent
Tryal, or Imitation of the Mira
Time he went to vifit the lat
Pruffia.—Mr. *Boyle* difcovered,
Oyl of *Anife* congeals in *Winte*
leaft Degree of Cold, and reco
tural Fludity with the leaft Degr
he adds, that a Liquor drawn
Benjamin Gum goes alternat
Fluidity to a Kind of Cryftalli
from this Cryftallifation to the I
Liquid.

At the Time our Author
ples, its Inhabitants were but
fuperftitious. There were an
many *Janfenifts*, and fome *Athei*
teftant Books were fold almof

(c) Remark of the Journalift.

It is to be fuppofed, that the *Spanifh* Government has cured them fince in this laft Refpect.

The *Grotto*, commonly called the *Dogs Grotto*, is well known, but our Author gives a new Explanation of this *Phænomenon*. Animals are choak'd, and lighted Tapers are extinguifh'd by a Vapour, which rifes about a Foot from the Bottom of the *Grotto*. It is commonly faid, that this Vapour is full of Brimftone, or is Arfenical; but our Author thinks it proceeds from its being fo light, that it cannot fwell the Lungs of Animals, ufed to a thicker Air. It is the *Phænomenon* of the Air-pump; for the Flame and Animals expire with the fame Symptoms, both in the *Grotto* and in the *Vacuum*.

The *Grotto* of *Pyrmont* (d) affords an Inftance of a Vapour confiderably lighter, and confequently of quicker Effect. It is without any Smell, without any external Mark of Brimftone; fo it's Effect can be afcribed to nothing, but to its being fo wonderfully light.

Mr. *Keifler* fpeaking of the Source of the *Naphta*, in the Dutchy of *Modena*, occafionally fhews by convincing Proofs, that

(d) In *Lorrain*.

that the yellow Amber owe:
to the Sea, but that it
Ground. No Print of Fish
terreftrial Animals are feen
of Amber was found on the
Bernftorf, whereon a Leaf
was imprinted, without havi
of its Fibers. It had only
drying.

The Catholics have infult
on the Subject of the A
They called his Account of
lumny ; yet our Author faw b
Relic ; it exifts, it is carr
Town ; it is worfhipp'd ; a1
then it happens, that fome
and Courage enough to defp
of Superftitions, that doe:
the Generality, much lefs c
the Church that encourages t1

The Lovers of Mufic fha
Article of *Venetia*, a Kind c
on the beft Voices in *Italy*,
where the *Italian* and *Frenc*
compared to the Advantage
mer.

Mr. *Keifler* relates fom
about *Porto-Re*, a Port wh
Emperor ordered to be built 1
of the Fleet he had refolvec
the *Mediterranean*. Unhappil

fiaftic was intrufted with the Management of the Money, and the Undertaking drop'd. Pofterity perhaps might have known nothing of this Attempt, if our Author had not preferved the Memory of it.——In vifiting the Works of *Porto-Ré*, he found a Kind of Mufcles alive, enclofed in rough Pieces of a brown-coloured Marble. How do thofe Animals get in that Marble? .What feeds them, how do they multiply in it ? We have Inftances of this Nature of Toads, found in Stones, but they are fo extraordinary, that they cannot be repeated too often.

The Lovers of Nature, will read with Pleafure, the natural Hiftory of the Dutchies of *Crain* and *Stiria*, it has fomething very furprizing. — The *Grotto* full of vegetating Stones, where the River *Poig* is loft under Ground ; — the *Grotto* of *Sta Magdalena* ; — the two Lakes of *Cirknitz*, the fmalleft of which is full in the rainy Seafon of the Year ; the greateft is perpetually hid in the inward Parts of the Earth ; — the Mines of *Mercury* in *Iftria*, where that dangerous Metal often penetrates through the Pores of the Miners ; all thefe Articles are not to be parallel'd.

PART II.   Q   The

The Author gives an adv:
Idea of *Vienna*. There are fewei
than at *Paris*, and they havi
grand an Appearance, but in Rei
are finer and larger. The I
Schwartzemberg, where two succe
feffors fpent 600,000 Crowns, r
do by much the Hotels in *P.*
gives a complete Defcription (
Eugene's magnificent Palace. T
a Report it had been deftroyed
heard fince it was only inconfid
maged.

One muft expect to hear ·
then of miraculous Images and
There are Abundance of them in
There you find the Tooth of *Sta.*
who in the Court-Chappel, has
one built by *Ferdinand* III. —
fhe faved the Arch-duke *Leo*,
fuffered much at the cutting o
Teeth —Our Author gives us
that Kind of Miracles.—*Cunigon*
teau is more fingular. This En
preferved her virginal Purity, th
married to *Henry* II. It is tru
accufed, whilft living, of Adul
the Emperor's bad State of He
contribute to let her die as fhe
But at leaft, no Body fhould ha
that the Manteau of a Princefs

praifed for her Chaftity, and certainly acknowledged as barren, fhould help to
eafe Women's hard Deliveries. Yet it is on
thofe Occafions, that Ladies of the firft Rank,
put on her Manteau, doubtlefs, without neglecting to make Ufe of a good
Man-mid-wife. It is in this Manner
that *John de Neopumuc* prefides over the
Safety of Bridges, tho' he was thrown off
one of them, and drowned.

The Particulars about the Imperial Family and the Miniftry of *Charles* VI.
fall a great deal fhort of our Expectation,
The Author writes to his Correfpondent,
that a common Friend is to give him a
faithful Account of it. Now that People
can fpeak without Danger on this Subject,
we fhou'd be glad to have a Share in that
Correfpondence. Strange Things muft have
happened at that Court, fince fo early as
1719. Prince *Eugene* wanted to refign his
Places, and retire to his Library, where
he ufed to fay, he was in no Danger of
not paffing his Time agreeably.

The Queen of *Hungary*'s Elogy, is but
of one Line. She was full young in 1730,
to difcover that Steadinefs, that fuperior
Genius, which have enabled her fince to find
Helps and Forces fufficient to ftand a-
gainft five Powers, united for her Deftruction, and one of which, had alone,

for-

formerly overthrown the Hou
tho' ſtrengthened with the
Spain, and the *Indies*.

The Library at *Vienna* is very
The Author found in it a N
Chancellor *Iſaia de Puffendor*
he gives to the Court of *S*
aɛt Account of the Imperial N
as it was in 1675. Nature
in this Piece ; in it are
plained the Cauſes of the We
Houſe of *Auſtria*, at the ſame
was in Poſſeſſion of a great Pa
and the *Indies*. A Power canno
midable, whilſt its Miniſters glo
ing the Finances, and whil
Fryars and *Jeſuits* have
Ear and the Miniſter's Vo
Diſpoſal.

The Particulars our Autho
the rich Mines in *Upper-Hun*
curious. The bad OEconomy of
has almoſt intirely deprived tl
of the Revenue of theſe Treaſ
nitz alone requires 8000 Wo
yet the clear Profit the la
had from all the Mines in *E*
not amount to above 60000
were immenſe, if all the Mi
reɛted with the ſame Regular

duſtry, which is admired in the Management of the *Hartz-Works*. ——The Ore
there is ſo rich, that at *Cremnitz* it gives
ſometimes 35 Ounces of Silver in the
Hundred ; and ſometimes the two Thirds
of thoſe 35 are Gold. The Curious,
and thoſe that underſtand that Trade, will
read with Pleaſure in this Book an Account of all the Methods made Uſe of
in *Hungary*, to make thoſe Minerals turn
out to the beſt Account.

The *Tocai* Vines are another rich Preſent of Nature, more profitable yet than
Cremnitz, *Schemnitz*, and the *Seven Towns*
on the Mountains. The Author makes it
of a larger Extent than is commonly
imagined, he fixes the Circumference at
ſeven *Hungarian* Leagues, or eighty-four
Engliſh Miles. What a Pity; that the greateſt Part of ſuch a rich Soil ſhould be
unmanured. The *French* better know how
to improve their Advantages. They make
more of their Vineyards, than the *Spaniards* of *Peru*. —— The Author
ſpeaking of the golden Grains found in
the *Tocai* Vines and Grapes, ſays he ſaw
in *Goſlar*, at Mr. *Schluter*'s, Braſs which
vegetated through the Holes and Pores of
an old Beam. The ſame is to be ſeen
in *Holland* at Mr. *Schlem de Clauſthal*, who
willingly ſhews it to Strangers. Theſe
Inſtances

Inftances add a great Strength
Mr. *Tournefort* gives of the
Stones.

Inftead of an Inquifition
Proteftants, they have in
Trials for Witchcraft. In va
Accufations banifhed from th
fonable World, that even in
were publickly profcribed b
they are yet fuffered in Count
norance is encouraged, and t
Reafons to do fo. The Judg
a Proteftant, was burned abou
ago with thirty-four Perfons,
Catholic gravely anfwered our
wondered at this barbarous E
the Man was certainly a
bulky as he was, he yet wei
Ounces and a Half. I fupp
weigh'd him in Water, acc
wife Method of *Adolphus S*
I obferve here with Pleafure
the many Bleffings the *Hun*
under their prefent Sovereig
is a Toleration of the P
ligion. They no more com
perfecuted in that faithful K
it is to be fuppofed, that th
cefs, in order to reward

(*r*) Remark of the Journalift.

fo well defended her, will confirm by juft and conformable Laws, the Toleration which they now enjoy only at Pleafure ; for good Laws can be expected but from good Princes.

. I cannot follow the Author in his Travels through *Germany.* Amongft other Places, he was at *Drefden,* where he faw the great Vault fo much talk'd of. There is a prodigious Quantity of Jewels, and Mafter-pieces of both Nature and Art. The Author gives the Preference to this Treafure over that of *Medicis,* for Pleafantnefs and good Order, and to the latter over the firft for the Value. ——The *Arfenal* excells as much in its Kind. They keep in it Arms for a hundred thoufand Men, and fifteen hundred Brafs-Guns.

Our Author gives other curious Particulars he has feen at *Leipfic, Halle, Nuremberg, Ratisbonne,* and in *Lorrain.* His Book certainly deferves to be tranflated into *Englifh* ; I wifh fome able Pen would undertake it. The Author's indefatigable Curiofity, his Veracity and good Tafte merits that more than one Nation fhould be obliged to him.

The Book has two Appendixes. The Firft is a military Topography of the *Black Foreft,* made by *French* Engineers. I hope
they

they will not want it any
the Entrance into *Germany*,
fhut to them. In the Secor
Author defcribes the Redi
Sweden, under the Reign
They ruined the Nobility
difing the Prince. The
their Turn; they lowered
thority, and put it as mu
ancient Limits, as it had got
under the two preceding R

A R T I C L I

The *Memoirs* of the *Roya*
the Year 1739, conti

MR. *Buffon* continues h
on Timber. He gav
Memoir on the Means of ;
for Service, ftrong and dur
now gives another, with a
Experiments he made in p
which I fhall relate in few
  He planted a Piece of L
eleven Acres; three of then

(a) See Part I. of this Journal, pag.
(b) Ibid pag. 13.

led, the reft was Plough-Land. He divided it into feveral Parts, each of which was managed in a different Manner. In fome, he only broke up the Ground, others were ploughed twice, others again three Times. In fome, the Acorn was fowed immediately after the Ground was broke up with a Hoe, and without ploughing; in others, the Acorn was carelefsly thrown on the Surface, or placed with the Hand in the Grafs. In feveral, he planted fmall Trees, taken out of his Woods; in others, he planted alfo fmall Trees of the fame Kind, but that were taken out of his Nurferies. Some were planted in Autumn, others in the Spring; fome an Inch, others fix Inches deep: In others, he fowed Acorns, which had been fteeped before in feveral Liquors, as in clear Water, in Lees, in Water drained of a Dunghill, or in Salt-Water. In fome of his Plantations, he fowed Acorns mixed with Oats; in feveral others, he fowed fome taken out of another Soil, where they were beginning to fhoot up. All of them were fowed one by one, and at a Foot Diftance from one another. Such were the Beginnings of this new Plantation. Here is the Condition it was in the Year following.

PART II,   R   In

In the Plantation from w
fon had the greateſt Hope:
had been ploughed three Ti
eſt Part of the Acorns ha
peared ; the young Oaks, wl
Acorns produced, appeared
later End of *June* ; they we
and the Leaf yellowiſh
ing.—That Part of the Pla
was ploughed but twice, a
alſo been ſowed before the
ceeded ſomewhat better tl
The Third that had only
broke up, was ſomewhat b
Second. By this Tryal, Mr.
that thoſe Soils that are ſtroi
with Clay, as this was, a
ploughed and ſowed before
is confirmed from the Conditi
Plantations were in.

Thoſe that had been ploug
ed in the Spring, were attende
Succeſs. But what ſurpriſed
was, that thoſe Places where
had been ſowed in the Grou
broke up with the Hoe, wer
better ſtored, than the others.
Places where the Acorn had b
yered with the Graſs, tho' Part
ied away by Winds, were)
well. The Plantations, where th
ſowed ſix Inches deep, had

than thofe where it was fowed an Inch,
or two deep. That Acorn that was kept
for a Week in Lees or in Water drained
off a Dunghill, fprung out earlier than
others. Of the Trees, which Mr. *Buffon*
had taken out of his Woods, very few
out-lived the firft, or fecond, Year, whilft
all thofe that were taken out of his Nurferies anfwered; few of the Seeds fail'd,
that were taken out of the Ground while
they were beginning to fhoot up and were
fowed in the Spring.

From this Mr. *Buffon* infers, that to fow
with Succefs in a ftrong and clayifh Soil,
the Acorn muft be kept during the Winter
in the Ground thus,—Firft make a Lay,
or Bed of Acorns about two Inches, and
then a Lay of Earth half a Foot deep, and
fo on alternately.—Then cover the Whole
with Earth a Foot deep, for fear of the
Froft. The Acorn muft be taken up in
the Beginning of March, and planted at
a Foot Diftance. Thefe Acorns fo prepared are already as many little Oaks,
and fuch a Plantation is in no Danger of failing. The Coft is not much,
as it required but a fingle ploughing.
Nay it would be attended with no Expence at all, if it were poffible to preferve from Birds, the Acorn placed under
Grafs with the Hand; for it finks of

itfelf.

itſelf, and ſucceeds even to a Wonder in un-
tilled Lands, that have a thick Sod, which
generally denotes, that the Soil is ſtrong,
and mixed with Clay.

I think (c) ſome Means may be contrived to ſave the Acorn from Birds. One
of the eaſieſt, and moſt obvious, wou'd
be to plant about each Acorn a few Thorns,
and interweave ſome more a-croſs the up-
right ones. The Fence ſhou'd be made pretty
ſtrong becauſe the Rooks, Jackdaws, and
Mag-pies, which in this Kingdom wou'd
be the chief, if not the only, Deſtroyers
of your Acorns, are ſtrong bill'd Birds.
The making of this little Fence wou'd be
indeed ſomewhat troubleſome, and expen-
ſive. But then there wou'd be no Occaſion ever to do it again, becauſe the very
next Year, your Seed being changed into
Trees, your Plantation wou'd not be expoſed
to the ſame Danger.

I believe the Labours, and Expence of
making up ſuch little Fences, wou'd not
be near ſo conſiderable, as giving the Land
even one ſingle ploughing.

Thoſe that are fond of the Natural
Hiſtory of Animals, will be pleaſed with
the Obſervations Mr. *Morand* has began on
the,

___

(c) Remarks of the Journaliſt.

the Anatomy of the *Leech,* and which are to be continued in other Volumes of these Memoirs. The Author passes by the Description given by others, and confines himself solely to the Structure of it's Parts.

He shews, that what has been taken by Anatomists for the Mouth of the *Leech,* is of no other Service to it but to cut the Skin of other Animals, and to suck their Blood. He takes Notice, that from the Extremity of the Body, which represents the Head, to the Entry of the *Oesophagus,* there are five different Parts that may be distinctly perceived, a Cavity, which is properly the Mouth,—Instruments to cut, — others to suck,—and a Gullet to swallow. Mr. *Morand* makes many curious Observations, on each of those Parts, and their Dependencies, but which cannot be made sensible unless the Figures be joined to his Descriptions, and on this Article I am forced to refer my Readers to the Book itself.

I may, however, without the Figures, venture to relate what he says on the Respiration of the *Leech.* According to our Author, there is Reason to believe the *Leech* breatheth through the Mouth, but what Part serves for the Lungs is yet unknown. All he could discover is, that they have Motions analogous

gous to thofe of Refpirat
this Difcovery, he purfue
Method. After having de
for many Days in cold
they were motionlefs, as i
placed by the Fire the Bot
were. As foon as they fel
began to recover and
Heat encreafing, all the *I*
then were fticking by the
the Bottle, loofed their He
faften'd by the Tail, and
Body alternate and *Ifochrone*
refembling much thofe of
and fuch as if it had fho
become uneafy in a warme

These Motions were ve
ftill regular, when the B
nearer the Fire, and when
further from it, they aba
Heat.

Here is a very curious
celebrated Mr. *Reaumur*,
Art of making a new Kin
Means extremely plain and e
form Glafs into China. I. M
in is examined the Naure an
the new China, *and a g*
given of the Way of m

_____

(d) *Ifochrone* equal in Time, in the fa

The cleareſt Notion we can have of the Nature of *China*, of its eſſential and diſtinguiſhing Quality, is to look upon it as a Matter half vitrify'd, a Medium between Earth-ware and Glaſs. This Notion is what led Mr. *Reaumur* into the true Way of making *China*, as he has explained it in ſeveral Memoirs preſented to the Royal Academy in 1727 and 1729. There he lays down two general Ways of making *China*. The firſt is to take a vitrifying Matter juſt at the Time that it begins to paſs from the State of Earthen ware into that of Glaſs, and when the Fire makes the ſtrongeſt Impreſſion upon it; in ſhort when it is but imperfectly vitrify'd. The ſecond Way is to make a Paſte of two pulveriſed Matters; the firſt of them to be able to reſiſt the hotteſt Fire, without being vitrify'd, the other to be eaſily vitrify'd

This Paſte ſo prepared is put into an Oven, where that Part of it which is ſuſceptible of being vitrify'd becomes Glaſs, whilſt the other only hardens, and the whole is *China*.

All the *China* that was made in *Europe* till now, whether at *St. Cloud*, at *St. Anthony*, at *Chantilly* in *France*, or in *Saxony*, was made according to the firſt Method. Tho' ſome Pieces of it are beautiful,

tiful, and equal to that
China, yet it is eafy to
a different Nature from th
ing to the fecond Method
Pieces of the firft to a ftr
that which made them v
vitrifies them intirely, and
they become Glafs. On
China imported from that
which it takes its Name
the ftrongeft Fire withou
into Glafs.

This Theory hath led M
Difcovery of the two
dients in *China,* and he has
are the *Petunfe* and the *P*
it is compofed.

He mentions in this A
Way of making *China,*
alone. If this *China* is n
old one (for the Author
this laft Experiment to P
has all the effential Qualit
even fome fuperior to it;
Advantage, that this *China*
more than bare Earthen-w
Ingredient to transform Gl
is *Parget* Stone, or *Talc.*
produce that Transformation,
a Mixture of white Sand, w
Stone; this Mixture, is pref

or Sand alone. The Sand, or the Mixture of both, muſt be well calcined and reduced into Powder, and this done, the reſt is very eaſy; here is the whole Myſtery. —Take one of thoſe large Earthen-Veſſels which the Potters make Uſe of. Put in that, or in any other Kind of large Crucible, the Glaſs which you want to turn into *China*. Fill your Glaſſes, and all the empty Places round about them with your Powder mixed of white Sand and *Parget* Stone. Take Care that the Powder touch the Glaſs Veſſels on all Sides; that is to ſay, that thoſe Veſſels neither touch one another, nor the Sides of the Crucible. The Powder being well preſſed hard, you muſt cover the Veſſel or Crucible with Clay. This being done, Fire muſt perform the reſt.—— The Veſſel muſt be carried to a Potter to be placed in his Oven, where the Fire acts with the greateſt Strength. When he takes his Earthen-ware out of the Oven take you alſo your Veſſel out, open it, and you will have the Pleaſure to ſee your Glaſs turn'd into a fine white *China*, which has this Advantage over all others that it holds any boiling Liquor, or may be put on the Fire without any Danger of it's breaking.—The above Powder may ſerve

PART II.   S   many

many Times. Mr. *Reaumer* is to continue his Obfervations on this Subject, of which I intend to give an Account in fome other Part of this Journal.

The laft Memoir I fhall mention for the Prefent comes from Mr. *Sauvages de la Croix*, and treats of fome venemous Plants, *viz.* the *Doronic*, the *Actea* of *Pliny*, or the *Chriftophoriana* of *Odonius*; the *Colchicum*, the *Belladona*, the *Cherry-colour Laurel*, the *Rofe-colour-Laurel*, the *Plumbago*, and efpecially, the *Coriaria*, called otherwife *Rhus Sylveftris Plin.* or *Rhus myrtifolia Monfpeliaca*. It is alfo called *Tanners-Plant*, becaufe the Tanners make Ufe of it to prepare their Leather. I fhall fpeak only of this laft, as being the moft dangerous.

The Ancients thought the *Coriaria* good againft many Diforders, yet it is one of the moft furprifing Poyfons, as it renders Epileptic thofe Men that eat of its Fruits, or caufes a fwimming in the Head of thofe Animals, which feed on its young Shoots. Here is an Inftance of it which I faw fome Years ago, " *fays Mr. Sauvages*, " in the Country in fome Kids and Lambs, " which at their Return from feeding were " ftaggering, and at laft fell down with excef- " five tremblings and convulfive Motions.
" They

" They rofe up again, but for fome Time
" held the Head down, and ran their
" Heads againft every Thing they met
" in their Way. They ufed to re-
" main for whole Hours in that Con-
" dition."

Some Shepherds being afked what was
the Meaning of this, anfwered, that thefe
Beafts had eat of a certain Plant (the
Coriaria) which had conftantly that Effect
on them;—that the young ones only were
effected in this Manner, the Old taking great
Care to avoid it. They added, that this
Drunkennefs was of no manner of Confequence. Mr. *Sauvages* had the Experiment repeated before his Eyes, and he took Notice, that thofe Animals eat only the
young and tender Leaves; the old Leaves
and the Fruits are a quick Poifon, but
the Shoots only caufe a Swimming in
the Head. This Obfervation confirms Mr.
Linnæus's Opinion, *viz.* That the young
Shoots of fome very venomous Plants may
be falutary. In *Lapland*, they eat by way
of Sallat the young Leaves of a very venomous Plant *(e)*, and in *France* they eat
the young Shoots of the *Clematitis five Flam-
mula repens* C. B. tho' Beggars make Ufe of

S 2

the

(e) Called in *French* l' *Aconit bleu*, or *Napel*, I believe
it is the *Hemlock*.

the old Leaves to caufe Ulcers in their Legs; for which Reafon, this Plant was called the *Beggars Plant*.

The *Coriaria* is as pernicious to Men as to Animals. To prove it, our Author relates the two following Facts.—A Child of ten Years of Age, eat by miftake fome of the Fruit of the *Coriaria* : He came home, fell fuddenly in Epileptic Fits fo violent, that he died the next Day, tho' all poffible Endeavours were ufed to fave him.———A Man about forty Years old, imprudently eat fifteen of thofe Fruits, and foon after he had two Attacks of Epilepfy. He was bled, but the Fits ftill continuing, he was carried to the *Hotel-Dieu*. Mr. *Sauvages* being called to his Relief, found him in Convulfions, having loft his Senfes, of a livid Colour, ready to fall from his Bed, thofe that were about him not having the Courage to help him. In the Interval between two of his Fits, he took the Emetic, and voided nine of thofe Fruits of *Coriaria*, but that did not prevent his dying towards the Evening, at the Fifteenth Fit. His Body being opened, they found in the Stomach five or fix Berries of that Plant, but perceived no Alteration either in the Brains, or in the Ventricle, nor any where elfe. Mr. *Sauvages* now fully convinced, that the *Coriaria* is

a

a moſt dangerous Poiſon, made this unhappy Accident as public as much as he could, and he now gives this Memoir as a Warning to the Public, to avoid that pernicious Plant.

ARTICLE VIII.

Ausfurlicher Bericht von der *Trankenbariſ-cben Miſſion :* Mit drey und funfzig Continuationen.

That is to ſay,

A full Account of the *Miſſions* in *Trankebar* in 4°. with fifty-three Continuations. *Hall* 1710—1743. In ſo many Volumes in 4° containing about 10000 Pages with Figures.

IF the Public has read with Pleaſure in the firſt Part of this Journal, the Relation of a Proteſtant Miſſion in (a) *Groenland*, I have Reaſon to hope, the Hiſtory

(a) The Reader, I believe, will be glad to know that the Miſſion ſettled in *Greenland* by Mr. *Egede*, has been carried on by the now reigning King of *Denmark*, with ſo much Zeal, that it has made a very conſiderable Progreſs.

History of a more considerable
the *East-Indies*, which is but
perfectly known, will be at lea
liked.

As to the natural, civil, o
History of the Coasts of *Malaba*
Topography of the little Ki
Tan-jaour, where the *Danish* N
chiefly reside, I think it needle
take any Notice of such Thing
them to Geographers, Historia
ralists, and Travellers. I shall alm
my self in this Abstract to what c
Religion.

Before I proceed to religiou
I think it worth while to ob
the Generality of the People o
of *Malabar* are black. But
mines, (c), and *Marattes* (d), a

(b) In my Abstract of the *Danish* Missio
I gave a pretty large Description of the Co
Inhabitants. The Reason of it was, that
and People, were but little known ; where
European Nations, and particularly the *En*
a considerable Trade on the Coasts of *Malab*
sufficiently informed of every Thing remark
kept the Progress of the Protestant Religio
and Travellers being generally little sollicit
sative about that.

(c) *Bramines* their Priests: —They are en
Profession by their Birth. But besides them,
Ministers of Religion, who have no other
their own will.

(d) *Marattes*, an eminent Set of People

brown and yellow; in a Word, very like a tawny *Portuguese.*

The *Pareics,* which is the lowest *Cast,* and do the meanest and most laborious Offices, are incomparably blacker than all the other *Casts* of the Nation. This, as my Author observes, confirms a very probable Notion, which some late Authors have taxed with Absurdity, *viz.*—That Men are all of one and the same Species, and that the Differences between the three general Sorts, or Classes, the White, the Black, and the Red, are occasioned by the Difference of Climate, manner of dressing, and rearing the Children, or, in short, by some Thing merely accidental.

Another Particular I think fit here to mention, is that they eat very little Flesh-meat. The *Europeans* themselves abstain from it. There are no Markets for Butchers-meat. They are satisfied with some Poultry, some Kids, and Fish. A *Metempsychosis,* or Transmigration of Souls, tho' generally believed by the *Indian Gentiles,* yet, says my Author, is not perhaps the true Reason of that Law, whereby they are forbidden to kill any Kind of Cattle. It may be, that Law was made by some wise ancient King, who considered the bad Effects of a Food, which in

that

that hot Country is fo liable to Putrefaction, or who thought it very advifeable, to fpare as much as poffible the
Beafts, that ferve in the neceffary Work
of Agriculture, fuch Beafts being hard to
rear in that Country, and never growing
to be bulky and ftrong. One Thing,
which confirms that Conjecture, is, that
of all the Beafts, a Cow is the moft re-
garded, and that the poor Fifhes are never the better for the Tranfmigration of
Souls. They do no Work for Man,
and Man eats them even in *Malabar*.

Thus our Authors. But their Conjecture
does not feem to me to be well grounded. It
is evident indeed, that their fpecial regard for
Cows, and other Beafts, which by their Milk,
or by their Labour in the Works of
Agriculture, are very ferviceable to Mankind, is to be accounted for from the
Inoffenfivenefs and Ufefulnefs of thofe
Beafts ; and thence it follows, that the
Malabares are much more averfe to the
deftroying, or hurting of that Sort of Cattle
than any other living Creatures : But it does
not follow, that the Law in queftion, is
not founded on their Belief of the Tranfmigration of Souls ; for it is well known,
that that Law or Scruple, extends to
all Kinds of Animals ; whereas, had it
ne

no other Foundation, or had it been made with no other View, than sparing the Lives of all serviceable Animals, which, from the Nature of the Climate and Soil, are scarce and lean in that Country, we may upon good Grounds conjecture it wou'd have been confined to them.

The Liberty allowed the Inhabitants of eating Fish, may be look'd upon as an Exception to the aforesaid Universal Law. And probably, the Reasons of that Exception are, First, that they look upon Fishes as the brutest Part of the Brute Creation, and Secondly, and chiefly, that when Rice, their chief Food, happens to fail, Fish, whereof they have great Plenty on their Coasts, is a great Relief to them. It is then a Kind of Necessity to feed on Fish ; and Necessity has no Law.

Besides their Belief of the *Metempsychosis*, they are remarkable for their Compassion, and Benevolence to every Creature, which they judge capable of any Degree of Pleasure or Pain. And that Principle alone carried to a great Length, and superstitiously spun out in minute Consequences, may make them too tender-hearted, nay, hospitable to all Sorts of Beasts, even to obnoxious Insects *(e)*.

PART II.   T   The

<hr>

(e) Remark of the Journalist.

The great Folks, and especially the *Marattes*, have not the same Regard for Beasts. They see them without any Scruple dish'd up, and served on their Tables.

Notwithstanding the tyrannical Government, and consequently the Poverty, and Dejectedness, those unhappy People live under, they addict themselves to Arts and Sciences, and are much more proficient in them, than could be expected in such Circumstances.

Their Religion is in some Things most admirable, in other Respects, strangely absurd.

What we call Charity, or the most extensive Benevolence, is their favourite Virtue. Even all Manner of Beasts, as has been occasionally observed before, are the Objects of it. It is by that they expect to be saved.

But the established, or reigning, Faith, and Worship, are the grossest *Paganism.* Yet a Kind of *Deism*, not very unreasonable, obtains among their Learned. When we upbraid them with the Absurdity of their Belief, and the foolish Idea they have of the Deity, they know very well how to distinguish between the Doctrine of the Learned, and the Doctrine of the Vulgar. They then tell you, that that same God, whom

whom they reprefent with five Faces, a Stag in his Hand, and fome other much more unbecoming Things about him, is in Reality, immaterial, invifible, omniprefent, and that his true Name is *The Supreme Being*. The Miffionaries met every where with Phyficians, Philofophers, (*f*) *Pandarams*, and even *Bramines*, who frankly own that their Gods, and their Idols, are only for the People; that all our Adorations are due to the true God alone; that legal Ablutions are utterly infignificant; that the only Means of pleafing the fupreme Being, is to follow the Rules of Uprightnefs and Charity. Their famous Poet *Tiku-walluwer* has wrote a Book of Morals, wherein he ridicules the Worfhip of the falfe Gods, and ftrenuoufly recommends Purity of Manners, and a profound Veneration for the one real God.

When the *Bramines* and *Pandarams* are obliged to confefs, that there is but one God; that confequently, he alone is to be adored, and are afked, why then they worfhip Idols, they hit upon the very fame Evafions, which are made Ufe of in *Europe* by a confiderable Church. We do not, fay they, worfhip a Marble

T 2 Block.

(*f*) A Set of religious and learned People.

Block. Thofe Figures ferve only to draw, and fix the Attention of the Vulgar, who are not capable of conceiving abftract Ideas of an immaterial God. 'Tis only in Appearance, or outwardly, that our religious Homage is offered to thofe Symbols. It belongs, and is intentionally directed, to the *Being of Beings*, the *Creator of all Things*, the *one only eternal God*.

Some of the moft refpected Sects among them, as their (g) *Gnanis*, or *Nianis*, their (b) *Tura-wark-bianes*, and their *Scaniacans* (i), far from paying to Idols any outward Homage, openly defpife the Gods, and Ceremonies of the Mob.

Other *Pandarams* find out fome Means to reconcile their Notions with Chriftianity. We have, fay they, three great Gods, who make but one God—There is your Trinity. The Second of thofe three Lords, thought fit to appear under a human Form—There is your Chrift. Upon

---

(g) *Gnanis*—learned Men, addicted to Contemplation, who profefs to defpife fenfual Pleafures, and are efteemed the moft perfect of Mankind.

(b) *Tura-wark-bianes*, a Sect deemed fublime, even among the *Gnanis*; or *Nianis*, and in the fame Principles.

(i) *Scaniacans* — The Word fignifies without *Blood*—whereby is meant, that they are, as it were, above Flefh and Blood.

on which my Author obferves, that that Parallel is very like the Explanations of the celebrated Prelate of *Condom*.

Some other learned Men go deeper in their Reafonings, and may juftly be compared to *Pirrhon*, *Montaigne*, *le Motte le Vayer*, and the like. However, Mr. *Ziegeubalg*, one of the chief, and lateft *Danifh* Miffionaries, to whom we are indebted for the freſheſt Part of this Account, affures us, that thofe Sceptics attack only fome difputable *Tenets* of the various *Malabarian* Sects; that they do by no Means deny a Deity, and that he did not meet with any *Atheifts* either among the *Hottentots*, or *Pagan* Authors in *Malabar*. But he has met with rakifh *Bramines*, who hoped for nothing after this Life, and made Happinefs to confift in gratifying our Senfes.

Their Authors, (I fuppofe my Author means fome of them) admit of a more than *Stoïcian Deftiny*, or *Fate*, which influences the Freedom of our Actions. They think that (k) *Bruma*, Creator of Mankind, has written on the Skull of every Man all his future Actions, and all the

(k) *Bruma*. That is the Name of one of their three great Gods.

the Events, which are to
They are fimple enough to take
Writing thofe little irregular I
are formed by the three princ
of the *Cranium.*

I muft confefs, when I re
of Divinity, I could not forl
into a loud Laughter. But i
lection, I foon grew grave aga
quickly into my Mind, that
Ages, we *Europeans* have ha
fomething fully as ridiculou
ought I know, ftill retain a
it in many Parts of *Europe*—
diciary Aftrology, *Chiromancy*,
Truly, it is lefs foolifh, to b
Man's Actions, and the Event
are engraved on his Head, tl
they are pictured in the Star
Palm of one's Hand (*l*).

Metemyfychofis is a fundame
their Religion. It has been
before any Thing we find re
Greek Hiftories, (*m*) and to
believed with the greateft Cr
Englifh Captain was convin
Strength of their Faith in

(*l*) Reflection of the Journalift.

(*m*) One wou'd be glad to know, whe
Author can make out this Point of Hif
logy.

by an Event well worth telling. He was trading along the Coast, and one Day, his Ship being becalm'd, he went a-shore to amuse himself with fowling. He unluckily shot a Bird they call *Perumal*, which has the Honour of serving one of their noblest Gods in the Quality of a *Saddle-Horse.*

A Man saw the Murder committed, and directly ran to alarm the neighbouring Villages. Crouds in an Instant gathered about the sacrilegious *Englishman*, seized him, and were going to put him to a cruel Death, when a *Mahometan* came nigh, and advised him to confess the Crime, and at the same Time, to alledge a good Excuse for killing the Bird. My poor Captain having received his Instruction, begged of the People to hear what he had to say. Silence being made ; *My Father*, says he, *died lately in a Voyage ; The Corps was flung over-board, and his Soul went directly into the Body of a Fish, which the* Perumal *was going to devour. Pray, good People, could I bear to see my Father torn to pieces ?*

The wise Men of the Place were struck with the Apology. They fairly acquitted him. And the Trial cost the Gentleman no more than some Pieces of
Gold,

Gold, wherewith he rewarded
Counfellor.

This *Metempfychofis*, is the
Purgatory. Aceording to the
cal Syftem, they, who have
formable to the Laws of N
rectly to a State of Happines
fay the *Malabarian* Divine
few. The far greater Part
have fome favourite Vice,
on their Souls after Death
ther Body. The Soul of an
narch into the Body of a H
Beggar. — The Soul of a
whofe Conduct did not anfw
ledge, into the Body of a
(*n*) I fuppofe the Reade
with me at the Punifhment
the vicious learned Man.

This Article of their Theo
have been fuggefted by t
they groan under, by the ju
have of the Bafenefs of Ty
probable Suppofition, that a l
be tortur'd with inward Ren
the proper Inference from i
withftanding his outward
his Enjoyment of fenfual P
but a contemptible, odious,
Man.

(*n*) Reflection of the Journalift.

At the great Day of Judgment, the Souls of the Impious are to come forth under the Form of a Worm, or some unclean Animal. In that Condition, they shall expiate their Sins, till by Amendment they deserve to be admitted into the Country of the Gods.

The *Malabares* (o), it seems, have, in a great Measure, the same Way of thinking with the famous *Origen*.

They are very desirous, and use their best Endeavours, to obtain a State of Bliss in another Life. To that End (and this, as has been said before, they lay the greatest Stress on) they do Abundance of Works of Charity, many of them for the public Good.

Such is their Opinion of the Excellency of Beneficence, that one of the chief Difficulties, which the *Bramines* oppose to the Labours of the Christian Missionaries, consists in representing to the People, that it is a Shame to give these Strangers an Opportunity of doing so much good as will entitle them to the most eminent Rewards. The Honour of Generosity, it seems, and the Blessings annexed to it, they are so jealous of, that they would keep it to themselves as much as

PART II.　　　　U　　　　　　they

(o Reflection of the Journalist.

they can of such invalu
tages.

(p) This Effect of national
Patriotism, has something in i
ly comical : But, however,
imply a noble Sort of P
shews, that some *eastern*
of a better Kind than many
nities.

Legal Ablutions are a sec
good Works. Penance is
this, they fairly outdo all E
all Proportion. I shall only
or two Instances among man
pose themselves quite naked
less, for a whole Month, to
Beams of the Sun. Others
or Arm, a-loft so long, that
having, by that constant Ina
their Power, the Member rem
stiff, useless, and cumbersome.

They have also a Notion
ring Sins. They clap them on
a Cow, and some good B,
unto himself both the Sir
Beast.

The thinking People a
have a pretty rational and c
tion of celestial Happiness. 7

(p) Reflection of the Journalist.

dife of the Vulgar much refembles the Paradife of *Mahomet*.

Their Hell is material, and very near the *fame as we fee it in many *European* Pictures: But what they call Hell, is in Reality, but a Purgatory; for, after three or four Centuries, the Souls get out, and come into this World again in the Body of fome Animal.

In my Opinion (q) there is here fome Confufion in my Author's Account. He told us, above, that after the Day of Judgment, the Impious under the Form of a Worm, expiate their Sins, till, by Amendment, they have fitted themfelves to be received among the Bleffed; and here he tells us, that after having undergone fuch Torments, as burning, or the like, they come into this World again in the Body of fome Animal.

Probably he means, that they have two different Hells—The one before the Day of Judgment—The other after; and, neither indeed is properly a Hell, but only a Purgatory. For from this Relation it is evident, they have no Notion of everlafting Punifhment.

It appears by their Books, that an Univerfal Deluge, a final Conflagration of the

U 2   World,

(q) Remark of the Journalift.

World, and a Day of Judgment, have been believed among them Time out of Mind.

They believe there are *Demons*, which may poſſeſs the Bodies of Men. Accordingly, they have proper Exorciſms to drive them out. Yet thoſe pretended *Demoniacs* are certainly no more than diſorder'd Perſons. The Impoſtures of the Exorciſts have been frequently diſcovered by the Miſſionaries.

(r) Strange, and cruel, are ſometimes the Effects of Ignorance. In the *eaſtern* Parts of *Europe*—On the Coaſts of *Barbary*—In the Kingdom of *Morocco*, and ſome other Countries, People are ſo infatuated with that Notion, that ſometimes they will not ſuffer a miſerable Creature diſtorted by Convulſions, or rack'd by ſome other violent Diſorder, to be attended by a Phyſician or Surgeon, becauſe truly where the Cauſe of the Evil is ſupernatural, it would be prepoſterous to employ natural, or phyſical Remedies (s). Thus it frequently happens, that a falſe Theory is

attended

(r) Remark of the Journaliſt.

(s) See Revol, of the Kingdom of *Morocco*, by Captain Braithwait.—*Anno* 1727.

See alſo—*Voyages de Tournefort au Levant*—and particularly, the Hiſtory of a Woman, who died of Convulſions. You may ſee alſo —*Voyages de Dermarchais, en Afrique,* &c.

attended with fad practical Confequences.

The *Pagans* in the *Eaft Indies* have no Books to rule their Faith : Nor is there a Head of the Church. And therefore, fays my Author, it is not furprifing. they are divided into 360 different Sects. It is true, continues he, Toleration reigns among them all ; and the reigning Principle is—*That Men, who obey the Law of Nature, fhall be faved, whatever Religion they may profefs.*

(t) I fet fo much value on that thorough Toleration, and that charitable Principle of theirs, that with me, I confefs, they do in fome Meafure make Amends for their grofs Superftitions. And their ridiculous (u) *Pagodas*, pompoufly fet up in our Temples, would not be a more fhocking Sight than a *Spanifh* Tribunal of Inquifition erected in this Kingdom.

They have what they call *Wedams*, four in Number, which contain their Doctrine. Thofe *Wedams* are not committed to writing. Their *Bramines* learn them by Heart, as did of old the *Druids* (w).

Six

(t) Reflection of the Journalift.
(u) *Pagoda*,—an *Indian* Idol.
(w) *Druid*, *Pagan* Priefts in *Gaul*.

Six Books of an inferior
them for a System of Div
the Doctrine of the *Wedams*
cally laid down.

Eighteen other Books a
Comments on the above
which, sacred Books they hav
treat of Morals and several S
all are wrote in what they
ed Language, a Language qu
to the Vulgar, and even
their learned Folks. Thereby
become absolute Rulers in N
ligion.

Here (x) my Author falls
ing Contradiction. First he
Malabares have no Books
Faith (See the preceding page)
informs us their *Wedam*, or
tain their Doctrine. It is tr
dams cannot properly be
because they are not in Writ
Effect is the same; and beside
mentaries are in writing; w
People have for those Book
or near the same, Regard,
our Holy Scriptures, does
fwer the very same End. No
blind Obedience to their Pr

(x) Observation of the Journalist.

pears, they have some such Regard. I
with my Author had better cleared up this
Matter.

Among those of their speculative Notions, which my Author justly calls dangerous, is their Opinion of the Origin of
Evil. They believe that Corruption, or
Vice, is born with Man ; that Wicked-
ness is in our very Essence ; that God
has imprinted the Characters of it on the
Body of every Child in the Mother's
Womb. But then they tell you, one may
get the better of it by Contemplation and
good Works.

Whether (y) they mean, that we are
very peaceable Creatures, and even naturally
very prone to Sin ; or whether they mean
that we are necessitated to do Evil, I cannot from the above confuse Phrases determine.

If they are consistent with themselves
they do not (and in Equity, we ought not
to) lay the utmost Stress on their Expressions, for from their observing and main-
taining, that by Contemplation, and good
Works, we can conquer that supposed
innate Viciousness, is evidently to be in-
ferr'd, they do not think we are under
the dismal Necessity of yielding to our
evil

(y) Observation of the Journalist.

evil Inclinations. So that
Tenet of theirs is not in R
rible, as it does at firſt appear
it produces very terrible Effe
my Author obſerves, it is the
monly alledged by vicious P
them, when cenſured for
duct.

(z) My Author never fai
Parallel between the *Malabar*
and the Doctrine and Worſ
tain famous Church in *Eu*
only here and there tranſlated
Strokes. I thought it prope
to the intelligent Reader, to
the Particulars of the Comp
ever it may hold. And it w
be wiſh'd, that ſame Parallel
any, even the minuteſt, Poi
Chriſtian Society, beſides th
Author had in View.

The Virtues chiefly recomm
them are the very ſame, wl
viour enjoins. They carry
ſo far as to condemn inter
which cannot be the Object
Laws.

Upon this, my Author ma
table Obſervation.——The Di

tween moral Good and moral Evil, muſt be very eſſential, and very eaſily diſtinguiſhed, ſince all Sects, and Nations, are ſenſible of it.

(aa) The *Indian* under the *Torrid-Zone*, —The *Groenlander* in the frozen Regions of the *Artick-Pole* —The *Hottentot* in a temperate Climate —The South and North *European*—all ſhew you the moral Senſe ſo interwoven in our Frame, ſo rooted in our Hearts, that under the ſtrongeſt Prejudices, and even in the hurry of violent Paſſions, it will not only ſubſiſt, and be felt, but frequently, maugre all Oppoſition, break forth in Acts of Sociableneſs and Generoſity.

To thoſe diſtant People, not to the Generality of *Europeans*, wou'd I apply for the true Knowledge of human Nature. From our very Cradle we, polite Nations, are ſo modell'd, and dreſs'd up, according to a Multitude of ſtrange Examples, Cuſtoms, and Prejudices, and ſoon after ſo diſtracted by claſhing Intereſts—ſo disfigured by filthy Exceſſes, and hoſtile Paſſions, that we muſt appear to one another, and even to our ſelves, under a frightful Aſpect : And when, by Dint of Thought and Labour, we have torn away

PART II. X the

(aa) Reflection of the Journaliſt.

the Difguife, recovered our
nefs and Benevolence, fmootl
tenances, or rub'd off the L
and improved our in-born r
then we are apt prefumptuc
gine it is not only our o
Superftructure, but forfooth
mental Work of the Creat
had the Wifdom and Glory
Very near as inconfiderate i
ments, as the Sages of *M*
Demoniacs, we fuppofe ten
chievous Events to be occa
nate Depravity, which are m
fult of critical Circumftances,
Negligence, or (the moft coir
all) hafty Determination.

Certainly the *Groenlander*'
tot's, plain Honefty and goo
form me of our primary Conft
better than the deepeft Sp
many of our Moralifts ever

In another Part of this Jou
to give an Account of the I
and it's Succefs.

A I

ARTICLE IX.

Lettres de Calvin *a* Jaque *de* Bourgogne *seigneur de Falais & de Bredam*, & à son Epouse Jolande de Brederode, 8° Amst. 1744.

That is to say,

Letters *from* Calvin *to* James *of* Burgundy *Lord of Falais and Bredam*; and to his Wife Joland *of* Brederode, 8° pag. 228. besides 24 for the Preface.

THOSE who are fond of Eclesiastical 'History, and in particular of the History of Reformation, will be pleased with these Letters. *Calvin* acted so considerable a Part in that great Event, that whatever may afford an Opportunity of knowing his Character thoroughly, cannot but be well received, even by those that have no great Veneration for his Writings.

There can be no manner of doubt about the Authenticness of these Letters. They are of *Calvin*'s own Hand-writing. This is asserted by People who know it and have compared them with other original Writings of his; and the Editor of them did not scruple send
in

ing his Manufcript to *Geneva* to be repofited in the Public Library, where the moft Part of *Calvin*'s Manufcripts are kept. They are befides fealed with his own Seal.

He has painted himfelf in them better than in any other of his Works, and even better than he was aware of. He ftill appears a great Man with great Faults. That he had excellent Qualities is what no Body can deny, and tho' he was grofly abufed by the Monks, whofe Turpitude he difcovered, yet he cannot but be admired by more reafonable People, for his Difintereftednefs, and Courage. He lived for many Years in a State of Poverty, and gloried in it. His endeavouring, at the Hazard of his Life, and with the Lofs of whatever is valuable in the World, to reclaim the World from Popifh Errors and Tyranny, is an Action truly Apoftolical. To afcribe it to any other Motive but the Defire of doing good would certainly betray a ftrong Biafs to Uncharitablenefs.—And yet this fame Man was withal of a choleric, revengeful and overbearing Temper, efpecially in religious Affairs.—This Character is drawn from the whole Tenour of his Conduct, and from the Letters I am abftracting.

The Gentleman, to whom they are directed, would be perhaps very little known were not his Memory preferved in them.

There

There is but one Author, that I know
of, that has made any mention of him,
and this Author is very little depended
upon, whether with Reason or through
Prejudice, is what I don't pretend to determine; I mean *Bolsec* in his Letters.——
The Historians of the low Countries say,
that *Philip* the *Good*, Duke of *Burgundy*,
had above twelve natural Sons and Daugh-
ters, who were educated with all the
Care possible; and many of whom were
legitimated; Bishops, Abbots, Abbesses, Am-
bassadors, Chevaliers of the Golden Fleece,
Governors of Cities and Provinces, *&c.*
and that the Family was allied by Marriages to the most illustrious Houses of
that Country. In 1501 *Baudoin* one of
Philip's natural Sons was put by the Emperor *Maximilian* in Possession of *Falais*,
a Fief of *Brabant*, situated on the Borders of the County of *Namur*. *James
of Burgundy*, Lord of *Falais* and *Bredam*,
Grandson of *Baudoin*, received his Education at his Father's, at the Court of the
Emperor *Charles* V. From his fifteenth
Year he took a liking to the Doctrine of
the Protestants: He afterwards married
Joland of *Brederode* descended from the
ancient Counts of *Holland*, and Aunt to
Henry of *Brederode*, one of the chief Supports
of the Reformers, and celebrated in Histo-

ry

ry for being at the Head of the Four hundred Nobles, who prefented to the Governefs of the Low Countries, in 1566, that famous Petition, by which the Foundation of the Liberties of the united Provinces was laid. This Marriage encreafed the Sufpicions already conceived againft his Religion, which made him refolve to leave his Country, where he did not think himfelf any longer fafe. Immediately after his Retreat he was out-law'd, and his Poffeffions and Goods were confifcated. He often changed his Place of Abode after his Exile, having fettled himfelf firft at Cologne; afterwards at *Bafil*, and *Strafbourg*, and at laft at *Geneva*. We may judge he was a Man of great Worth by the Encomiums *Calvin* paffes upon him in his Dedicatory Epiftle at the Head of his Commentaries on the 1 Epiftle to the *Corinthians*. They kept up a clofe, friendly, and familiar Correfpondence together for near ten Years, and *Calvin* conftantly figned himfelf *his true Friend for ever*.

Neverthelefs this Intimacy did not laft *for ever*; fo far from it, that it turn'd into a moft inveterate Averfion.

The Difpute which one *Bolfec* a Phyfician had with *Calvin* was the Occafion of the latter's falling out with *Monfieur de Falais*. *Bolfec* difliked *Calvin*'s Doctrine on Predeftination;

tion; he constantly opposed him, and at last carried Matters so far as to attack him publicly when he was preaching. *Calvin* was not of a Temper to bear such a Contradiction. His Passion was raised to such a Heighth, that he aimed at causeing his Antagonist to be either put to Death, or at least kept for ever in a Dungeon. This, which bears so hard on *Calvin*'s Character, is plainly inferred from these Words in one of his Letters to the Churches of *Switzerland*, to whom he applied for their Approbation of his cruel Resentment, against *Bolsec*, as he did afterwards with respect to the unfortunate *Servetus* : " We are willing, says he, to " purge our Church of this Plague, and " to remove it in such a manner, that it " should not be in his Power to hurt " other Churches (a). *Bolsec* was put in Prison at *Calvin*'s Solicitation the 16th of *October* 1551. The Reason alledged to arrest him was, *that he had opposed Calvin's Doctrine, and occasion'd a great Scandal.* *Monsieur de Falais*, tho' *Calvin*'s intimate Friend, did not approve his revengeful and persecuting Disposition. He resolved

(a) *Calvin. Epist.* 133. *Ministris Helvetiis.*—" Nos vero " sic Ecclesiam nostram cupimus hac Peste purgari, ne inde fu- " gata vicinis noceat."

folved to fave, if poffible, I
was his Phyfician. The firft S
was, to endeavour to prevail o
drop his Purfuit, alledging for I
that as he (Mr. *Falais)* was
and as *Bolfec* was the only one
his Conftitution, he could not
Calvin was deaf to his Friend'
tation. Upon this *Monfieur de I*
to the Churches of *Switzerlan*
Friends he had among them,
ed their giving their Sanctio
Calvin had refolved to do. Th
er complains of this in ano
he wrote to the fame Churcl
he fays, that *the Anfwers he r*
them were not fo full and plai
expected and wifbed for. (*b*)
time *Calvin* broke with *Mon*
lais, and even perfecuted and
to withdraw from *Geneva,* a
the *Pays de Vaud. Let* Falais
fec, fays he, in one of his L
him write over to you that B
a bad Man; in that be onl
own Reputation to fave a Rog

(*b*) *Calvin. ep.* 134. *Miniftris Bafilienfibu*
" de quæftione nobis propofita dediftis min
" quidum, quam vos forte poftulabat, cert
" taque noftra ferebant."

does not know (*c*). He had dedicated to *Monfieur de Falais* his Commentary on 1 *Corinth.* but afterwards he took out that Name which had been formerly fo dear, and was now become fo odious to him, and dedicated the Commentary to the Marquis *de Vico*, with thefe words ; " O that I " had never known that Man, whofe Name " I am now forced to take off this Work " of mine ; or rather why did not I know " him " — What Spleen in a Man who every Day ufed to preach on Charity and Forgivenefs !

It is faid in *Bayle*'s Dictionary, (*d*) that " *James of Burgundy* Lord of *Falais* be- " came a Proteftant, but that being fcan- " dalifed at the Difputes that arofe at " *Geneva* between *Bolfec* and *Calvin*, the " Year 1551, he went aftray, as well as his " Wife, and left the Doctrine of the Reformed, " and their Church alfo." This Mr. *Bayle* copied from *Beza*, whom every Body knows to have been partial in favour of *Calvin*, who fpoke very ill of *Bolfec*, and who confequently was not inclined to fpeak advantageoufly of *Monfieur de Falais.*

From Mr. *Bayle*'s Words one would infer, that *Monfieur de Falais* went over

PART II.   Y   again

(*c*) *Epift.* 134. *Miniftris Bafilienfibus.*
(*d*) Article de Philippe de Bourgogne ; Remarque G. & Article de Calvin. Remarque FF.

again to the *Roman* Catholic Party ; yet
it is probable *Beza* meant only, that *Falais*
had forsaken the Church of *Geneva* to live
somewhere else, or that he had departed
from some of *Calvin's* favourite Tenets, which
he might well do, and be still a very good
Protestant. Had Mr. *Falais* turned Roman
Catholic, *Calvin* would not have slipt the
Opportunity of abusing him, nor would
the Writers of the Church of *Rome* have
neglected to transmit their Triumph to
Posterity ; and yet they are all silent a-
bout it : *Calvin* only says, " that *Falais*
" had withdrawn himself from him, and
" from the Church of *Geneva*."

From this we may infer, 1. That because *Calvin* had been publicly opposed
by *Bolsec* on the Article of *Predestination*,
he wanted either to put him to Death,
or to confine him for ever. 2. That he
fell out with one of his most intimate
Friends, because he hindered him from
acting such a bloody Scene, as that which
he acted some years after, in causing *Servetus* to be burned.

Castalio a good natured, pious, worthy
Man, and who knew by Experience this
fatal Disposition in *Calvin*, knew also how
to paint it, and did it in a very mild Manner considering the Times : Speaking of
the Church of *Geneva*, and of some others

in

in *Switzerland*, which were influenced by the same persecuting Principles, he expresses himself thus (e): " As they have a " greater Esteem for that uncharitable " Doctrine of their Church than for Cha- " rity itself, they decree as a certain and " undeniable Principle, that to recede from " the Doctrine is a greater Sin than to " do immoral Actions.—Therefore, tho' a " Man among them be very vicious, cove- " tous, a Backbiter, slanderous, deceitful, " envious, passionate, spiteful, provided he " agrees with them in their Opinion about " Baptism, — Predestination.— Free-will— " and the like ;—provided he resorts to Ser- " mons and Sacraments,—and has a great " Veneration for Preachers,—he is a Christ- " ian : Christ did wipe off his past, " present, and future Sins.

" But let a Man be free from all those " Vices, and put it out of their Power to " upbraid him with any Fault, if he only " differs from them in any of their Tenets, " as Baptism, Predestination, Free-will, or " *Persecution* ; he is an Heretic, and rot- " ten Member ; he must be cut off from " the Body of the Church. There is " no Charity, no Obedience to Christ's

Y 2 " Com-

(e) *De Hæreticis a Civili Magistratu non puniendis pro Martini Belli farragine adversus libellum Theodori Bezæ,* libellus MS.

" Commandments, no inoffensive Beha-
" viour, (which are the true Fruits of
" the true Doctrine, for the Tree of im-
" moral Doctrine cannot bear moral good
" Fruits) *nothing of the kind* shall recom-
" mend him to them, but he shall be re-
" jected as a Devil." *Then the Latin
adds*; . " We have many Instances of this,
" but especially in the Person of *Mon-
" sieur de Falais*, who, after he had been
" extolled to the Skies by *Calvin*, was
" by him sunk into Hell, as soon as he
" began to differ from him on Account
" of persecuting *Jerom* the Physician ;"
and in another Place he says, that on the
same Account, " *Calvin* proclaimed *Mon-
" sieur de Falais* an Heretic in a public
" Congregation *(f)*." By this Account of
Calvin's persecuting Spirit, not to mention
other Faults, which he might be accused of,
and wou'd also have prompted him to cruel
Deeds) few People, I believe, will doubt
his been afterwards the chief, if not the
only, Author of the unfortunate *Servetus's*
Death. This Point is very well cleared up in
several *(g) English* Writings, and for that

Reason,

(f) In publica Congregatione à Calvino judicatus est He-
reticus.

(g) See *Memoirs of Literature* Vol. IV.—*Benson's* Account of *Calvin* burning *Servetus*,—and *Chandler's* History
of Persecution.

Reafon, I fhall fay very little about it, tho' the Editor of thefe Letters mentions it, as well as the Author of *La Bibliotheque raifonnée*, who at the fame Time anfwers fome Things faid in the fame Journal to juftify, or excufe, *Calvin*'s Proceeding in that Refpect,—I think it appears by his own Writings, and by thofe of Cotemporary Authors: 1. That *Servetus* was condemned at *Grenoble* on the Evidences taken from Letters, which *Calvin* had fent to his Judges, and that he would have been put to Death there had he not made his Efcape. 2. That *Calvin* was *Servetus*'s Accufer and Profecutor at *Geneva*. 3. That when he undertook to profecute *Servetus* he knew, that, if his Charge of Herefy was proved, the Laws were fuch that he muft have fuffered Death. 4. That when it was moved in Council that the Laws againft Heretics fhould be repealed, or at leaft fufpended, the Motion was oppofed by his Friends, and that he himfelf fpoke publicly againft it. 5. That there had been for many Years a great Animofity between them, as appears by feveral abufive Letters they wrote to each other. 6. That at the Time of the Trial he was in hopes *Servetus* would not efcape Death (b).

7. That

(b) Spero capitale. faltem fore Judicium, pœnæ vero atrocitatem remitti cupio.

7. That confequently he prof
with a fixed Refolution to tal
away. 8. That before this
ever after, it was his conftan
that Heretics are to be punifhed
Death.

It is proper thofe Faults in
Reformer fhould be known, i
fhew that tho' he was a grea
he was but a Man, and a very
in fome Refpects; and by that
too great a Refpect being paid
of thinking, which has been u
done ever fince he flourifhed
chief Aim is to fhew, that tho
mation has delivered us from a
ber of Errors and Superftiti
has but faintly touched the ch
all, that which is the Founda
others, that which alone makes
gerous, I mean fpiritual Tyrani
wanted not to deftroy it, but
move it from *Rome* to *Geneva*
Pope to *himfelf*. The *Pope*
burn'd *Calvin* at *Rome*; and *Ca*
have burn'd at *Geneva* either th
any one that happened to fu
his Decifions. Confequently
Churches of any Denominat
foever, which have imbibed t
ciples of Perfecution, ftill wa
mation, and it is what every

that has a Concern for the Members of Chrift ought to wifh moft fincerely, and to promote by all the proper Means in his Power. If we are once well convinced, that fomething remains to be done, there will be great Hopes of our fetting about it earneftly, and very foon ; one is the Confequence of the other.

After having dwelt fo much on the Reflections, the Editor of thefe Letters makes, I ought now to proceed to the Letters themfelves ; but this Article is already drawn to a fufficient Length. I may perhaps continue it in fome other Volume.

ARTICLE X.

A Treatife concerning the Senfes, by Mr. *Le Cat*. II. Abftract *(a)*.

Of Smelling.

THIS Senfe, according to the Author, is only a Branch of Tafte, which he confiders as refiding in the Stomach, Gullet, Mouth, and Nofe, tho'
it

(a) See the Part I, of this Journal, pag. 96.

it exerts itself with some Variety in each. This is certainly an Error, as I observed in my last Abstract—'Tis confounding the natural Distinction between one Sensation and another.——But it becomes a happy Error, since it has engaged the Author to observe, with more than usual Accuracy, the mutual Relation and Subserviency of those several Sensations, which he conceived were Modes only of a general one.

The pitituatory Membrane, which is the immediate Organ of Smelling in the Nose, extends a great deal farther, and lines successively the Mouth, the Gullet, and the Stomach, and is in each of those the Organ also of their respective and particular Sensations. Hence the mutual Influence, which Smells and Tastes have on each other, and the more extraordinary Power, which belongs to them in common, of exciting Appetite, or creating Loathings and Disgust in the distant Organs of the Stomach. The Continuity of the same Membrane sufficiently accounts for the Correspondency of the Sensations, excited in the several Parts of it. It would be an unnatural Alliance, if one Extremity of the same Organ should convey Pleasure to the Mind, while the other suffer'd Pain, or was, as it might

happen,

happen, essentially injured. A Syftem put together, with so little Dependence in the Parts, could not subfift for any Time.

By a general Law, which prevails in the Animal OEconomy, the Nerves and their Papillæ lose something of their Flexibility, as they recede further from the Brain. Their Coats grow thicker, and themselves more clumsy and more stubborn. They require stronger Impreffions to affect them, and feel less acutely and less perfectly. Hence the pituitatory Membrane admits, according to the Author, of different Modes of one original Senfation ; according to the truer Syftem, of Senfations specifically different.

As it issues immediately out of the Brain with all its Senfibility entire and unimpaired, it is fitted to receive Impreffions from the moft subtle and minute Effluvia——from the volatile Salts of Bodies, which alone are Odoriferous. —— Their groffer fixed Salts are referved to act upon it at a greater Diftance from the Brain ; Where something is abated of its original Quicknefs of Senfation, and thefe are tafted in the Mouth. — The Solids themfelves exert their Action laft, and only in the Stomach, when the fame Membrane has contracted by its Progrefs a

PART II.   Z.   greater

greater Confiftency, a firmer Tone, and requires more forcible Impreffions.

I have obferved already from the Author, that volatile Salts alone are properly the Objects of this Senfe. Their Vehicle is Air drawn by Infpiration within the Sphere of Action of the Organ. We fmell only when we breath freely thro' the Nofe, and a Cold, which prevents the one, hinders the other in the fame Degree.

The Nofe is no very complicated Organ. There is, however, more Contrivance in the Difpofition of its Parts, than is ufually obferved. The two Cavities, which are called Noftrils, are both lined with the pituitatory Membrane. 'Tis of a fpongy Nature, and, in Effect, a Wreath of Nerves, and fecretory Veffels wove into one another; therefore of quick and ready Senfibility. Its Surface is loaded with Papillæ very fmall, becaufe the Objects are minute which are to act upon them, and very numerous, that every odoriferous Particle may meet with a Papilla to receive it. They are befides fofter than thofe of other Organs, more lightly cover'd; —and, that the leaft Impreffion may affect them, they are kept flexible and pliant by a liquid oozing out of the fecretory Veffels, and by the Difcharge

befides

befides of the lachrymal Ducts into the Nofe. Thefe Cautions were all neceffary, confidering the Finenefs of their Object, but alone, they would not have been fufficient. The Air, in a rapid Paffage thro' the Nofe, would not have depofited odoriferous Particles enough to affect the Organ fenfibly, fomething was wanting to detain it. Accordingly, it is retarded in its Motion by the Structure of the Noftrils. They are each of them provided with two irregular hollow Cones, which advance far into their Cavities, contract them greatly, and leave only a narrow winding Paffage for the Air. Thefe hollow Cones in thofe Animals, which have the keeneft Smell, are remarkably larger than in Man, and this is the only difcernable Advantage in the Structure of their Organs. Their Ufe appears from thence, and that no more has been afcribed to them, than they are in Effect intended for.

Of Hearing.

NOISE is the Object of this Senfe, and it is then called *Sound*, when it is fo modified, as to become agreeable to the Organ. Under thefe Modifications, it

has

has been made the Object of an Art, and
improved into an Inftrument of exquifite
Enjoyments, and under thefe Modifications it beft deferves to be confidered.

Sound in the fonorous Body is a Vibration, or rather a Series of Vibrations, which,
communicated to the Air, and propagated
by it to the Organ, produce a Senfation there
which we call *Hearing*.

This Vibration in the fonorous Body
muft be attended with a tremulous Motion of its Parts, without which, tho'
the Body vibrates, no Sound will follow.
Thefe two Motions confpiring together
produce *Sound*, and its Tone arifeth from
the Velocity of the Vibrations in the
Whole, and in the Parts. Slow Vibrations
give deep Tones, and quick Vibrations
fhrill ones. The Meafure of the Vibrations is determined by the Nature of
the fonorous Body. Elaftic Bodies vibrate
fmartly, and thofe among them moft,
whofe conftituent Parts are fmalleft. In
Strings, on which accurate Experiments
may beft be made, the Deepnefs of the
Tone depends upon their Length and
Thicknefs, and inverfly on their Elafticity
and Tenfion. Or in other Words, the
thickeft, longeft, flackeft, leaft elaftic Strings
yield the deepeft Note ; and by varying
judicioufly

judicioufly thefe Qualities, or Circumftances in the Strings, every Note may
be produced in the whole Scale of
Sounds.

By the Vibrations of the fonorous Body
thofe in the Air, are excited and determined. · The Air, which immediately fur-
rounds the Body, is compreffed by its
Vibrations. It afterwards expands itfelf by
its own Spring, and compreffeth that beyond it, while it reftores itfelf to its
original State. This new Portion of compreffed Air acts, in the fame Way, on
the next Ring of Air, and, by thefe fuc-
ceffive Stops, an undulating Motion is excited, and *Sound* conveyed from the Body to
the Organ.

Mr. *Le Cat* fuppofeth, that it is not
the whole Mafs of Air, which is affected in this Manner ; but the moft fubtle
Part only of that Fluid. The Effect of
Sounds, according to this Gentleman,
would be more confiderable than they are,
if the whole Mafs were moved, and a
Candle might be blown out, for Inftance,
by ringing a Bell at a fmall Diftance. ——
But not to mention the amazing Effects
of *Noife*, —— fhaking Houfes, —— breaking
Windows, when it is violent, and not too
diftant, Mr. *Le Cat*'s Argument appears to
me defective from another and a better
Reafon,

Reafon. The Force exerted
againſt any intervening Obſtac
meaſured by the Weight of
of it only, which acts upon
cle multiplied into its Velocit
Sound, where the Air moves
and fucceffively, is certainly
than one Half of the Wa
which is form'd by every Pu
as in Winds an immenſe Bulk c
together and at once, and
gainſt the Obſtacle with
Wheight.

There is a more plauſible
methinks, in Favour of th
Notion.——Different Tones rec
ent Undulations in the Air
whole Maſs therefore undulat
how can different Tones be hea
Can the whole Air undula
Ways at the ſame Time ? W
ſtronger Pulſe abſorb the weaker
will they not modify each other,
pound Pulſe ariſe, and conſeq
a new and compound Tone in
tradiction to Experience ? Su
ſome Parts only of the Air a
ed in propagating Sounds, the
is conſiderably leffened ; but it i
if you ſuppoſe that the Partic
by their different Size and Ela

each of them appropriated to a peculiar Tone, and do not undulate, till they are called upon by their own Note. This is an Hypothefis ingenioufly invented, but countenanced by no Experiments, and befides, entirely infufficient to account for the Phænomena, which it is intended to explain. It will be neceffary, notwith-ftanding, to admit different Undulations in the fame Mafs of Air, fubfifting to-gether at one Time, and conveyed to the Ear without Confufion. When feveral Inftruments ftrike an Unifon, there are feveral Undulations form'd, beginning from different Centers, and fpreading Unifor-mly round, without deftroying one ano-ther.

These by the Hypothefis, fince the Tone is in each Inftrument the fame, are excited in a Fluid, confifting of Particles the fame in Kind, which therefore muft admit of diftinct Undulations at one Time in different Directions. I fhall add, that Mr. *Le Cat* himfelf mentions a curious Obfervation not eafily reconciled methinks to the Hypothefis he has em-braced. Befides its Note, a String yields to a nice Ear fome harmonious Tones at the fame Time. An attentive and fkilful Hearer, perceives diftinctly the Octave, the fifth and third join'd with the fundamental

tal Tone, which is heard alone by thofe unexercifed in Mufic. Thefe therefore exift together in their Caufes, and different Undulations arrive at the Ear without Confufion : Nor is there in a Pulfe of Sound that choice of Particles obferved, which he fuppofeth, fince three or four Sets of them at leaft conftantly move together.

I do not mean to ridicule Mr. *Le Cat's* Opinion, that the Air confifts of Particles of different Sizes, and different Degrees of Elafticity, and confequently fitted to admit of different Vibrations, there is *no* Improbability to me, certainly no manifeft Abfurdity in that Opinion ; But that in a Wave of Air, all the Particles of any given Tone fhould be exactly cull'd, and the reft remain immoveable, feems entirely unmechanical. A String in Motion cannot make thofe nice Diftinctions. It exerts itfelf upon every Thing it meets, and it meets with every Species of Particles at once.

I have been particular upon this Part of Mr. *Le Cat's* Treatife, becaufe the general Theory of Sounds, which he has endeavoured to improve, is ftill, as I conceive, in a very great Degree imperfect, and becaufe even the falfe Conjectures of great

Men,

Men throw light upon a Subject which is but little underſtood.

What the Author ſays of the Proportions between Strings of different Tones, of Concords, of the Velocity of Sounds and of other Articles of the ſame Nature, may be read with more Advantage in many other Works, and is indeed generally known. I ſhall therefore proceed to his Obſervations on the Structure of the Ear.

The Ear conſiſts of two Parts ſeparated by the Drum, and denominated from their Situation. The External performs the Office of a Tunnel, and conveys the Vibrations of the Air, collected into a ſmall Compaſs by numerous Reflections, and therefore more intenſe, to the internal Ear, which is properly the Organ. The Structure of this Part admits of unlimited Variety, and differs from itſelf in almoſt every Species of Animals; but it anſwers the ſame general Purpoſe in them all, tho' not in the ſame Degree. In thoſe Animals, which are of quickeſt Hearing, this Tunnel is remarkably capacious, and is fitted beſides with Muſcles to diverſify its Poſture, and direct it to the Sound. The Air collected in this Tunnel falls upon the Drum, a Membrane, which cloſeth its Extremity obliquely, and excites in

PART II.　　A a　　　　　it

it the very fame Vibratio
had itfelf received from
Body.

That the fame Membran
of different Vibrations, and a
different Tones ; its Tenfior
ferent. Accordingly the Dr
tural Situation is very flack
Tenfe, only , when the Ton
and by a curious Piece of Mecl
the Author thus explains.

Behind the Drum, and
Ear, there is a Cavity fuppl
thro' a fmall Communicati
Mouth, firft difcovered by *1*
containing an Apparatus of
connected with each other 1
cles, and therefore moving
as it were upon feveral Hing
three in Number, and callec
mer, the *Anvil*, and the
articular Bone, which fom
reckon as a fourth, being in
Head only of the Stirrop. 1
is fuch, that the Extremity
mer, adhering to the Drum,
ed by a fmart Vibration, g
tires into the Cavity, and
Membrane after it, ftrains it
Pitch. In a flow Vibration,
and fcarce recedes from its n

on; the Drum of Confequence remains as it was, relaxed, and fitted to receive the graver Tones.

This Membrane, tho' thus curioufly adapted to vibrate Unifons with the fonorous Air, is not, however, the immediate Organ of Hearing. It ferves only to excite regular Undulations in that Air, which as I have obferved already, is contained in the Cavity behind it. The Drum has been burft in Dogs, without the immediate Lofs of this Senfation. They grew deaf indeed in Time, the real Ear being deprived of its Defence againft Accidents and Injuries. But they heard without this Membrane, which cannot therefore be the Organ. It lies ftill deeper in two Cavities, more remote from Injuries, and of more exquifite Contrivance; communicating with the former, each of them by a fmall Orifice, and with each other by a Third. Thefe Cavities are both completely lined by the auditory Nerve, in its moft flexible and fofteft State, at its firft Iffue from the Brain, and provided therefore, as the immediate Organs of Senfation. Of thefe Cavities, the one is called the *Labyrinth*, the other is the *Cochlea*.

Their Structure is fo different, that the Author has been tempted to conjecture,

A 4 2   that

that their Purpofes alfo are different, that the Labyrinth is, according to the juft Diftinction he has made between them, affected by Noife only, and the Cochlea by Sounds.

The *Labyrinth*, is a little Cavity, into which three femicircular Canals are inferted like fo many Handles of a Veffel, both Orifices of each Canal opening into the *Labyrinth*, and communicating with nothing elfe.

From this Conftruction, fmart Vibrations, and a ftrong tremulous Motion of its Parts, may be excited in the Air contained in it. But there is nothing to modify them into Tones. The Canals may ring, but how they fhould change their Pitch is entirely inconceivable.

It is otherwife in the Structure of the *Cochlea*, which has a Membrane vifibly adapted to vibrate Unifons with every Tone.

The *Cochlea*, is a Canal of a fpiral Form, confifting of four Rings, according to the moft acute Anatomifts, and refembling in its Shape the Shell of a fmall Snail. In this winding Cavity, there is a nervous Membrane, fufpended thro' the Middle of it, and dividing it according to its Length into two equal Parts of the fame Shape and Size, In this Situation, not

not unlike that of the Spring of a Watch roll'd up, it is impoffible, the different Portions of this Membrane fhould have equal Degrees of Tenfion. In the wider Rings of the Spiral, it defcribes by its Pofition, it is neceffarily flacker,—grows tenfer by imperceptible Degrees,—and is moft fo at the Apex of the *Cochlea*, whatever Tone happens to ftrike the Ear. Some Portion therefore of this Membrane has the requifite Tenfion to receive it and in fome Part or other of its length every poffible Vibration may be fucceffively excited.

This Opinion of the Author's would perhaps be more confonant to Truth, if it were a little qualified. There is no Noife without a Tone, and therefore there cannot be an Organ appropriated to the one in Contradiftinction to the other. It feems rather, that the *Labyrinth* is defign'd to perform the Office of an Echo, to encreafe the Sound which has previoufly received its Pitch from the Membrane in the *Cochlea*. Without fome Suppofition of this Kind, it will be difficult to affign a Reafon why the *Cochlea* fhould be divided into two feveral Cavities. — Why one of them fhould open into the Cavity behind the Drum, and the other into the Labyrinth,—or why the Labyrinth itfelf fhould be broken into fo many Windings by the femi-circular Canals—But confider it as an

Echo

Echo to the *Cochlea*, the whole Structure. is accounted for.

By one Orifice the *Cochlea* receives the Sound—It communicates it to its Echo by the other—and the femi-circular Canals reflect and encreafe it when received.

The Neceffity of this little Alteration in the Author's Syftem will be very much confirm'd, if what *Schelhammer* affirms, be true, that there is no Communication between the Labyrinth and the Cavity behind the Drum.—The Foot of the Stirrop which lies upon the oval Hole, by which alone they could communicate, covering it always, and fo clofely, that no Air can make its Paffage thro' it. Mr. *Schelhammer*'s Authority is of great Weight upon this Subject; his Treatife *de Auditú* being very much efteem'd—But future Enquiries and Experiments muft ultimately decide the Queftion.

There are fome incidental Obfervations in Mr. *Le Cat*'s Treatife, which it cannot be expected, fhould be taken Notice of in a Work of this Kind. The Reader will find it worth his while to perufe the Book itfelf, not only for the Sake of thofe, but alfo, and efpecially, to inform himfelf to more Advantage, than he can do from this Abftract, in the curious Structure of the Ear.

[*To be continued.*]

ARTICLE

ARTICLE XI.

La Sainte Bible, &c.

The *Holy Bible*, by *Charles Le Cene*. II.
Abftract. (*a*)

ACCORDING to the Plan, I laid in
my former, I am to give an Account
of feveral of the moft remarkable *Additions*
and *Omiffions* in the New Teftament according to Mr. *Le Cene's* Opinion. I begin by
the *Additions.*

Matth. Chap. III. between the 12th and
the 13th. Verfe Mr. *Le Cene* puts this
Sentence taken from St. *Jerom*, (*b*) who
faid he read it fo in *St. Matthew's Gofpel
to the . Hebrews :* " At this time the
" Lord's Mother and his Brothers faid to
" him ; *John* the Baptift baptifes to pro-
" cure the Remiffion of Sins ; let us go
" and be baptifed by him : But he an-
" fwered to them ; what Sin have I com-
" mitted

(*a*) See Part I. of this Journal, pag. 121.
(*b*) Hieronym. Dialog. III. in Pelagianos. Many learned
think, that what St. *Jerom* calls the *Gofpel to the Hebrews* is
the fame and the only one that the *Ebionites* received. But
this is only a Conjecture ; and I believe it is not yet decided
whether *St. Matthew* wrote in Hebrew or in Greek.

" mitted to go and be baptif(
" unlefs what I now fay fhou
" ed an Error."———It is ge
and I believe with a great dea
that the Quotations of the F
Scripture are not much to I
upon. Yet I Believe this ⋅ Ru
fome Reftriction. They quote
ture for the moft part *ex n*
then they often fell into grea
this Obfervation is enough
their various Readings of Pa
are, in part at leaft, really cor
oldeft Manufcripts; but does
hold in ⋅ fuch a Cafe as this
could not be a *lapfus memoric*
had never read the Words i
of the Scripture? He pofitiv
read them in the *Gofpel to th*
and there is no Room here
a pious Fraud, becaufe the
no manner of Reference to any
Point of Divinity. From th
conclude—that in the time of
there was a Gofpel wrote in I
called the *Gofpel to the* He
that in this Gofpel was co
Sentence related by him. I
thefe Words *unlefs what I now*
deemed an Error, muft be I
as an Irony, as if Jefus Chrift I

to his Relations, whether they ever faw him do any thing that might be called a Sin.—To join this Sentence with the following Verfe, Mr. *Le Cene* renders the Greek Word τοτε, by *yet*, or *neverthelefs*; inftead of, *at this time*, as all our Verfions have it.

Matthew XX. after the 28th. Verfe. Our Author inferts the Words contained in *Beza*'s Manufcripts, which are the fame that are related in *Luke* xiv. v. 18. with this Difference, that here they are thus introduced; *Endeavour therefore to exalt yourfelves above what is little, and to appear little with Refpect to what is* called *great* (c).

Mark xvi. after the 8th. Verfe; Mr. *Le Cene* receives the Reading of a Manufcript, (d) as follows : " They only told in few " Words whatever had been declared to " them about *Peter* : And after this, Jefus " himfelf fent by their Miniftry, from Eaft " to Weft, the holy and incorruptible " preaching of eternal Salvation." Part of this Addition feems to contradict what is faid before, *neither faid they any thing to any*

　　PART II.　　　B b　　　　*Man,*

(c) Vid. Bezæ N. Teft.—Colomefii Obfervationes facræ—pag. 80. & 81. Synopf. Crit. IV. pag. 500.—Nov Teft. Gr. cum variant. lection. 12°. *Amft.* 1735.—Mr. *Le Clerc* thinks, that *Beza*'s MS. is only a Paraphrafe, but I would not chufe to affirm that the *Proofs be alledges*, are fufficient.

(d) *Wechelii* five *Franc. Junii* Lectiones. Vide Id. N. Teft. Gr.

Man, for they were afraid ;
fuppofe, that the firſt T
after being fomewhat recc
Fright was what is here c
I leave entirely to the L
Readers.

Mark xvi. After the 15th
Cene alſo inſerts theſe Wor
very much like an Addition
Commentator : " But they
" ty faying, this World is n
" quity, and Incredulity, v
" allow impure Minds to
" true Virtue of God ; ther
" one now manifeſt his Rig
They did their Duty ; this I
with Reference to what Jeſus
them with in the foregoing
Meaning is, that tho' the Diſcip
of Incredulity on this Occaſi
wards they did really deſerve th
of the Lord.—Mr. *Le Cene*
tion the Manuſcript from whicl
Addition. (*e*)

Luke vi. between the 5th. an
the Author inſerts theſe Wo
Cambridge Manuſcript (*f*). "
" fome Body working that l

(*e*) See the Greek Teſt. quoted above.
(*f*) That belong'd before to *Beza.*

" Sabbath Day, he told him ; O Man
" thou art happy if thou knoweft what
" thou doft ; but if thou knoweft it not,
" thou art curfed, and a Tranfgreffor of
" the Law.". *Grotius* doubts not of this
Addition being fpurious ; yet I do humbly
think it worthy of Jefus Chrift, and entirely confiftent with his Refolution of abo-
lifhing the tirefome Ceremonies of the
Law. Why fhould we not fuppofe that
fome attentive Difciple of Jefus Chrift
found out this Defign, and acted accordingly ?

Luke xxiii. in the 43d. Verfe the fame
Manufcript (g) has the following Words
which Mr. *Le Cene* receives : " As he was
" in a cruel Anxiety Jefus told him," *Verily
I fay unto thee, to Day fhalt thou be with
me in Paradife.*

Luke xxiii. v. 54. I do not know where
Mr. *Le Cene* found thefe Words, " And
" he *(Jofeph of Arimathea)* roll'd a large
" Stone, which Twenty Men fcarce could
" have moved, to the Door of the Se-
" pulchre."

John vi. v. 56. Here is another confiderable Addition, of which Mr. *Le Cene* gives
no manner of Account, nor does he fay
from whence he took it : (b) " As my
B b 2 " Father

_____

(g) See the fame Greek Teft.
(b) It is taken from the *Cambridge* MS. See the Greek
Teft. above.

" Father is in me, I am also in my Fa-
" ther. Verily, verily I say unto you,
" that if you do not receive the Body
" of the Son of Man, as a Bread which
" gives Life, you shall not have Life by
" him."

The Author leaves us also in the dark
as to the following Addition :

Acts v. 38. " Take Care, *says Gamaliel,*
" you do not to others what you would
" not have to be done to you."—This
looks like the Reflection of a Commentator—So does the following.

Act. vi. 10. *(i)* " He would convince
" them with Freedom, and no Body could
" resist Truth."—I cannot help having the
same Opinion of what is inserted in

Acts x. v. 41. *(k)* " We have conversed
" with him during forty Days."

Acts xi. v. 1. I do not know what to
think of the genuineness of the following
Sentence : " For some time before *Peter*
" was wishing to return to *Jerusalem:*
" Having then called the Brethren toge-
" ther, he confirmed them by a long Dif-
" course, and preached in their Countries,
" and after he told them the Favour, God
" had granted" *to the Gentiles.*

Acts

(i) This is found in the MS. of the *Bodleian* Lib. Ibid.
(k) Idem & ibid.

Acts xv. v. 20. 29. The following Addition authorised by the *Cambridge* MS. (*l*) feems to me to be very important and worthy the Attention of the juftly celebrated Council of *Jerufalem*, the only one, whofe Decrees are binding. 'Tis a glorious Affertion of the religious Liberty every Man ought to enjoy: After defiring the new Converts to Chriftianity to *abftain from Meats offered to Idols*, they add, " and " take Care not to do to others what you " would not have to be done to you; but " be led by the Holy Ghoft." That is, " Take Care not to take from others that " Liberty of Confcience, the Freedom of " thinking and acting which you feel is your " undifputable Right, but follow rather the " mild and peaceable Directions of the " Spirit of God, fuch as they are to be " found in the Gofpel, and in your own " Hearts."——What a glorious Example! Why was it fo ill followed! Here is a Council of Apoftles, who declare they have no Power over People's Confciences, but only to advife them to do what they would require from others in the fame Circumftances; whilft all the Councils, Synods, &c. that met fince, in Imitation of this (as they pretended,) have, more or lefs, in a manner

conspired

(*l*) See the fame Gr. Teft.

conspired againſt the Liberties of Mankind, and eſſentially injured them.

(*m*) *Rom.* xi. v. 1. Mr. *Le Cene* receives theſe Words from the *Alexand.* MS. in the King's Library, *Hath God caſt away his People,* " which he had *approved* before." (*n*) So does he tranſlate conſtantly the Greek Word προγινώσκω ; eſpecially in *Rom.* viii. v. 29 and 30. where this Tranſlation makes a very different Senſe from that which the common Reading offers.

Rom. xiv. v. 24. Here Mr. *Le Cene* places the three laſt Verſes of the following Chapter, according to the Manuſcript of St. *Paul's* Epiſtles kept in *Emanuel's* College at *Cambridge.*

1 *Tim.* iv. v. 1. Our Author adopts theſe Words of *Wechelius's* Manuſcript: (*p*) " For they will be Worſhippers of the " Dead, ſuch as were worſhipped in the " Land of *Iſrael.*"

1 *John* ii. v. 23. Mr. *Le Cene* took the following Addition out of the *Alexand.* Manu-

---

(*m*) I paſs over the Additions contained in the following Places, as being of no Conſequence, and for which I refer the Reader to the Greek Teſt. above quoted. *Acts* xvi. 10. 35. 39. 40.—xviii. 8. 27.—xix. 1. 5. 9. 14.

(*n*) See the ſame Gr. Teſt.

(*o*) See the Greek Teſt. above quoted——Synopſ. Critic. ſol. V. pag. 305. 327, 328.—& Knatchbul pag. 102.

(*p*) *Wechelii* five Fr. Junii Lectiones.

Manufcript: " Whofoever acknowledges,
" *or receives*, the Authority of the Son,
" acknowledges alfo that of the Father."

1 *John* v. ver. 20. He alfo adopts, from
the fame valuable Manufcript the Word
God which fixes better the true Meaning
of this difputed Paffage : It runs thus in
his Tranflation : *We know that the Son of
God is come, and that he has given us Intelligence to know the true* God ; *and we
are devoted to this who is the true one, by
his Son Jefus Chrift ; That one is the
true God, and the Author of eternal Life.*

Jude v. 22 and 23. I do not know from
whence Mr. *Le Cene* took thefe Words.
" There are fome, whom you are to con-
" vince they are already condemned."
*Save the others with Fear, pulling them
out of the Fire :* " Have Compaffion of
" others, and Fear for yourfelves."

Revelat. iv. v. 8. The Words Holy—
Holy—Holy, are repeated twice more,
that is nine Times in all, in a Manufcript which Mr. *Le Cene* follows here.
I fuppofe it is from thefe three Times re-
peating thefe three Words that they have
been look'd upon as a ftrong Argument
in Favour of the *Trinity*, in the common
Way of explaining it.

I intend

I intend to give in fome oth
this Journal an Account of the
in Mr. *Le Cene*'s New Teftaı
fhall clofe this Abftract with t
vation.——The fmall Number
tions, for the moft Part very
able, which are found in fuch
of ancient Manufcripts, difcover
rent Times, and in different P;
World, muft be to every unj
Mind, an undeniable Proof that t
fcripts are genuine. *(q)*

(*q*) See this more enlarged upon pag. 24
Journal.

A R

ARTICLE XII.

Literary News.

MUSCOVY.

PETERSBOURG.

AS I had not room in the I. Part of this Journal for an Abſtraꝶ of the Memoirs of the Royal Academy of this City for the Year 1738, mentioned in my laſt, I ſhall barely give the Titles of the Articles contained in it.—This Volume is compoſed of 24 Memoirs,— 16 of Mathematics, — 4 of Natural Hiſtory,—3. of Hiſtory and Criticiſm — and one of aſtronomical Obſervations.—Here are the Latin Titles of the Memoirs of Mathematics. 1. Georg. *Wolfg. krafft.* Obſervatio ſolſtitii Æſtivi, faꝶa Petropoli Anno 1730.—2. *Ejuſdem* de Ungulis Cylindrorum varii generis. — 3. Leonhardi *Euleri* Solutio ſingularis Caſus circa Tautochroniſmum. —4. Jacob *Herma-ni* de ſuperficiebus ad æquationes locales revocatis, variiſque earum affeꝶionibus.—5. Leon. *Euleri* Me-thodus generalis ſummandi progreſſiones. — 6. C. G. Criteria quædam æquationum, quarum nulla radix rationalis eſt.—7. Leon. *Euleri* Obſervationes de Theo-remate quodam Termatiano, aliiſque ad numeros primos pertinentibus.— 8. Dan. *Bernoulli* Theoremata de Oſ-cillationibus Corporum filo flexili connexorum & ca-tenæ verticaliter ſuſpenſæ. — 9. Leon. *Euleri* Proble-matis Iſoperimetrici in latiſſimo ſenſu accepti ſolutio generalis — 10. Georg. Wolf. *krafft,* de Lunulis quadrabilibus, e variarum curvarum combinatione Or-tis. — 11. Leon. *Euleri* Specimen de conſtruꝶione

æquationum differentialium, five indeterminatarum fe-
paratione — 12. *Ejufdem* de folutione Problematum
Diophantæorum per numeros integros —13. Jac. *Hermanni* de quadratura curvarum Algebraïcarum, quarum Æquationes locales coordinatas fibi invicem per-
mixtas involvunt. — 14. *Ejufdem* Supplementum ad
fchedam in Menfe Augufto Actorum Eruditorum,
1719. circa problemata a Taylero Mathematicis non
Anglis propofitum, editam. — 15. Leon. *Euleri* de
formis Radicum æquationum cujufque ordinis conjec-
tatio— 16. Ejufdem conftructio æquationis differentia-
lis $a \times n \, d\times = d Y + Y_2 \, d\times$.

The Memoirs of Phyfics are the following, 1. I. G. D.
— de mutilatione Brachiorum in puero, cujus Tom.
III. Comment. facta eft Commemoratio, Differtatio
Anatomico—Phyfiologica.—2. Jos. *Weitbrecht*, de Cor-
dibus villofis. — 3. *Ejufdem* de Circulatione fangui-
nis Cogitationes Phyfiologicæ. — 4. I. G. D. Aortæ
& Spinæ dorfalis mira Corruptio: præmittuntur animadverfiones generales fuper Spinæ dorfalis ftructu-
ram. ———— The Memoirs of Hiftory and Criticifm, are all three of the late Mr. *Bayer*. 1. De
Litteratura Mangiurica. 2. De Lexico Sinico eù
guéy. 3. De Ruflorum prima Expeditione Conftan-
tinopolitanâ.

The Aftronomical Obfervations for the Year 1738,
are of Mr. *de l' Ifle*, Profeffor in our Univerfity.

Mr. *Siegefbeck*, M. D. has publifhed his Botanofo-
phiæ varioris brevis Sciagraphia, &c. 4°.

This Univerfity has fuffered a great Lofs by the
Death of Dr. *Amman*. He was born at *Schaffaufen*
in *Switzerland*, had ftudied at *Leyden*, and had the
Happinefs of living fome Years at Sir *Hans Sloane*'s
in *London*, Botanicks were what he excelled in.

S W E D E N.

S T O C K H O L M.

They are reprinting here a Work of M. *Magnus
de Bromell*, intituled, Mineralogia & Lithographiæ
Suecenæ, 8°.

U P S A L.

UPSAL.

On the Reprefentations of Profeffor *Andrew Celfius*, the late Diet made a confiderable Correction to the Kalendar.

We forfake the cyclic Computation to find out *Eafter*, which is to be fixed according to the true Æquinox of *Eafter*, as determined by aftronomical Calculation. *Eafter* being in this Manner fixed to the firft Sunday after the Full Moon, which follows immediately the vernal Æquinox, we fhall keep it the fame Day as other People ; the Date only fhall differ as long as the old Stile fhall be in Ufe in *Sweden*.

DENMARK.
COPENHAGEN.

Mr. *Pontoppidanus* is going to print a confiderable Work of his, in *German*, on the ecclefiaftic Annals of *Denmark*.

Knitlinga-faga ; that is to fay, the Hiftory of the Pofterity of the Canuts, by Mr. *Gramm* in the *Icelandifh* Tongue, with a *Latin* Tranflation found in the Papers of the learned *Arnas Magnæus*, and revifed by the Author.

Young Mr. *Tycho Hofman* has publifhed a Collection of the Lives of fome illuftrious *Danes*, — The I. vol. contains four Lives, with this Oddity, that each of them is written in a different Tongue — I. The Life of Admiral *Troile*, in *Danifh* — II. Of Count *Annibal Scheftedt* Great Treafurer, in *French* — III. Of the Great Admiral *Cort-Adeler*, in *German*, and IV. Of *Peter Laffon* Counfellor, in *Latin*.

Nicolai Klimii Iter fubterraneum, novam Telluris Theoriam ac Hiftoriam quintæ Monarchiæ adhuc nobis incognitæ exhibens, e Bibliotheca *B. Abelini*. 8vo. — This Work is already tranflated into *French* and into *German*.

The Court has given the proper Orders for a new *Danifh* Verfion of the Bible ; and all the Learned of the Kingdom are invited freely to give their Advices. — I wifh this noble Example may be followed in other Countries.

Mr.

ALTENA.

Mr. *Bernard Clement Mettingh* a Civilian of this City, has given a confiderable Work intituled, De ftatu Militiæ Germanorum Principalis & Accefforiæ Veteris & Medii Ævi.

PRUSSIA.
DANTZIG.

Mr. *Schott* is going to give the fecond Part of his Chriftian Pruffia, and is about publifhing a Periodic Work intituled, Acta Polono — Boruffica.

Mr. *Lengnich* has publifhed the I. Vol. of his Public Law of *Poland*.

THORN.

Profeffor *Schultz*, has publifhed a confiderable Work on the Chancellors of *Poland* : — Commentarius de Cancellariis Regni Poloniæ, 4to. with the Literary Programma of Chancellor *Andr-Zaluski*. To which is added a fmall Treatife which was very fcarce : — Reinold Heidenftenii folefcis fecretarii Regii Cancellarius, five de dignitate & Officio Cancellarii Regni Poloniæ.

KONIGSBERG.

Mr. *Hilienthal* is about giving a Book intituled Bibliotheca exegetica; or the Commentators of the Bible; as a Supplement to *Fabricius*, *Thomafius*, *Reimmann*, and *Stolle*.

They print here the I. Part of the V. Vol. of *Pruffia* illuftrated.

GERMANY.
VIENNA.

Two excellent MSS. of *Hippocrates*'s Works being fallen in the Hands of Dr. *Make* he refolved to make ufe of them for a new Edition of thofe Works, with various Readings and the Notes of Meffieurs *John Cornaro* and *John Sambucus*, two learned Phyficians, to whom thefe MSS. did formerly belong. They fay this Edition is to exceed in all refpects any of thofe we have already.

Mr. *Phil. James Lambacher*, has wrote a curious Pamphlet on the Time that the Collection of Laws ftiled fpeculum fuevicum, was compiled.

Mr

HOFF.

Mr. *Longolius* has given us a new Edition of *Aulus Gellius*, with a copious Table and a Preliminary Differtation.

ALTORF.

We are printing here Mr. *Schwartz's* large Commentary on *Pliny's* Panegyric, 4to.

Mr. *John Heumann* wrote lately a Differtation on the ceremonies to be obferved at the Death of an Emperor, entituled, de Imperatore mortuo.

MEMMINGEN.

Mr. *Schelborn* is giving a new Edition of a Work firft printed in 4to at *Ingolftatd* in 1618; but extreamly fcarce, becaufe all the Copies were taken up by Emiffaries from *Rome*: It is the Defence the Emperor *Lewis* of *Bavaria* made againft *Bzovius*, as it was written by Counfellor *Chrift. Gewold*. The Calumnies of the Continuator of *Baronius* are invincibly confuted in this Book.

NUREMBERG.

Mr. *John James Schubler*, a celebrated Mathematician, died here lately.

Mr. *Doppelmayer* another Mathematician, is writing a Book on the Phænomena of Electricity after the Difcoveries of *Hauksbee* and *Gray*; and the Experiments of Mr. *Du Fay*; —alfo an Introduction to Aftronomy.

FRANCKFORT on the Mein.

They have tranflated here into *German* the Sermons of Mr. *George Whitefield*.

The Bookfeller *Hutter* is printing by Subfcription an Abridgment of the Theatrum Europæum, which contains in 21 Vol. Fol, with a great number of Figures, the Hiftory of what paffed in *Europe* from 1619 to 1718.

Mr. *Falken* hath not yet found a Bookfeller willing, or able, to take upon him the printing of his Traditiones Corbeienfes.

Regefta Chronologico-Diplomatica, in quibus recenfentur omnis generis Monumenta & Documenta publica,

publica, &c. by Mr. *Peter Georgifch.* —This work bears a good Reputation in *Germany*.

GIESSEN.

Flores fparfi ad Jus Auftregarum, tam legalium quam conventionalium ; — a long Differtation by Mr. *Senckenberg*, wherein he makes many learned Obfervations on the Origin and Hiftory of thofe Arbiters called *Auftregæ*.

Mr. *Neubauer* is carrying on a Work began by Mr. *Mofer*, and with his Approbation, viz. An Hiftorical Dictionary of the learned yet alive, both among the Reformed and the Lutherans of *Germany*.

WETZLAR.

Tractatus Juridico-Hiftoricus de Matrimonio Principis, Liberique Domini cum Virgine nobili Inito.— This queftion has been long debated in *Germany*, and has been attended with ruinous Law-fuits, viz. Whether the Children of a Prince by a Wife not born a Princefs, tho' of noble Defcent, may inherit of their Father's Eftate and Privileges. —Mr. *Ludiger de Mansback* the Author of this Book endeavours to folve this puzling Queftion.

MARPURG.

De Lingua Novellarum Juftiniani Originaria, —by Mr. *Hombergh*.

Mr. *Cramer* hath given a Pamphlet on this Queftion. What punifhment a young Woman under Age deferves, if engaged by her Mother to deftroy her own Child.

Mr. *Hartman* has given the 1ft. Vol. of his Hiftoria Haffiaca, 8vo.

JENA.

They are printing here an Hiftorical Dictionary of learned Phyficians, 4to. by Mr. *Chr. Will. Keftner* ; alfo an univerfal Law Dictionary in 2 Vol. fol. by Mr. *John Jer. Hermann.*

ERFURT.

Dr. *George Helmerfhaufen* has publifhed a very curious Academical Differtation on the Archi-Chancellors of the Empire.

COBURG.

They have reprinted here a Work grown very fcarce, written

written in the 15th. Century by one *Andrew Guarna* an *Italian* : —Bellum grammaticum Nominis & Verbi Regum de obtinendo in Oratione Principatu, The Editor has added to it the following Piece : —Duellum de Orthoponia & Orthodia Græca.

L E I P Z I G.

Mr. *Huhn* has given a Diſſertation —de Conſcientia Dei ; wherein he treats this Queſtion ; —whether we can ſay, that God has a Conſcience, and in what it conſiſts. The Author is for the affirmative.

De Profeſſoribus veteris Eccleſiæ Martyribus. —Mr. *Rivinus* the Author of this Diſſertation ſpeaks only of thoſe Martyrs that went of their own accord to accuſe themſelves before the Judges appointed to condemn them to Death, and he endeavours to vindicate this Behaviour againſt the Objections of Mr. *Le Clerc, Barbeyrac,* &c.

Hiſtoriæ Provocationum & Appellationum apud veteres Romanos Specimen.—A ſhort but well wrote Pamphlet, by Mr. *Kiſner.*

Theoria Radicum in Æquationibus.—An Academical work of Mr. *Kæſtner.*

De Natura Quanti. —Philoſophical Theſes, by Mr. *Bærmann.* Here is his Definition :—Quantitas eſt homogeneitas, Multitudo, & Contingentia, eorum, quibus Ens conſtat.

Artis Medicæ per Ægrotorum apud Veteres in Viis publicis & Templis Expoſitionem Incrementa ; by Mr. *Hundertmark.*

Commentarii de rebus Imperii Romani a Conrado I. uſque ad Obitum Henrici III. —by Mr. *Maſcou.* 4to.

De Victu & Regimine Lactantium, by Mr. *Pauli.*

The Magiſtrate of this Town has a Greek Work wrote in the XII. Century and complete. It is a Ceremonial of the Court of *Conſtantinople* compoſed by the Emperor *Conſtantine* Porphyrogeneta. It contains all the Ceremonies practiſed at *Conſtantinople* during the IX. and X. Century, and is the only one in the World, ſince neither *F. Montfaucon* nor any other Bibliothecarian have mentioned it. A Gentleman of this Univerſity intends to give this Work to the public; with a Latin Tranſlation, —ſeveral Remarks —and a Greek

Gloſſary

Glossary of 400 Words deficient in *Du Fresne's*—
The Edition is to be in fol. and shall be equal in Size
and Beauty to the *Louvre* Edition of the Constanti-
nopolitan Historians.

Reflexions Philosophiques, &c. or Philosophical
Reflections on the Immortality of the reasonable Soul.
12mo. 1744. —This Book is well wrote but very ab-
struse.

Richard's Leben, &c. or the Life and memorable
Actions of *Richard* elected Emperor of the *Romans*,
Earl of *Cornwall* and Count of *Poitou*, by *Geo. Chr.
Gebauer*, 4to. with Cuts.— I intend to give an Ac-
count of this Book in some other Volume of this
Journal.

G O E R L I T Z.

Historia Doctrinæ recentius controversæ de Mundo
optimo ; by Mr. *Baumeister*.

W I T T E N B E R G.

The celebrated Dr. *John Will. Hoffmann* died here of
an Apoplectic Fit.

Primordia superioritatis Saxonicæ, ex antiquis Saxonum
& Francorum Rebus eruta ; by Mr. *Hanack*.

Historia Astronomiæ ; sive de ortu & progressu Astronomiæ Liber singularis, a 4to. By Professor
Weidler.

L U B B E N.

Here is a curious and instructive Pamphlet by Dr.
Adami : De materia calcaria post Diuturnam Arthri-
tidem per vias urinarias educta, observatio singularis.

L A U B A N.

Mr. *Gude* has given a Collection of Tracts on Ecclesiastical History, especially on the Means *Julian* the
Apostate made use of to favour Paganism.

H A L L.

Dr. *Baumgarten* has published some Dissertations,
De Legione Fulminatrice, in answer to *Woolston*.

The celebrated Mr. *Wolff*, who had left this University about fifteen years ago, because some Divines
had been pleased to misrepresent his Philosophical Way
of

of Thinking to our late King, and had settled at *Marpurg*, is come hither again at the desire of his *Prussian* Majesty.

FRANCFORT on the Oder.

De Caufis præcipuis hodierni frequentioris Polyporum proventus. —— A long Diſſertation by Mr. *Ebert.* He imputes the Polypus to two different Caufes: I. To the ufe of ſtrong Liquors. II. To the Jefuit's Bark.

A Phyſician is generally look'd upon as a Man engaged by his Profeſſion to follow Nature; here is a Man who pretends to maſter it. —— De Medico Naturæ Magiſtro; — an Academical Diſſertation by Mr. *Ochme.*

BERLIN.

The very learned, and juſtly celebrated, Mr. *Alph. Des Vignolles* died here lately, aged 94 years and fome months. We are to have foon an Account of his Life written by a Gentleman of this City, of which I will give an Abſtract when it comes over; I ſhall confine myſelf for the prefent to the Catalogue of his Works taken from a Manuſcript wrote with his own Hand.

I. The Hiſtory of Pope *Joan* by Mr. *Lenfant*: the fourth Part by Mr. *Des Vignolles*, with the Life of Pope *Joan*.——An hiſtorical Liſt of 150 Witneſſes, and feveral inconſiderable Articles—— Wrote in 1694.

II. Diſcuſſio Chronologica de periodica Revolutione Cometæ annorum 1668. 1702. inferted in the I. Tom. of Mifcellanea Berolinenſia, Anno. 1710.—— Wrote in 1707.

III. Epiſtola Chronologica adverfus Harduinum; added to Vindiciæ veterum Scriptorum, againſt the fame by Mr. *La Croze* 1708.——As foon as Father *Harduin* faw this Work he fent his Retractation to *Amſterdam*, where it was inferted in a new Edition of his Works.

IV. Difcours, &c. or, a Difcourfe on the Time of *Nero*'s Perfecution againſt the Chriſtians. The Author fixes it to the 64th year of Jefus Chriſt, the 15th

PART II.   D d   No-

November. The Differtation is inferted in *Hifoire* critique de la Republique des Letters, Tom. VIII. and was wrote in 1713.

V. Extract of a Book of Cardinal. *D'Ailly* on the Calendar, inferted in Mr: *Lenfant's* Hiftory of the Council of Conftance.——Wrote in 1713.

VI. A Letter to Mr. *Maffon* on a Medal of *Augustus.* ——1713.——Hift. Crift. Tom. IV.

VII. Critical Remarks on the Pythic-Games. Hift. Crit. Tom. V.——1713.

VIII. A Differtation on the fame Subject. —— Hift. Crit. Tom. VI.——1713.

IX. Two Latin Letters to the learned Mr. *Liebe,* of *Leipzig,* on a Medal of *Lewis* XII. with this Motto, Perdam Babylonis Nomen.——1714.

X. Two Difcourfes on the Birth-Day of *Augustus.* —Hift. Crit. Tom. XI. and XII.——1714.

XI. Remarks on a Paffage of *Lactantius* on *Nero's* Perfecution againft the Chriftians.——1715.——Hift. Crit. Tom. IX.

XII. Extract of a Letter to Mr. *Maffon* on a Paffage of *Pliny.*——Hift. Crit. Tom. X.——1715.

XIII. A Differtation on Chriftmafs-Day. —— The Author fixes it to the 20th of May.——Biblioth. Germanique. Tom. II.——1717.

XIV. Remarks on a Memoir of l'Abé *Renaudot* on the Origin of the Sphere, the firft of l'Academie des Infcriptions & Belles Letters.——Bibl. Germ. Tom. V. ——1719.

XV. An Anfwer to what concerns the Author in a pretended Paftoral Letter of Mr. Dartis. This Anfwer with thofe of Meffieurs *Lenfant* and *de Beaufobre* make a Volume 4to. printed at *Berlin* in 1720.

XVI. A Plan of the Author's Treatife of Chronology, began in 1713 and publifhed in 1738. Bibl. Germ. Tom. III.——1720.

XVII. The Elogy of Mrs. *Kirch,* and of fome other Ladies renown'd for their Knowledge in Aftronomy. Bibl. Germ. Tom. III.——1722.

XVIII.

XVIII. Three Differtations on the Eclipfe in *China* at the Time of our Saviour's Death ; —— in which the Author difcovers a Cycle of 60 Days, the Ufe of which is manifeft in Chronology. —— Biblioth. Germ. Tom. V.——1722.

XIX. The Adventure of a Dog which fwallow'd fome Rags wafh'd with Soap, and threw them up at feveral Times in eight Days.——Bibl. Germ. Tom. VII.——1723.

XX. A Letter on the Chinefe Chronology in an-fwer to Mr. *Kaes* Profeffor at *Kiel*—Bibl. Germ. Tom. XIV.——1725.

XXI. Abftract of the firft Memoirs of the Academy, at Peterfbourg.——Bibl. Germ. Tom. XIII.

XXII. Two Anfwers to Mr. *Kohlreiff*, who had attack'd the Author's Plan of Chronology No. XVI, and one of his Differtations on the Eclipfe at *China*, No. XVIII.——Bibl. Germ. Tom. XIV.——1726.

XXIII. An Abftract of Tom. III. of Mifcellanea Berolinenfia for the Year 1727.——Bibl. Germ. Tom. XIX.——1728.

XXIV. A Letter with an Abftract of the Work of Mr. *Kirch.*——Bibl. Germ. Tom. XX.——1730.

XXV. De annis Egyptiacis. — Mifcell. *Berol.* Tom. IV. Anno, 1734.——1731.

XXVI. De Cyclis Sinenfium Sexagenariis. — Mifcell. Berol. Tom. IV.——1732.

XXVII. A Relation of two Cataracts the Author had, and how he was cured of them.——Mifcell. Berol. Tom. IV.——1732.

XXVIII. Parergon Sinicum; or Explanation of a *Chinefe* Calendar for the Year 1654. — Mifcell. Berol. Tom. IV. ——1733.

XXIX. Abftract of the Tom. IV. of Mifcell. Berol. for the Year 1734.——Bibl. Germ. Tom. XXXI.

XXX. A Letter concerning young Mr. *Baratier.*——Bibl. Germ. Tom. XXXII.——1735.

XXXI. A Defence againft the Ariftarchus's of *Tre-voux*, who had attacked the Plan of Chronology of the Author.——Bib. Germ. Tom. XXXII.——1735.

XXXII. A Conjecture on the IVth. Eglog of *Virgil*, intituled Pollio.—— *Bibl. Germ.* Tom. XXXV.——1736.

XXXIII. Supplementum ad Difquifitionem de Cyclis Sinenfium. N°. XXVI.——Mifcell. Berol. Tom. V.——1736.

XXXIV. Obfervationes ad Epiftolam Gaubilii, A Miffionary of *China*, who had attacked the foregoing Differtation.—Mifcell, Berol. Tom. V.——1736.

XXXV. Abftract of Tom. V. of Mifcell. Berol. —*Bibl. Germ.* Tom. XXXVIII.——1737.

XXXVI. Remarks on the return of the Comets, which Mr. *Caffini* had foretold, and yet did not happen. —*Bibl. Germ.* Tom. XXXIX.——1737.

XXXVII. Chronology of the facred Hiftory, and of the foreign Hiftories relating to it. From *Mofes* to the *Babylonian* Captivity.——Quarto 2. Vol. ——*Berlin*, 1738.—(This Chronology bears a very high Character abroad).

Mr. *Hen. Pott* has publifh'd one Vol. Quarto, of Chymical Obfervations :—Obfervationum Chymicarum, præcipué circa fal commune, acidum falis vinofum, & Wifmuthum, verfantium, Collectio prior. —— The Second Vol. is impatiently expected.

Mr. *Jordan* has Publifhed Mr. *La Croze's* Letters on feveral Branches of Learning——Thofe of his Friends to him, (except Mr. *Cuper's* printed elfewhere [a], —— and feveral Remarks of Mr. *La Croze*, on the Greek and Latin Authors.

The Life of *Cicero* by Doctor *Middleton* was tranflated here into *German*.

B R E S L A U.

Dr. *Kundman* publifhed an Hiftory of the Univerfities, Colleges, and Schools, of *Germany*, Quarto.

Silefia Diplomatica, Quarto, 2. Vol. by Dr. *Walther*.

S T E T-

[a] See p. 233. of this Journal.

S T E T T I N.

Differtatio Hiftorico—GenealogicaSiftens gefta notatu digniora Imperatorum Gentis Auftriacæ inde ab Interregno Magno ad Carolum ufque quartum ex Diplomatibus, Scriptoribufque coævis eruta —————by Mr. *Ewald Fred.* de *Hertzberg.*

J E V E R N.

Hiftoriæ Medicinales, by Mr. *Moehring*————It is a Collection of Cafes which happened in the Courfe of his Practice—The Book is well wrote.

R O S T O C K.

Animadverfiones Philologico-Criticæ, or a Collection of Errors committed by the Learned in Point of Rabbinic Erudition ; ————by Mr. *Carpou.*

H A M B U R G.

Confpectus Bibliothecæ Chronologico—Diplomaticæ ; or a Collection of Diplomas concerning 1. The Empire in general. 2. It's Temporal and Spiritual Princes. 3. It's Nobility. 4. The Cities of *Germany,*—a confiderable Work by Mr. *John Paul Fincke.*

Here is a Work of Algebra in which it is faid Mathematicians will find fomething curious and new — Specimina Algebraica, Methodo Mathematica pertractata. Primum de permutationibus & combinationibus Quantitatum, in genere vero, Variationibus : Alterum, de natura Æquationum a priori quoque demonftrata ;— by Mr. *Ludolph Fred. Weifs.*

Jo. Winckteri Dieferici Difquifitiones Philologicæ, Scripturæ facræ quædam loca, & Antiquitatis, tam Ecclefiafticæ quam profanæ monumenta illuftrantes, Octavo.

The Antiquitates Selectæ of *Briffonius,* were reprinted here with fome Remarks of the Editor Mr. *Trekell.*

Profeffor *Reimari* is going to publifh a new Tranflation of *Dion Caffius,* with feveral Remarks of the late celebrated Mr. *Fabricius.*

W O L-

WOLFENBUTTEL.

Traditiones Corbeienses, illuftrationi obfcuræ Doctrinæ dePagis *Germaniæ*, & imprimis *Saxoniæ* infervientes, Quarto, by Mr. *Falken.*———— He had the Advantage of examining the Archives of that famous Abby (*Corvey*), a Permiffion which the late Mr. *Leibnitz* could never obtain.

HILDESHEIM.

. They have printed here lately the Memoirs of *Col. Chrift. Wriſsberg*, wherein many Tranflations of the XVIth Century are illuftrated, by Mr. *Loſius.*

HELMSTADT.

Mr. *Schlager* has given us the two following Works, which are much efteem'd here.—Hiftoria litis de Medicorum apud veteres Romanos degentium conditione— De Debitore obærato, fecundum jus Hebraicum & Atticum Creditori in fervitutem adjudicando,————

. De Imperatoris Capitulatione Difquifitio,—by Count. *Joſ. Anth.* of *Oetingen.*

GOETINGEN.

. Specimen Jurisprudentiæ Confultatoriæ de abufu Juramentorum e Republica profcribendo ; by Mr. *Winckler*, Quarto.

. Profeffor *Haller*, hath juft publifhed a confiderable Work of Botanicks, Folio; he acknowledges his having received confiderable helps from Meffieurs *Stæhelin, Koenig, Geſner, Divernoi, Huber, Schollen*, & *Gagnebin.*

. The Thefaurus Antiquitatum *Germanicarum*—by Mr. *Trever*, is foon to come out.

. Mr. *Guden* has given a very ufeful Work for the Hiftory of *Germany* : Codex Diplomaticus exhibens anecdota ab anno D CCCLXXXI ad M CCCC Moguntiaca, Jus *Germanicum* & *S. R. J.* Hiftoriam illuftrantia.—It may ferve as a Supplement to the Scriptores Rerum Moguntiacarum.

. Elementa Juris Canonico-Pontificio Ecclefiaftici tum Veteris tum Hodierni; — a confiderable Work by Mr. *Kahl.*

B R E M E N.

Hiſtoria Fiſtulæ Euchariſticæ, by Mr. *Vogt*.——It is the Hiſtory of an antient cuſtom of ſucking the Wine out of the Euchariſtic Cup by a Pipe made of a ſmall Reed.——This Cuſtom ſtill prevails in ſome *Roman*— and alſo in ſome *Luthern* Churches.

L E M G O.

. De Juriſdictione Germanica : A Work of Mr. *If. de Puffendorf*, reprinted by *Meyer*.

Pharos, or an account of ſome Ægyptian Antiquities, Quarto, by Mr. Koch.

D U I S B U R G.

Jus Pagaſianum, ſive ea Juſtiniani Pandectarum Capita quæ Pegaſi ICſulti ſententias, & opiniones de Jure referunt; — a Quarto by Profeſſor *Pagenffecher*.

S W I T Z E R L A N D.

L A U S A N N E.

I ſaid in the firſt Part of this Journal (b) that the new Edition of Sir *If. Newton's* Opuſcula, which they are printing here, was undertaken with the approbation of the Royal Society in *London*. So it was affirmed in the *Bibliotheque raiſonée*, and the Nouvelle Bibliotheque at the *Hague*. But I have ſeen ſince in La Bibliotheque Françoiſe, a Letter of the Editor, wherein he diſclaims all Pretenſion to ſuch an Approbation of the Royal Society, and ſays that he did not even aſk it ; being not ſufficiently known by the Members that compoſe that illuſtrious Body to take ſuch a Liberty.

B A S I L.

The Bookſeller *Imhoff* has reprinted *Cave's* hiſtoria Literaria, according to the *Oxford* Edition of 1740.

B E R N.

Tentamen Theologiæ dogmaticæ methodo ſcientifica pertractatæ, by Mr. *Wythenbach*, who profeſſes himſelf an Imitator of Meſſieurs *Leibnitz*, and *Wolff*.—Shou'd the Apoſtles of J. Chriſt ſee what is here called his Religion appear in that ſcientific Dreſs, they wou'd, I believe, be much ſurpriſed.

N E U-

NEUFCHATEL.

The celebrated Mr. *Ostervald* has just published a new Translation of the Bible. He has added to each Chapter a reasoned Summary of what it contains, and moral Reflections at the End of it. It must be taken notice of, that this Edition is the only one that deserves the name of *Ostervald's* Bible ; that of *Amsterdam*, which bears that Name, being really Mr. *Martin's* Translation, to which the Editor added Mr. *Ostervald's* Reflections, such as they had been printed separately, and to which the Author makes several Amendments for this Edition. Mr. *Ostervald* also gives this further Notice, that he disavows the following Books printed in his Name in *London*, at *Amsterdam* and at the *Hague* ; viz. *Ostervald's* Compendium Ethicæ, 8vo. — *Ostervald* Theologia, 4to. — and *de l' exercice du Ministere sacre*, 12mo. — he chiefly complains of this latter, in which some Disciples of his, who are the true Authors of the Book, make him say almost at every Page, what he never dream'd of.

PARIS.

Mr. de *Jonquieres* has translated into *French* a considerable Work of his Highness *Demetrius Cantimir* Prince of *Moldavia* ; it is an History of the *Ottoman Empire*, in 2 vols. 4to. — of between 500 and 600 pages each vol.

Father *Charlevoix* already known by his Histories of *Japan*, and of the Island *Hispaniola*, has published an History of *New France*, in 3 vol. 4to. or 6. vol. 12mo. with Geographical Maps.

M. *Philippe* has given a beautiful new Edition of *Lucretius* in 12mo. with Cuts, a well wrote Preface, and a Catalogue of the former Editions of this Poet, which are 55 in number.

Recherches, &c. or Critical and Historical Enquiries into the several States and Progresses of Chirurgery in *France*, 4to. 1744.

La Chyrurgie Complete, &c. or a Complete System of Chirurgery ; the modern way of explaining it. 12mo, 2 vol.

Entretiens

Entretiens Mathematiques, &c. or Mathematical Difcourfes of Father *Regnault.*

Le parfait *Cocher*, or the perfect Coachman 12mo.

UNITED PROVINCES.
HAGUE.

Eman. Swedenborgii Regnum Animale 4to.

Supplement aux Memoires de *Condé*, &c. A Supplement to the Memoirs of Condé, with the Anti-Cotton, &c. The whole Work is in 7 vol. 4to.

LEYDEN.

The Bookfeller *Leuzac* intends to print by Subfcription, a new Tranflation of *Job* by Mr. *Ruchat* a Profeffor of Laufanne.

AMSTERDAM.

The *Roman* Hiftory by the late Mr. *Rollin* is continued by Mr. *Crevier.* The 10th Tome is out ;—as well as the 6th of *Drakenborch*'s Livy, 4to.

Inftitution, &c. or, Military Inftitution of Vegetius, 8vo. fig. a very fine Edition.

L'Art de trouver la *verité*, or the Art of difcovering truth, by F. *Regnault*, 12mo.

Le Guide d'Angleterre, or, the Guide through *England*, &c.

The Bookfeller *Wetftein* has added 3 vols. to the 12 he publifhed fome time ago, of *Baronius*'s grand Collection. Annales Ecclefiafticæ Cæfaris *Baronii*, Card. cum critica fubjecta Antonii *Pagi*, Continuatione Odorici *Raynaldi*, Notifque Dominici *Georgii* & P. Joannis Dominici *Manfi*, &c.

Sermons de Mr. *Henry Chatelain.* 8vo. 2 vol.

GREAT-BRITAIN.
LONDON.

They have printed here in French, the Memoirs of *Count de Guiche*, to ferve as a Supplement and a Continuation to d' *Aubberry*'s, *Du Maurier*, and Count *D' Eftrade*'s Memoirs. 12mo. 1744.

What Mr. *Fofter* fays on the Theocracy of the *Jews* (Vol. III. Serm. XV.) hath been attack'd by Mr. *Lowman.*

An Addrefs to Deifts, &c. by *Eben. Hewlet*, 8vo.

Mr. *Warburton* is (they fay) writing the Life of his good Friend Mr. *Pope.*

Mr. *Lockman* has tranflated from the French of *La Fontaine* ; the Loves of Cupid and Pfyche, &c.

Germana quædam Antiquitatis eruditæ Monumenta : quibus Romanorum Veterum Ritus varii tam facri quam profani, tum Græcorum atque Ægyptiorum nonnulli illuftrantur. Romæ olim maxima ex parte collecta ac Differtationibus, jam fingulis inftructa, à Conyers *Middleton*, 4to.

A Continuation of the Life and Adventures of *Don Quixot* ; by Mr. *Baker*, 2 Vols,—Cuts.—

The Juftice of Peace, by Mr. *Barlow*, Fol.

Excerpta quædam ex Luciani operibus, by Mr. *Kent* ; 2d, Edit.

A Paraphrafe and Notes on the II. of S. *Peter*, and the Epiftle of S. *Jude* ; after Mr. *Locke*'s manner.

Seed's Sermons at Lady's *Moyer*'s Lecture ; 2 Vols, 2d. Edit.

An Account of Commodore *Anfon*'s Voyage to the South Sea, by *Pafcoe Thomas.*

Columella's 12 Books of Hufbandry, 4to.

The Bifhop of *London*'s laft Charge to his Clergy.

Dr. *Mead* on Poifons. 3d. Edit.

Pococke's Defcription of the Eaft; 2d. Vol. Fol.

The Life of *John* Duke of *Argyle*, by *Robert Campbell*, Efq;

The 4th Vol. of Cardinal *Wolfey*'s Life is come out.

Difcourfes on Trade and other Matters relating to it ; by *J. Cary*, Efq;

The prefent Practice of Conveyancing by *J. Mill.*

Nelfon's Juftice of Peace, 12th Edition, continued to the prefent Time.

The Ground and Foundation of Morality confidered, by Mr. *Chubb.*

Dialogues concerning Education. 4to.

EDINBURG.

Meffieurs *Mc Laurin* Profeffor of Mathematics, and *Andrew Plummer* Profeffor of natural Philofophy, were

appointed

appointed Secretaries to the new Society erected here for the Improvement of natural Hiſtory. All the Learned in *Europe* that have any thing to communicate to the Public, by the means of this Society, are deſired to direct their Letters to either of the two above-named Gentlemen.

An hiſtorical and critical Commentary on *Euſtachius*, by the late Dr. *George Martin*, and publiſhed by Mr. *Munro*, Profeſſor of Anatomy.

DUBLIN.

Mr. *Hawkey* is going on with his beautiful Edition of Latin Claſſics, undertaken by the Approbation of, and promoted by Encouragement from, our Univerſity, and printed in the College. *Virgil* is already come out, and fully anſwers the Expectation of the Public. *Horace* is now in the Preſs.—A few Setts are printed on Royal Paper for the Curious, and will exceed any thing of the Kind publiſhed in this Kingdom. Each Subſcription for common Setts is a Britiſh half Crown.

A

A
TABLE
OF
CONTENTS,
AND
An INDEX of the Authors quoted.

A Table of Contents.

A Table of Contents.

Conſtans

A Table of Contents.

A Table of Contents.

F.

A Table of Contents.

PART II,   F f   *Le Com*

A Table of Contents.

Maximilian

A Table of Contents:

Patriarch;

A Table of Contents.

Rotari,

A Table of Contents.

A Table of Contents.

F I N I S.

www.ingramcontent.com/pod-product-compliance
Lightning Source LLC
LaVergne TN
LVHW012207040326
832903LV00003B/174